A Practical Introduction to Survey Design

A Practical Introduction to Survey Design

A Beginner's Guide

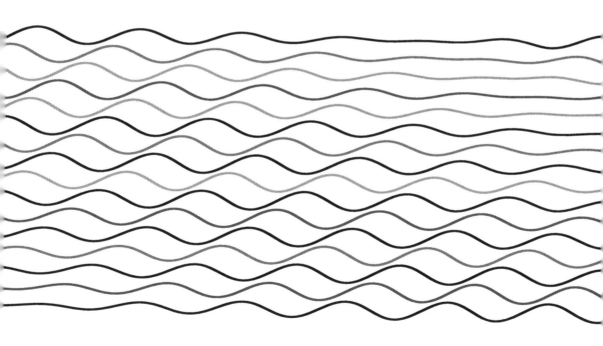

Haydn Aarons

Los Angeles | London | New Delhi
Singapore | Washington DC | Melbourne

Los Angeles | London | New Delhi
Singapore | Washington DC | Melbourne

SAGE Publications Ltd
1 Oliver's Yard
55 City Road
London EC1Y 1SP

SAGE Publications Inc.
2455 Teller Road
Thousand Oaks, California 91320

SAGE Publications India Pvt Ltd
B 1/I 1 Mohan Cooperative Industrial Area
Mathura Road
New Delhi 110 044

SAGE Publications Asia-Pacific Pte Ltd
3 Church Street
#10-04 Samsung Hub
Singapore 049483

Editor: Jai Seaman
Assistant editor: Lauren Jacobs
Production editor: Martin Fox
Copyeditor: Neville Hankins
Proofreader: Christine Bitten
Marketing manager: Ben Griffin-Sherwood
Cover design: Shaun Mercier
Typeset by: C&M Digitals (P) Ltd, Chennai, India
Printed in the UK

Library of Congress Control Number: 2020938963

British Library Cataloguing in Publication data

A catalogue record for this book is available from the British Library

ISBN 978-1-5264-6029-5
ISBN 978-1-5264-6030-1 (pbk)

At SAGE we take sustainability seriously. Most of our products are printed in the UK using responsibly sourced papers and boards. When we print overseas we ensure sustainable papers are used as measured by the PREPS grading system. We undertake an annual audit to monitor our sustainability.

For my family

Brief contents

Detailed contents

About the author

Haydn Aarons is a Senior Lecturer in Sociology at the Australian Catholic University in Melbourne, Australia. He has taught research methods including survey research and quantitative methods to social science and humanities students for over 20 years. He has worked on numerous survey design research projects for industry, government, and academic research. His research in sociology covers topics in health, religion, cultural consumption, and military sociology.

Preface

Welcome to *A Practical Introduction to Survey Design*. There are many good texts that cover surveys, but few that promote an in-depth understanding of the key contexts and components of survey measurement, and few that instruct readers in developing knowledge and skills in survey design through a systematic and applied process. This text aims to contribute to the enhanced learning and teaching of survey research to help meet important aspects of present and future social science research needs.

Today the social sciences are as vital to an informed and functioning society as ever, in addressing complex social changes and problems. Their importance is strongly evidenced by the relevance of empirical patterns produced from quantitative methods to understanding behaviour and experience, and as a tool informing better governance and decision making. There is a consensus in many countries, however, acknowledging the current gaps in the quantitative research skills of many students and graduates. Responses to this crisis, such as the UK's Q-Step program, are an excellent example of redress, but data analysis skills are only one side of the coin. Informative and useful data analysis – no matter how sophisticated – relies on high data quality. High data quality is a direct consequence of good data collection methodologies such as survey design. Knowledge and skills in data collection, therefore, must prefigure data analysis. A further aim of this text then is to contribute to the continued development of learning and teaching in quantitative methods through comprehensive knowledge and skills in survey design.

This book has three broad aims: (1) to introduce and initiate readers to the world of survey research; (2) to guide readers through a systematic process that informs about key knowledge and skills associated with survey design; and (3) to enable and encourage readers to apply what has been learned through designing their own survey. Introducing and initiating readers to the world of survey research involves a discussion of the appropriate contexts and uses of surveys and survey data (Chapter 1), positioning survey design within the frameworks of the research process and survey design process to promote a systematic approach to survey design (Chapter 2), and setting specific research goals for a survey through the development of precise research questions (Chapter 3). Guiding readers through survey design as a systematic process involves a deep consideration of what exactly a survey should aim to measure (Chapters 4 and 5), and how exactly to measure it with well-constructed survey questions (Chapter 6). After a survey has been designed, how to put it into the field, which respondents to ask (Chapters 7 and 8), and then how to manage and prepare the data ready for analysis (Chapter 9) are important practical concerns complementing planning phases. The final chapter (Chapter 10) provides an in-depth example that ties all of the various components together to illustrate how a survey research instrument is designed and executed, and how the data it collects are used to produce high-quality research.

How to read this book

The book presents survey design sequentially through the key stages of what I term the 'survey design process'. Each chapter articulates in depth the various stages in the survey design process sequentially to build knowledge and skills. Survey design entails intellectual and practical components relating to the planning and then the execution of a survey. Survey researchers necessarily must plan before they can execute. Therefore, the text is best read from start to finish, so that knowledge and skills are built on a developmental process of staged learning and application, replicating the way in which professional researchers organize a survey research project. The chapters outline the purpose and content of each stage, and the key challenges and specific problems associated with each stage. Research methods are best learned by 'doing', however, so each chapter has a 'YOUR SURVEY' section that invites and encourages readers to apply what they have learned in the design of their own survey.

The book is accompanied by a suite of online tools and resources housed in the book's companion website. Web resources include reflective questions on the topics of each chapter, templates for various aspects of the development of a survey, and videos providing examples, hints, and tips concerning various aspects of survey design. There are web links to publicly accessible resources such as professional large-scale surveys, international statistical agencies, and to survey question banks. The website also includes links to various further learning resources associated with surveys, such as the main scholarly journals for survey research methodology as well as the SAGE Research Methods database. For tutors or instructors there are also prepared PowerPoint slides for each chapter.

Acknowledgements

The labour involved in writing is solitary; however, there are always people who either are in the background or travel with you as you write and who have influenced and inspired you to do so. To them my acknowledgements and thanks. Firstly, I would like to thank SAGE for the opportunity to promote the learning of something that I am passionate about through this book. In particular, I would like to acknowledge and thank Jai Seaman and Lauren Jacobs at SAGE for their gentle patience, professional guidance, and encouragement over the course of the book's development. Secondly, I have used my honours thesis in this text as an example of what can be achieved with a humble student survey. The honours year was a wonderful awakening to the possibilities of survey research. A huge debt of gratitude therefore must go to Dr Timothy Phillips, who, as my honours thesis supervisor, introduced me to the world of survey research and nurtured my continuing interest in the method. Tim has been a key mentor for me as a student and as a researcher. Finally, as a teacher of survey research and quantitative methods I would like to acknowledge and thank the many students I have taught over 20 years, many of whom, like me once, felt dread about the prospects of having to do a quantitative research methods unit. Every year that I teach survey research and quantitative methods, however, I encounter 'converts' as I call them. These students often start my unit with fear, loathing, and dread, but end it with respect, knowledge, and, for some, even a love of survey research and 'quants'. This change in demeanour is one of the great rewards of my profession; this text is for them, and anyone potentially like them that may read it.

Online resources

A Practical Introduction to Survey Design: A Beginner's Guide is supported by online resources, which are available at: https://study.sagepub.com/aarons

For students

See surveys in action with a selection of **sample completed surveys** and **codebooks**.

Assess your skills with **reflective questions** for each chapter.

Deepen your understanding with a set of curated **weblinks** to journal articles, data agencies and other useful content.

Plan and create your survey with a selection of handy **templates** and a **checklist** to get you started.

For lecturers

PowerPoint slides for each chapter featuring figures and tables from the book, which can be downloaded and customized for use in your own presentations.

One

Surveys: Data, Uses, and Contexts

This introductory chapter sets the scene for survey research and survey design by giving an overview of their key components and contexts. This chapter covers the following:

- To learn what a survey is
- To appreciate how surveys are used in research and for what purposes
- When to use surveys in research
- Types of data collected from surveys
- Types of research questions surveys help answer

Research is the means by which many organizations and enterprises function effectively, understand and manage change, and maintain quality. This is true be they academic, governmental, commercial, or community based. Research is the art and science of asking questions about a series of relevant unknowns. Data are the means by which those questions are often best answered. Organizations of all kinds require valid and reliable data to meet their needs which are driven by the research they set out to do. This has always been true but is perhaps even more relevant and necessary in the present contexts of mass societies, rapid change, and increasing complexity. There are numerous ways of researching, and various forms of data employed to meet the needs of organizations. These needs are reflected in research questions. Data are observations relevant to these questions and come in different forms such as text, image, sound, and numbers. Research methods (the means of data collection) are more or less appropriate to the needs of the research. Survey research therefore produces data that meet specific types of needs; that is, it answers specific types of questions and is appropriate to a specific research context, and not others. That context is research that requires mostly quantitative data (numbers, statistics, percentages, rates, and levels), is often social in nature, (that is, it collects data about people and their behaviour), and is mostly concerned with groups and **populations** rather than individuals alone.

The relevance of survey research and survey data is evidenced by the sheer breadth of organizations that use it, the number of educational institutions that teach it, and the fact that survey research has developed over the last century to the point where it very much constitutes its own science (Converse, 1987; Weisberg, 2005). Further testament to the importance of survey research – if dollar values impress you, at least – is the estimate by *Fortune* magazine (Fortune, 2016) that the public opinion research industry (of which survey design is a very important part) is a $20 billion industry. Estimates such as this signal the fact that the scientific as well as practical need for such data is integral to how societies and groups are organized across numerous domains. As all aspects of societies continue to evolve and change, survey research will be of increasing importance to meet the data needs of organizations and societies, as will its associated skills in survey design and administration.

Surveys, often referred to also as 'questionnaires', are a ubiquitous research instrument used to collect mostly quantitative data to answer research questions. The data they collect are used for a staggering assortment of purposes from tracking consumer trends to gauging satisfaction with a product or service, from planning and evaluating complex social policy to assisting in diagnosing mental illnesses, from assessing why voters voted the way they did, to why they do not vote at all. They are profoundly useful instruments, crucial for the practical applications of knowledge creation, evaluation, planning, and resource allocation. They also contribute substantially to our attempts at theoretical understanding of a vast array of human activity associated with a range of academic disciplines, government services, and economic and commercial interests. In many respects they represent still, despite changes in technology and the advent of other forms of data collection, one of the most efficient and effective means of collecting relevant data of high quality for groups for use in research. An understanding of the key components of survey design, then, is crucial to understanding how a lot of research from a wide range of different disciplines is conducted, and consequently an important aspect of the decision-making processes for larger populations and groups. At some point you may have to design a survey with the aim of collecting data to answer a research question, interpret data from a survey that someone else has designed, or critically assess research using empirical evidence derived from survey research. This book guides you through the process of survey design, assisting you in designing a survey yourself, and/or appreciating and understanding the process behind how someone else did. Either way, you will come to understand survey methodology and the quantitative and qualitative research in the social sciences that is dependent upon it a lot better after reading this book.

What is a survey and what is its role in research?

In the most broad and elementary terms a survey is a schedule, or many schedules of questions designed to collect mostly quantitative data (but they can also collect qualitative data), given to a **sample** of respondents to complete. The actual data it collects are the recorded marks, circles, ticks, and clicks in the numerically scored answer formats to the questions on each page. No doubt you have at some point for some reason taken part in completing a survey and are familiar with this part of the process. Data are banks of raw numbers that are collected and transferred into statistical software (it is difficult to imagine how researchers did this before computers), organized into meaningful analytic categories, analysed, applied, discussed, and acted upon.

That all sounds very simple, but it belies a much deeper and complex process of planning, design, consultation, and context. An apt metaphor here is a clock. While a clock face may be simple and purposeful, underneath the surface are a complex series of cogs, wheels, gaskets, and pins that are arranged and ordered in sequences giving the mechanism its precise movement to produce a reading of the time. It is this mostly occluded process of planning, design, consultation, and context that this book is concerned with. If this is done poorly the data the survey collects will be useless. Planning and design for many survey research projects take time and effort; a lot of work goes into the 'front end' of survey research before any data are collected or analysed. Given that survey research is so widespread and that the design and planning process is so important, a lot of attention on the various components of the survey design process to improve data quality and the usefulness of surveys is necessary.

Surveys as instruments for research are more than just a set of questions on a piece of paper or a website, however, and therefore constitute different forms of critical and vital communication for the purposes of scientific knowledge. Survey research is also a reflective and ethical field of enquiry and a science, subject to theories, empirical evidence, and change much like any other area of knowledge. The survey instrument is a product of the researcher and reflects the contexts, biases, and assumptions that the researcher brings to the research. So, the art of survey design is not just a matter of learning how to ask a few questions, but involves delving deeper into the theories of how people behave and perceive, and how research represents those phenomena it seeks to measure to generate knowledge and understanding.

How surveys are used in research

To gain a better understanding of how surveys work and of survey research in general we need to consider the survey in its context of research tool embedded within the research process, as an instrument that is designed to perform a task but is also an idea within other ideas. The best way in which social science research learns about people is to ask them questions and collect observations, but what do the questions represent? Which questions does a researcher ask? How does a researcher ask such questions? Who does the researcher ask? And what do the answers respondents give really mean? These are all very important considerations to survey design and are more complex than you might have imagined.

Like an image shown on a screen from a projector, the survey instrument projects key aspects of the story the researcher is trying to tell. The survey represents the deeper thought associated with a research problem. For example, to measure a phenomenon such as depression in a survey, which many researchers seek to do (with survey questions such as those that comprise psychometrics such as the Beck Depression Inventory (Beck, 1972)), researchers need first to have an idea of what depression means, how it manifests in people, what it feels like, and what its components are; only then can they attempt to measure it and see how it might be communicated back to the researchers through a questionnaire from those they sought to question.

A survey that seeks to measure depression has to project the idea or concept of depression through a series of questions. Where does this meaning, manifestation, and communicative ability come from, so as to make the survey useful, however?

We all have theories or ideas about behaviour but those are not necessarily tested or debated beyond our own experience or imaginations. Scientific disciplines such as psychology will combine theories about experiences such as depression from observations, then seek to test and refine those theories with further observations. Through the time spent on numerous rounds of theorizing, observation, and refinement, understandings about complex human experiences such as depression take shape, change, or remain the same. How researchers think of the phenomenon to begin with is how they portray it in a survey, which feeds back to them in the form of data or observations, which they then interpret. To test or measure a phenomenon such as depression the survey instrument is designed to house the idea or concept, projecting to the respondent through the questions the researchers' own thinking about it, which is often further reflective of much other previous work.

Again, the example of a clock is instructional here. A clock is an instrument that collects and displays its own kind of data (time) and is designed to measure time as a theoretical construct in terms of data (in seconds, minutes, and hours). You can now see that a questionnaire is but the tip of the iceberg of changing ideas, theories, and experiments. Surveys therefore need careful planning because the collected data are the result of a predetermined set of questions that reflect or project a series of ideas, constructs, or concepts that are the conduits for understanding the relationship between people, their behaviour, its explanations, what we know already, and the researchers' own imagination. And when we consider a topic as consequential as depression, the process of survey design can take on a heightened importance because serious decisions about people's lives are made with the results.

Beyond their mere utility as instruments that collect data, surveys also represent different means of communication often with meaningful and powerful consequences. Through questions and data, surveys assist in communicating ideas, experiences, emotions, and beliefs between researchers and researched, between populations and people with power, and between businesses and clients. Surveys are a crucial mechanism communicating relationships between ideas and concepts to establish and clarify causes, associations, and correlations between behaviours and experiences. They also communicate sets of values of how we think about experiences, and how we think others think about experiences. Importantly they convey various perceptions between researcher and researched. What a researcher might think of as an aspect of someone's life and what that aspect of someone's life is really like may or may not actually reflect any truth or **plausibility**, so the need for a survey design process outlining prospects and pitfalls is crucial.

Research methodologies are a means of attempting to map scientifically and understand human experience, albeit somewhat remotely and indirectly. This holds for any discipline that has people as its main concern. This attempt is often imperfect and our knowledge consequently inconclusive, despite the many insights we do gain. Surveys are also susceptible to various limits in their effectiveness to answer questions therefore, but they are one of the most effective means available to us to understand diverse patterns of human behaviour for large populations. Being properly informed about the process of design and planning a survey therefore guides us in trying to map human experience better, solve problems, and gain understanding within a range of limitations.

Deductive and inductive research and reasoning in survey research

Deductive

Theories → concepts → surveys → empirical observations (data)

Inductive

Empirical observations (data) → surveys → concepts → theories

Surveys are also then a crucial form of scientific communication. And this context is important because it connects our research imaginings to a formal process to attempt to ensure that we strive to understand with a series of checks and balances. In any of the social sciences we attempt to understand human experience beyond that of our own personal limitations and for more than just the few but the many, yet we derive our observations often from our own experience and ways of seeing; in this way we are empirical, and being empirical can assist us in overcoming forms of misunderstanding and bias. Yet just being empirical is not enough: how do we know what we know is accurate? How we know what we know, and if it is worth knowing, is a crucial question accompanying such activities as survey design, because human experience is complex. **Deductive research** and **inductive research** are two distinct ways in which surveys can contribute to a scientific understanding of human experience. Empirical research can proceed from a series of theoretical propositions or statements, from which key ideas or concepts are then measured in a survey from which we gather observations in the form of statistical data. The analysis of the data then assists in supporting or refuting the **theory** in question. In reverse order we can use observations derived from surveys and build theories from the statistical patterns that occur.

Weber's *Protestant Ethic* as inductive
and deductive survey research

As an example of the differences between inductive and deductive survey research consider one of the most famous works in sociology: Max Weber's *The Protestant Ethic and
the Spirit of Capitalism*.

You may have heard the term 'Protestant work ethic', or at least the more contemporary
phrase 'work ethic'. This comes from Weber's famous study of the religious differences in
socio-economic status he observed in Germany around the turn of the twentieth century.
Weber starts his famous work with an analysis of the German census data in which he
finds a striking pattern between Protestants and Catholics in Germany. Many of the 'business leaders and owners of capital, as well as the higher grades of skilled labour, and even
the more higher technically and commercially trained personnel of modern enterprises
are overwhelmingly Protestant' (Weber, 2001: 4). *The Protestant Ethic* then proceeds to
explain the statistical patterns with a theory of how religious changes in Germany arising
from the Protestant Reformation in the sixteenth century facilitated certain kinds of economic behaviour change as distinct forms of cultural approaches to work and economic
life leading to the specific statistical patterns of Weber's own day.

Following Weber's famous work, there have been many attempts to replicate his findings in countries outside Germany such as in France, the UK, and the United States,
countries that also have Protestant and Catholic populations. These replications have
used survey data deductively, however, commencing with Weber's theory and using the
survey data to test the theory (Bouma, 1973).

Contexts of surveys and survey research

To get a clearer picture of what surveys are and how they are used, let's consider some
examples of specific contexts of different aspects of survey research impacting survey
design. The first context that defines survey research is the nature of the data it collects –
quantitative data. While I have stated that surveys can also be used to collect qualitative data (that is, textual data such as a personal description, recount, observation, or
testimony such as you might encounter in an interview), the overwhelming majority
of data that surveys collect is quantitative. Statistics are ultimately the language of surveys and they are the means by which researchers answer their questions when they
conduct survey research. Surveys are therefore subject to particular rules so as to be
valid and useful means of data collection and communication. Much like a language,
the words have to make sense to both communicating parties through the shared rec-
ognition of symbols and their meaning. How a survey is designed and administered
entailing the questions that are asked, the way they are asked, the order in which they
are asked, the ways they are answered, and who is asked all impact on what kinds of
statistics are derived and therefore what can be known from them.

Quantitative data used in the social sciences are radically different from qualitative
data, although they are both employed as tools to address similar topics, they are

different data, and they are used to answer different types of questions (Figure 1.1). They can, however, complement one another superbly. Quantitative data gathered through research instruments such as surveys are most effective in counting, numerically classifying, and relating experiences, attitudes, opinions, values, actions, and attributes for larger populations. A key strength of survey research is the breadth and prevalence of opinion, experience, and attribute, but not so much depth. Surveys mostly collect data about individuals; these data are then analysed in aggregate at the sample population level, which then stands as evidence for patterns and regularities in the wider population. An appropriate context for a survey then is an enquiry that seeks to know about broader patterns, contours, outlines, and the overall shape of experiences, more so than the many nuanced details.

While this is a limitation, it should not be seen as a weakness; it simply is a means of ascertaining this level of information, which has a power and utility of its own. For example, we certainly want to know in great depth and detail what depression feels like for an individual, but we also need to know how widespread it is within a population, which segments of the population might be more or less affected, what the essential symptoms and affects are in common, and the levels of intensity for those who indicate its presence in their lives across the broader population – how else do we plan larger scale solutions in mass contemporary societies such as ours?

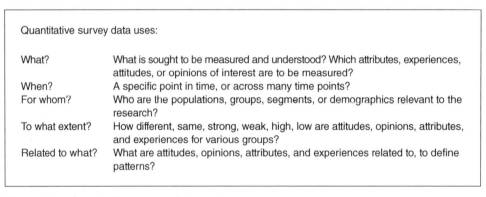

Quantitative survey data uses:

What?	What is sought to be measured and understood? Which attributes, experiences, attitudes, or opinions of interest are to be measured?
When?	A specific point in time, or across many time points?
For whom?	Who are the populations, groups, segments, or demographics relevant to the research?
To what extent?	How different, same, strong, weak, high, low are attitudes, opinions, attributes, and experiences for various groups?
Related to what?	What are attitudes, opinions, attributes, and experiences related to, to define patterns?

Figure 1.1 Quantitative survey data uses

Rate, level, correlation, raw number

Statistics derived from surveys numerically inform us about rates, levels, strength and weakness, group patterns, and relationships between sets of experiences, attributes, and achievements that can indicate causes, **correlations**, and associations, present situations, and changes over time. We plan research questions and set problem solving goals around these limits/advantages. Peruse projects like the national census of your country through your country's national statistical office or bureau, or large national or international social, economic, or political surveys such as the Afrobarometer, the General Social Survey in the United States, the Asian Barometer, or the European Social Survey, and you will find therein questions asked to gauge sets of individual responses that are inferred back to the larger population. They capture quantitative data for sets of experiences and attributes that give us broad statistical portraits and contours of many of the key dimensions of populations, such as educational achievement, income levels, household composition, employment status, use of services, market share, and feelings about political systems, but usually do not go into any depth about these experiences.

Further, survey data are capable of providing sophisticated layers of such experiences and their specific sites by including demographic measures which tap the differentiating aspects of a population such as:

- gender
- age
- ethnicity
- religion
- geographic location
- family relationships
- workplaces
- household composition
- sexualities
- civic associations

We can learn a lot about the social or demographic distribution of a particular behaviour, experience, feeling, and attribute through layering and specification. In doing so we can compare and contrast levels, rates, and frequencies of experiences, attitudes, and opinions between different groups. We can do this with surveys at one point in time in one place by using what is known as a case study, or over time to assess change through a longitudinal approach, and/or comparatively by using the same or similar surveys in more than one place at more than one time, just like the World Values Survey or the International Social Survey Programme does.

So, surveys produce particular types of data, and are therefore appropriate to certain kinds of research questions and are further designed for particular types of respondents, and, as we will see, the data are also put to certain kinds of uses. Survey data allow us to discern broad patterns of variation of experience based on particular defining attributes. This is the type of knowledge we gain from surveys through the data they collect. Where is change, differentiation, or sameness? What or who is responsible for this variation or lack of it in a population? Understanding the types of data surveys collect and the types of questions that survey data can answer gives us a strong grasp of when to employ them and when perhaps to pursue another methodology. Let's look at a few examples in depth to make these points clearer.

---------------- Survey design and big data ----------------

Perhaps you have heard the term 'big data', a term that describes the immense volume of data that are available to researchers through various forms of digital presence online. One of the key problems with big data is how to analyse them, discern their relevance to research problems, as well as assess the quality of the data. Big data have enormous potential for researchers, but one of the key problems of big data is that they may not be at all relevant to a project's research questions. Twitter and Facebook for example are great sources of public big data about a range of topics, but the researcher is at the mercy of what people post and there is no guarantee that such posts will translate into relevant data. Further, they only represent data for those who have active accounts, and who might post opinions or experiences about the topic of interest. Given that estimates of active accounts (those which can be verified as belonging to actual people) of some social media sites such as Twitter for a large population such as the United States are around only 20%, of whom most users are under 40 years of age, data from Twitter cannot possibly be representative of the broader US population. Surveys, however, are designed with a specific research purpose in mind, and with good sampling techniques can be representative of the broader population. Special or unique populations who use social media, however, can be targeted for a survey.

Types of questions, types of answers, types of knowledge

Story telling is a human universal, and different stories serve different purposes; however, they do all have something in common: understanding and relating to others and ourselves. For example, if we want to know what it is really like to be a surgeon, an astronaut, a movie star, or an Olympic gold medallist, surveys are not able to give us much insight in terms of the richness of experience we might want to know about these people. We can certainly ask questions about these professions or achievements, but the data will not give us a lot of depth compared with, say, an interview that generates qualitative data. What might we ask an Olympian in a survey?

How does it feel to be a gold medallist?

a   Great
b   Fantastic
c   Amazing
d   Awesome
e   Relieved
f   Other (please state)..

Or:

On a scale of 1 to 10 please indicate how happy you were with winning the gold medal at the recent Olympics in event.... With 1 meaning 'just happy' to 10 'out of my mind happy'.

Compare what we might receive from asking these questions about winning a gold medal with the descriptive depth entailing the emotional contexts of family, national expectation, and personal pathos conveyed in an interview such as that of Felix Sanchez, the Dominican Republic's only Olympic gold medallist to date (take a look at the YouTube video on the companion website), and you can appreciate the limits and purposes of statistical communication that is derived from survey research.

So, do you see what I mean? We could certainly gain some insight into what it is like to win a gold medal at the Olympic Games if we were to ask Felix Sanchez to complete a questionnaire about his performances, but it does not really compare with the textual description of his experience that he offers. On one level we connect much more readily with that kind of story telling: we get closer to the specific human experience of winning a gold medal with qualitative data than with survey questions and statistics. Intuitively, however, we do know that an athlete will be happy to win a gold medal, but we may not know the whole story. The personal endeavour entailing years of preparation, training, sacrifice, and dedication, and the glory, accomplishment, fame, and fortune that accompany a gold medal, can be imagined and discerned if not experienced by many of us. We do not really learn anything from survey questions such as these, so we tend not to use them for such research questions.

We can still learn an awful lot about Olympians by shifting the focus of the questions. The use or not of a survey is a matter of purpose, context, and research question type, remember. While still curious about what it is really like to win a gold medal, we might further be interested in why those who win them, win them. Sport is big business and a source of national pride these days, especially global events such as the Olympic Games; consequently there is a lot of research done on how to win. What differentiates those who win from those who do not, and not just for one athlete but for many? In addition to mere biological or physiological factors, we might theorize that winning and losing have something to do with the mind sets and emotional experiences of athletes. How then do practice regimes, injury rates and types, diet, and coaching styles impact upon the emotions, attitudes, and general motivation of athletes, which in turn then impact on performance, and for many athletes, not just one athlete such as Felix Sanchez? These are things interviews can certainly tap, but a survey can accurately gather these kinds of data for hundreds if not thousands of athletes in a very short time, relatively cheaply, and be used effectively to improve performance as well as plan the management of athletes into the future.

Better still, the data from a survey of a sample of Olympic athletes can assess the strength of relationships between these many different potential causes or drivers of winning and losing. We may find that coaching styles impact the emotions of athletes, thereby affecting an athlete's motivation and consequently having an impact on performance, much greater than the training regime of that athlete. Further we might want to know the effectiveness of specific training regimes on an athlete's performance through either biological assessment or attitudes towards how that training is aiding or hindering techniques. We can readily appreciate the effectiveness of a survey therefore in discovering the causes or correlations of better or worse performance of athletes to inform an athlete's optimum performance and how gold medals might be won and lost. All this can be learned through the language of statistics derived from survey data to tell us a particular kind of story, complementing that of the personal journey an athlete may take on the road to a medal.

Let's consider another example to illustrate further the point about surveys and their use. Migration and seeking asylum are important topics for many social and political researchers, as well as governments. The reasons why people leave a country to come to a new one are complex; how migrants and refugees adjust to new countries, cities, and communities and what established people make of them are key questions that researchers interested in migration and government officials charged with the task of administration often ask. We might want to know what it is like to be a migrant or asylum seeker. What are the feelings and experiences of those who try to establish new lives in new contexts? Why do people migrate or seek asylum? Again, we can ask migrants or asylum seekers themselves a range of questions in a survey to gauge a response.

What is it like to be a migrant or asylum seeker?

a   Fantastic
b   Quite good
c   OK
d   Difficult
e   Horrible
f   Other...

Why did you decide to migrate, seek asylum?

a   War
b   Unemployment
c   Lack of opportunity
d   Family reasons
e   Better lifestyle
f   Other...

And a range of other questions. Now compare this with the testimony of telecommunications entrepreneur Tan Le whose family migrated to Australia from Vietnam in the late 1970s and who expresses with depth and richness what it is like to be a migrant, and why her family decided to migrate (again, the video can be accessed on the companion website).

Again, there is no comparison in terms of gaining specific personal and emotional insight into the experience of leaving one's home, between a few survey questions and the textual response such as Tan Le's. Yet for the impact and knowledge we gain from listening to stories such as Tan Le's, we can really only say from this testimony that these experiences are hers and hers only; we cannot say if all migrants or most migrants have the same experiences from this excerpt. Perhaps some do, but we cannot know for sure. And for many researchers it takes hundreds of interviews to establish that there is a common pattern that we can attribute to such an experience as migration; interviews such as this take immense amounts of time and money.

Again, like the case of an Olympian, we can intuit, empathize, if not perhaps perfectly understand what the experience of migration is like, even if we have never experienced such a phenomenon ourselves. But as much as we may learn from accounts such as this, personal accounts of what it is like to migrate are not the only questions researchers have concerning the phenomenon of migration or asylum seeking. Other important questions need answers, especially in our current times when migration and asylum seeking are global phenomena often involving millions of people and numerous societies, and not confined to mere individuals.

Through survey data we can gauge how well migrants settle in different societies through data on employment rates, educational experience, health, well-being, community networks, and other measures. And we can do it for thousands of people who have migrated. We can mark out the deficiencies in resource allocation or settlement processes, note the differences in the experiences of different migrants, gauge the opinions of a population about migration policies, and track the political mood for a whole nation or a group of nations around such complex human movements. With survey data we can connect the larger social, economic, and political patterns across a number of different aspects of the greater migration experience. This is precisely what is happening in Europe right now with the aid of surveys such as the European Social Survey. The data will assist the governments, researchers, policy analysts and publics to understand the complexities, challenges, and patterns of the collective migration experience. The diverse statistical data on different dimensions of complex topics such as migration, and many other issues besides, have the potential to contribute to an informed public debate, a rational political discourse, and a just decision-making process despite the ideological divisions associated with such issues. How else can contemporary societies deal with such complexities of governance than with an empirically sound set of observations that are derived from instruments such as surveys?

Vinyl records?

People are dedicated to material consumer objects, as we know, and as sociologists such as Ian Woodward (2007) and others have pointed out, the love of the tangible material object is still a very real phenomenon for many. Consider some material object you love – a mobile or cellular phone, a car, a dress, a book, a piece of furniture. You could easily express in words how you feel about this object, why it is special to you, and what about it specifically you love. This phenomenon has economic and commercial consequences, as many companies know and are realizing. Let's consider the materiality of music as another example of the contexts of survey data. Despite the rapid and profound changes in technology that have afforded astounding access capability to the world's historic corpus of music through such electronic formats as Spotify and Apple Music, vinyl records – yes those large cumbersome tyre-looking relics – are, in numbers of sales, rising rapidly and phoenix-like from the digitally induced ashes of technological change. For those that cannot conceive of the evolution, or perhaps should I say latter-day devolution, of musical recording technologies it looks something like Figure 1.2.

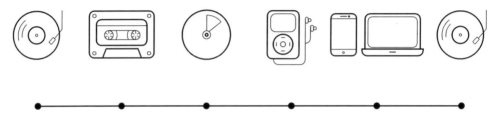

Figure 1.2 Evolution of music recording

(If you have not seen a vinyl record and don't know what a cassette tape is, Google it or ask an older family member.) According to the *Guardian* newspaper (Ellis-Petersen, 2017) sales of vinyl records in the UK in 2016 were up over 50% on the previous year. Over 3.2 million LPs (that is, 'Long Playing') had sold in 2016 in the UK, and over 4 million in 2017. LP records are now 10% of the UK music market. Data such as this have caused companies such as Sony to re-establish production factories for vinyl after 30 years of closure as consumer demand for vinyl records is set to increase further. Similarly, the Kindle and other compact electronic reading devices have not killed off books, as many in the publishing industry thought they would. Hard copies of books (such as this one!) are still around, and maintaining their share of the market.

For researchers and analysts interested in such consumer patterns large-scale data from surveys complementing other data are vital information leading to informed commercial decision making. We have statistics on the levels of sales and market share for vinyl records but how do we explain this revitalization of vinyl and for whom? We can learn from sales figures that the purchase of vinyl records and books is not confined simply to a few hipsters in places such as Hackney in London, Williamsburg in Brooklyn, or Kreuzberg in Berlin. For consumer patterns such as these, commerce and marketing researchers want to know a range of population-level details accompanying insight into how and why the resurgence and continued increase in sales of vinyl records have occurred and what sections of a population are purchasing them. What are the demographic and social backgrounds of people who buy vinyl records and are these changing? Why do people buy them? Conversely, what is the future of electronic or streamed music? What is its relationship to vinyl records and CDs

(Compact Discs)? How many units of vinyl should a company produce? How should they be marketed? ICM Unlimited asked these questions in a survey for the British music recording industry.

Beyond specific consumption practices survey research is a mainstay method of discerning household economic patterns, the data from which are crucial to economic policy. Government routinely relies on such survey data to discern consumption patterns for large populations, with a view to understanding a range of financial, economic, and cultural behaviours impacting on business and industry such as spending patterns, household budgets, and consumer confidence. Marketing and commerce research also rely heavily on surveys to gather data on general consumer behaviour, brand strength, and brand loyalty.

—————— The problem with Chardonnay ——————

The region where I live in Australia is a successful wine-grape-growing area. Many growers used to grow Chardonnay grapes for wine production. At one-point Chardonnay held around 40% of the total wine market sales in Australia and a lot of the variety was exported overseas. Almost overnight, however, sales of Chardonnay plummeted, causing chaos in some sections of the wine grape industry and a huge drop in revenue (wine is big business in Australia and internationally). The Foster's Group commissioned extensive research into the problem and their surveys revealed a variety of factors that accounted for the rapid decline of Chardonnay. While cheaper high-quality imports of white wine from places such as New Zealand accounted for some of the decline, the main reason Chardonnay fell out of favour was cultural according to the data. The cultural factor was a very popular television sitcom called *Kath and Kim*. Part of the comedic appeal of *Kath and Kim* was that they displayed decidedly bad taste. Chardonnay was a drink associated with the pair, who often mis-pronounced the variety as Car-don-ay. The association of Chardonnay with *Kath and Kim* was too much for many consumers who promptly stopped buying the variety!

Health

Ever been sick? No doubt you have. Your own experience of illness, no matter how serious, is your own experience of illness. As with the example of depression earlier, researchers and health professionals are certainly interested in the detailed descriptions people like you provide to gather data so as to offer relief or a cure for whatever has ailed you. The description you gave the doctor or other health professional hopefully allowed them to diagnose accurately – with the aid of physiological tests – what was wrong and prescribe a medication or course of therapy that assisted you back to health. So much for the individual, but what about the experience of illness across a whole society or even globally, especially pandemics? How do health authorities and health researchers, in part, learn about the spread and determinants of diseases through large groups or whole populations so as to inform the general public and plan health policy? The answer? Surveys. Nearly all countries and many regions have population health surveys measuring important aspects of health and illness across various social demographics.

Health and illness patterns are different around world. Different diseases affect people at different rates in different countries, although there are similar health and illness patterns in similar countries based on particular characteristics. Health and illness everywhere, however, are distributed through a population along the lines of different social attributes: illnesses are fundamentally socially determined, as well as genetically and biologically determined. In the societies of North America, Western and Northern Europe, and increasingly in the richer parts of Asia (Van de Poel et al., 2009) a leading cause of death is cardiovascular disease such as heart attack. This is often cited as a disease of affluence (Burkitt, 1980) because it is strongly associated with lifestyle choices afforded by wealth. Cardiovascular disease we have learned is essentially a cultural problem, related to poor diet, lack of exercise, sedentary lifestyles and work practices, as well as genetic factors. Compare this with diseases of deprivation and poverty such as malaria that affect many in poorer parts of the world.

Survey data inform us of the rates of exercise people undertake, the amounts and types of foods people eat, the levels of alcohol people consume, and the types of work people do. Combined with a series of other measures these data provide us with a powerful empirical tool informing the probability of a disease such as a heart attack occurring and hence how to arrest the potential of one eventuating. We see the results of such data in the many public health campaigns that various health authorities promote through television commercials, the internet, and other literature. Moreover, survey data can accurately inform us which sections of a population are most susceptible to which diseases, allowing health planners to attend to those groups especially. For example, being male or female, younger or older, wealthier or poorer, more or less educated, and living in one place or another can have radically different impacts on your health.

Politics

You may or may not purchase vinyl records, be a candidate for heart disease, or have won a gold medal at the Olympic Games, but you are without choice, subject to the influence of politics. Like it or not, even a cursory glance at the daily papers, internet, or television reveals a saturation of political content in most countries around the world these days. This is to some extent to our benefit of course, to know how our leaders lead and why they make the decisions they do; to have access to details of the issues affecting lives through the political machines that circumscribe them is important. Again, you can reflect on your own experience of politics: perhaps how you voted, and why in the last election you voted, if you voted. Which issues are relevant to you and why? Which leaders mean the most to you and why? These are questions the answers to which can predict elections when asked of a representative sample. They are important in politics because they relate crucial data about power and decision making for whole societies.

Most political activity, but especially elections, is of intense interest of course to a citizenry, to pundits, and to those at the coal face of formal politics such as political party members. Policy and political issue analysis and speculation are hotly debated and discussed dimensions of politics. Surveys are an integral part of the political process of most countries and most modern electoral races, usually in the form of polling, but also in larger extended questionnaires that aim to cover a range of possible factors that assist analysts to connect issues with voters to explain election results and election patterns over time. Surveys are well suited to political issues and electoral analysis given the mass nature of political representation and society-wide impact of policy. Surveys have been excellent research instruments for a variety of political analyses associated with electorates because they cover large populations and measure opinions.

Many surveys are used to try and predict political events such as the outcome of an election. They are mostly excellent predictive instruments, but they failed miserably and spectacularly on two very important occasions recently: the 2016 US Presidential election and the Referendum for the UK's withdrawal from the European Union or 'Brexit'. Virtually no one predicted that Donald Trump would become President of the United States. In the aftermath of President Trump's unlikely election win, the media, Clinton voters, and a score of other interested parties wanted to know how (aside from foreign interference). Who voted for him, who did not, and why? Making sense of elections is a great exercise for surveys because voting is distributed socially through a population and patterned by sets of opinions, experiences, and attributes related to demographic groups and experiences. Who voted for Mr Trump (or indeed any candidate in any election) and Brexit, and why, are questions for a population and not so much for an individual. While polling was not able to predict clearly Mr Trump's electoral victory or support for Brexit, surveys have been the best way to describe empirically which kinds of voters voted for him, such as white voters, male voters, rural voters, poor voters, or white, male, rural, poor voters vs non-white female, metropolitan, wealthy voters.

Migration, politics, commerce, public health, and athletic performance are all important topics that surveys significantly contribute to the understanding of at national and international levels, but surveys are also an excellent methodological tool for the data needs of smaller organizations and local communities. Smaller concerns such as local businesses, schools, sporting clubs, welfare and community service agencies, and local councils all have data needs to assist how they function and to meet the needs of clients and members. A range of specific and tailored information can be ascertained from local or communal settings such as these. People's strongest connections and everyday practical affairs are often within their own communities. Survey research often guides local authorities and expresses the wishes, desires, and attitudes of residents, clients, and members. Often these groups are not on the radar of researchers and often local authorities in community settings do not have the expertise to conduct the research needed to plan at the community level. Skills in survey design and data analysis can empower local community settings and provide relevant data to these organizations.

Table 1.1 Summary of survey contexts

For whom?	Types of questions	Types of data	What is measured	Data communicates	Conditions
Populations	Frequency of a behaviour, action, value, opinion, or attribute	Quantitative	Breadth of:	Patterns of:	Valid and reliable
Nations		Statistical	Attitudes	Frequency or prevalence	Representative
Communities		Numeric	Opinions	Relationships	Different cultural, social, political, and/or economic contexts
Client lists	Descriptive	Relational statistics	Attributes	Associations	
Specific groups	Explanatory	Qualitative	Values	Correlations	
Large groups	Relational		Behaviours	Strength	Representative sample
Small groups	Hypothetical		Experiences	Direction	
			States	Significance	
			Facts	Accuracy and error	
			Theoretical or abstract concepts		

Uses	Theory	Levels	Contexts	Purposes	Ethics
Prediction	Inductive: data first, theory second	Rates	Basic research	Theory building	Confidential
Evaluation		Rankings	Academic	Theory testing	Anonymous
Distribution and frequency	Deductive: theory first, data second	Levels of agreement	Governmental and policy based	Government policy	Secure
Gaps, issues, problems,		States		Industry and agency guidelines and practice	Voluntary
Decision making		High to low	Industry and agency based		Objective
		Strong to weak			Value neutral
Policy provision		More to less			Transparent
Comparative					Consultative

So, from the preceding discussion we can learn three things. (1) That surveys are specifically for researching groups, large or smaller (not too small, though); individual experiences are in there somewhere, be they as a consumer hunting shops for a new-found love of vinyl records, a voter in an election, or someone who has been sick.

However, an individual's own experience is like that of so many other people so that with survey research we can learn about how you and your experience relate to specific patterns in a larger population – in many ways individuals are not that unique actually, although groups differ. From there we can learn about patterns, causes, and influences to predict, inform, and act. (2) These experiences are related to the specific research needs of organizations, governments, businesses, academics, and community services. We know that surveys are subject to limits and appropriate contexts: that is, they measure certain things in certain ways and produce particular types of data to be used in specific ways to answer certain kinds of questions. (3) Surveys are used in loads and loads of settings but they are used as part of a research process within a scientific paradigm to test and/or build theories within a range of academic disciplines. Table 1.1 summarizes all of that.

Key knowledge and skills

This introductory chapter has introduced you to the contexts and uses of surveys. The key knowledge and skills presented in this chapter are as follows:

- Surveys are research instruments that collect mostly quantitative data relating to specific types of research questions.
- Survey data are intimately related and orientated to theory, through either inductive or deductive research.
- Survey research is usefully applied to a variety of important research settings and topics that contribute data to real-world problems.

Further reading

Most social research methods texts have brief but useful overviews of survey research contexts within a 'quantitative methods' section. A good discussion of the contexts of surveys and data for research can be found in Chapter 7 'Nature of Quantitative Research' of Bryman's *Social Research Methods*.

Full text reference:
Bryman, A. (2015) *Social Research Methods* (5th edn). Oxford: Oxford University Press

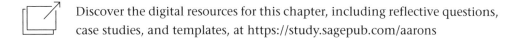 Discover the digital resources for this chapter, including reflective questions, case studies, and templates, at https://study.sagepub.com/aarons

Two

Types of Surveys: Components and Limitations

This chapter outlines the key components of the research and survey design process. The chapter covers:

- Types of surveys
- Components of survey design
- Limitations
- Total survey error

Components of a survey

So, we have the details of what surveys are used for, how they help research human problems and concerns, why this is important, and how it is great but limited. But how do researchers get from asking questions to making informed decisions with survey data? What are the components that make up a successful survey? This section heralds what will be covered in the remainder of the text and glimpses the iceberg under the surface of the water relating to what survey design entails.

Research is planned with contexts, purposes, and limitations in mind. When to use a survey, what type of survey is needed, how a survey is designed, and what questions it will answer are all part of what is known as the research process. This process is not particular to survey research – all methodologies are associated with it – but survey design has its own version. The research process is a bit like a blockbuster film with a cast and crew that play different roles. Surveys are best thought of as a supporting actor – they are not necessarily the glamorous lead, which is usually the findings or theoretical frameworks that explain the observations that the data report; however, they are indispensable to the story, much like Edward Norton is to *Fight Club*, even though most movie goers only seemed to have noticed Brad Pitt.

In broad terms then you start at the beginning. You need a topic; topics are broad areas of enquiry such as health and illness, education and poverty, or consumer confidence and business performance. Topics are then refined into research questions based on how the given topic has been researched previously. What do we know about it, how has it been studied, and what do we need to learn about it still? Crucial to this phase are theoretical and previous forms of empirical enquiry on the topic of interest. You map out your research journey with a research design (Figure 2.1). Then you need a methodology to collect the data to answer your questions (enter surveys) and enter the survey design process (Figure 2.2): we need to consider how to design, administer, and execute the survey, and who to ask to answer the survey's questions. Once the data have been collected they are analysed, the results reported, and a discussion and conclusion reached feeding back into the broader topic.

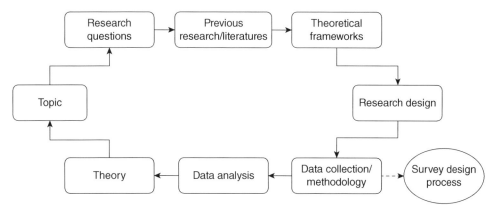

Figure 2.1   Research process

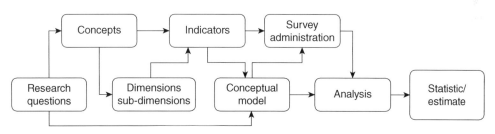

Figure 2.2   Survey design process

Types of surveys

While surveys of different types all have the same uses, capabilities, and limitations relating to research in general, they necessarily differ in their design to meet the specific research purposes of the projects that utilize them. One of the main distinctions between surveys impacting data is time. Research designs are set to consider problems in different contexts over time or as a once off. The majority of survey research projects are one-off events, a snapshot of a set of people and behaviours at one place in one point in time. We call these kinds of survey projects a '**cross-section**' or a 'case study'. They adequately serve the need of the researchers with a single effort, or a one-off study is all that can be achieved with the resources available.

In addition to a cross-sectional survey or case study, a number of survey research projects are **longitudinal**: that is, they are repeated over and over, until the needs of the project have been met or the research is completed, or, indeed, until the project's funding runs out! Longitudinal surveys are advantageous in a number of ways. Firstly, they afford the research a reliable means of comparison over time. Often researchers are interested in how things change, or remain the same for larger populations; longitudinal surveys allow this comparison by means of asking the same questions in each wave of the survey. Surveys can also be comparative, allowing researchers to assess opinion, values, and attributes across numerous different communities and publics. This comparative capability is another great advantage of survey research. Comparative surveys can also be longitudinal. Some examples of influential comparative longitudinal research include the European Social Survey, the World Values Survey, and the International Social Survey Programme.

Beyond their temporal differences survey designs differ depending on the types of data they are employed to collect. While surveys can be employed for a variety of study designs and to measure a vast array of interested and specific constructs, we can identify five broad types: (1) the social survey; (2) the poll; (3) an evaluation survey; (4) a census; and (5) a referendum or plebiscite (additionally a ballot used to elect an official could also be called a survey). They are all very similar in their general aims and function within the research process but have different specific aims which are bound to the contexts of the research, the resources (time, money, and expertise) afforded a researcher, and the needs of the project/situation. All of these types of survey, however, have similar aims: to collect mostly quantitative data, be social in nature, and collect data for large populations.

Social surveys

A social survey is usually a long-form survey (it can be either cross-sectional, comparative, and/or longitudinal), with an extended series of question modules on a variety of topics, designed to collect data on a number of attitudinal and attributive states and hypothesized relationships between variables. Social surveys are often 'general' in the sense that they include a range of social issues that are of public interest and of interest to a wide range of researchers. Some notable examples include the General Social Survey in the United States, the British Social Attitudes Survey in the UK, and the Japanese General Social Survey, but many countries have general social surveys. A feature of these surveys is that they can include and suspend topics as needed, and researchers can opt in and out of these surveys depending on their needs and what is important for a given society at a given time. For example, if an issue has risen in importance or awareness such as migration has for European countries, then these surveys can respond by including measures, and then as the issue subsides (in a public policy sense at least) leave them out, or include others that might capture other aspects of public opinion. Another great feature of these types of surveys, providing they are longitudinal (which most are), is that they can measure social change and assess causes for this change. Included in the notion of a social survey are surveys that are designed with more specific aims than a general social survey but whose measurement ambit is nevertheless quite comprehensive. Examples of such social surveys are election studies that aim to understand voting patterns and intentions, and population health surveys whose aims are to measure standards of health and illness, yet canvass a wide range of demographic features, work experiences, family life, income, location, and a host of others.

Polling

Even if we do not care much about politics, most of us are, I am sure, familiar with **polls**. Although they are used for a number of different purposes, they are frequently employed in assessing how an electorate thinks about political issues or political leaders, potential or incumbent. They are generally shorter in length (usually around 1–10 questions) and the questions are confined to a very focused agenda – a political issue of the day that is prominent or a scenario that gauges how people would react. Polling is often used to measure public perception towards the performance of a political party, leader, or minister or secretary. Polling is also used to gauge opinion about a contemporary issue that is in the news or has the attention of the public at a particular time – this is often related to the political climate such as immigration, health spending, taxation, same-sex marriage, gun control, or censorship of films. A poll's focus on one issue only is quick to complete and allows (if publicly available) researchers, journalists, and other interested parties to have a clear idea of what a population thinks and can communicate this in the news cycle while the issue is still of interest. Polls often collect various demographic data so as to allow the data on political issues to be possibly matched to specific segments in a community thereby revealing population patterns about issues. During an election campaign, as I am sure you have witnessed, or even been a part of, polls come thick and fast from numerous outlets as the debate about leadership and policy intensifies. You may be familiar with some of the larger polling companies that undertake such work, including Gallop, Neilsen, and Pew.

Evaluations

One especially important and practical task that surveys are employed for is **evaluations**. If you are a student, then you will be very familiar with evaluation surveys. They are deployed in many different contexts, however. Evaluation surveys, in combination with other forms of data collection, are mostly used to assess the effectiveness of a government policy, intervention, or programme related to some area of governmental, agency, institutional, or organizational activity. Most forms of social or client services, or government programmes, are required to be evidence based to justify scientific expenditure and/or improve, replicate, or replace whatever it is that they do. Evaluations will target the effects of the programme or service and assess whether it met its stated aims and improved some aspect of performance or state of being. Evaluative surveys may be one-offs but are often longitudinal (and at times can be within a short time frame of before and after an event) and comparative.

Census

A census is a survey that has ancient antecedents. The ancient Egyptians and Romans used censuses for taxation purposes. Most national governments conduct a census every 5 to 10 years for the purposes of tracking demographic, economic, and social change, and to assist planners and governments to allocate public resources accurately and efficiently. A **census** is a survey that is social but differs from a social survey in that it does not seek to measure attitudes, opinions, and values. Its focus is squarely on a series of attributes of a population that relate to a household and its members. A common list of measures on a census form includes profession, employment status, income, educational attainments, number of people in a dwelling, marital status, number of children in a household, type of dwelling, gender, and age. The attributes sought in the census do not include physiological features such as height, weight, and blood type. Another significant difference about a census compared with other forms of survey design is that it seeks to include every member of the population, within reason. This is achievable in countries like Australia or the Netherlands that have relatively small populations. In countries such as the United States that have over 300 million people, however, a census is far too costly and demanding. The United States Census Bureau therefore relies on a sample of the population effectively to collect such data for its long-form questionnaire (short-forms are sent to or accessed by every household). Many countries have been conducting them for over a century, giving researchers a tremendous source of national longitudinal demographic data.

Referendum/plebiscite

Finally, a very short but immensely consequential survey design is the referendum or plebiscite. Governments of various countries put referenda to their citizens to gauge what individuals want relating to a specific issue. It is a feature of many countries with a parliamentary democracy as the form of government. Referenda or plebiscites typically only ask one or two questions. There have been some very newsworthy referenda in recent times. Of these recent referenda, perhaps the most notable has been the question concerning continuing British membership of the European Union. The British public were asked one question: 'Should the United Kingdom remain a member of the European Union or leave the European Union?' The two response categories were: 'Remain a member of the European Union' or 'Leave the European Union'.

The difference between a referendum and a plebiscite is different in different countries. In some countries both plebiscites and referenda are used to change some aspect of that country's constitution; in others it is the means to change legislation only. In any case it is a survey usually of all eligible voters of a country on a single issue. Another recent referendum/plebiscite was the Australian marriage law postal survey vote on whether the law on marriage should be changed to allow Australian same-sex couples to marry. The Australian survey contained one question: 'Should the law be changed to allow same sex couples to marry?' The survey was run through the Australian Bureau of Statistics. While both surveys were short, direct, and profound in their consequences, the collected data launched fascinating debates in both countries because they could be matched with other forms of quantitative data such as census and social survey data related to geographic regions. Scholars, journalists, and analysts were able to discern what demographic, social, cultural, and economic factors might have been influential in determining patterns of preference around which sections of society voted which way on both issues.

Key components of survey design

Concepts, dimensions, and indicators

Surveys are constructed using a conceptual framework. Questions do not just appear from the aether and the process of survey construction is not random. The key function of a survey is to measure something through the questions it contains; this requires careful deliberation and planning. What a survey measures ultimately through a series of questions is a **concept** or construct. Concepts are the building blocks of theories and are embedded in research questions, such as what is the relationship between education and income? A concept, however, is often vague and incoherent, yet if I ask you what education and income are, you will have some idea because both concepts are familiar and you will have at least some experience of them. Both concepts are nevertheless quite complex, for example there are many forms of education and income. A key problem associated with concepts that survey design must contemplate is how to overcome vagueness and incoherence of concepts such as education and income, health, community, and others commonly measured. What exactly do we mean by these terms? This is crucial to survey design because if we have a loose or vague definition of these concepts then our data will not accurately measure the concept.

Complex concepts such as education have what are knowns as dimensions. A **dimension** of a concept is a form of it or classification within it that we can discern and has meaning. For example, in education we identify a number of dimensions such as primary or elementary education, secondary education, and tertiary or higher education. Further there exists technical or vocational education and so on. Identifying dimensions of concepts assists researchers to focus their research and then to design more accurate surveys that produce valid and reliable data.

From concepts and dimensions **indicators** are developed. Indicators are the actual questions in a survey that measure the concept in question. Indicators are many and varied and measure concepts in different ways depending on the needs of the research. For example, questions are employed that seek simply to measure if a respondent has an attribute such as being employed, for which a respondent may indicate 'yes' or 'no'. However, other indicators measuring a concept such as employment might want to know about the experience of a job and require more nuanced indicators such as how satisfied a respondent is with their job for which a greater range of responses are necessary to give a more accurate record of what the respondent feels. For example, a survey might offer a respondent a question on job experience that allows the respondent to answer between 'completely dissatisfied' and 'completely satisfied' and other meaningful points in between the two extremes. Indicators with various answer formats are scored and this provides the survey with the quantitative data to discover patterns during analysis. The simple 'are you employed?' question might be scored 1 for yes and 2 for no, yet the employment experience question might be scored 1 for completely dissatisfied through to 10 for completely satisfied. Another important consideration of indicators is question wording and phrasing. Some pitfalls can occur in how you ask a question which can confuse potential respondents. Indicators should aim to avoid ambiguity, confusion, and wordiness, or verbosity. In addition to question formats, the positioning and arrangement of sets of questions in a survey can affect the way in which respondents answer.

Concepts, dimensions, and indicators represent what is called operationalization. **Operationalization** is a process of defining and clarifying a concept precisely to the point of arriving at a question in a survey that aims to provide valid and reliable data. The process of operationalization is one of moving from the abstract (vague concept) to the precise (indicator).

Units of analysis

Surveys, as I have stated, are a social phenomenon, meaning they aim to assist understanding of a number of things about people. However, we can observe people and attempt to understand their behaviour in many different ways with the use of surveys. What researchers have to decide when designing research that involves a survey is at what level of analysis should the research aim? The research questions will demand a unit of analysis associated with this research aim. In other words, how should the data collected in our survey represent the people we are interested in? Or, at what level of human life do we count and analyse? We call this 'level of human life' the '**unit of analysis**'. Its distinctions carry important differences in how we pursue our research and what our findings will look like. Typically, most survey research aims to understand the characteristics, behaviours, and attitudes of individuals. For surveys such as the General Social Survey or the British Social Attitudes Survey the unit of analysis is the individual. When we begin to analyse the data we are comparing sets of individuals (with similar and different demographic characteristics) across different measures, or recording different levels and rates of a variable for individuals in aggregate.

Yet we may want to go beyond the individual depending on the aims of the research. Many researchers aim to collect data from a household, for example (such as a census or the other household surveys). In such studies a whole household completes the survey or is represented in it and researchers can make comparisons between whole households across different measures. Beyond the individual and the household, researchers use surveys to analyse comparisons on zip or postcode, cultural groups, religious identities, and nations depending on the questions that need to be answered. To enable these kinds of analyses, however, the survey instrument needs to include measures of them, therefore the researchers need to be mindful of the types of analyses they desire for the research based on the kinds of statistics they need.

Modes

Survey design is beset with not only philosophical and intellectual questions concerning its nature and the type of knowledge it assists in generating, but a series of practical questions and considerations also. Among its most important practical considerations is what mode the actual survey needs to take effectively to ask a sample of respondents a series of questions and gather the necessary data in order to do the research. In other words, how do you get the survey to the people you need to fill it out and how do you get them to fill it out accurately? This is far more complex than you might imagine and its fortunes wax and wane with the tides of technological change, people's attitudes towards being respondents, and a range of other obstacles. How respondents receive the questionnaire can produce varying results in terms of **response rate** and **data quality**. The mode of administration can also determine who actually receives it and who does not, which has consequences for how representative the data are, further impacting the research. Researchers use different means to administer a survey in the field; these means are subject to resources such as time, money, and labour. There are four modes of survey research that researchers typically use: face-to-face, telephone, mail-out and return, and more recently web-based surveys. These modes can be thought of as assisted (face-to-face and telephone) and self-completion modes (mail-out and return, and web-based).

The gold standard survey mode is the face-to-face interview, wherein a trained interviewer meets a respondent at an arranged time and place (usually the respondent's home) and conducts the survey there and then. A similar assisted mode is a telephone interview. This survey mode collects the data via a phone call with a respondent. The most common form of self-completion is the mail-out and return mode. This mode relies on a survey reaching a potential respondent by post. The respondent then fills out the survey which is usually in the form of a booklet by circling, marking, or crossing the answer categories; when complete the survey is returned to the researcher via return post. Increasingly researchers are using web-based self-completion survey modes that can be completed on a variety of web-capable devices such as a PC, mobile or cellular phone, and tablet via email, social media, website, or app.

Each mode has advantages and limitations in terms of effectively reaching potential respondents. Many larger academic, industry, and government surveys are experimenting with multi-mode survey administration to try and ensure better coverage of potential respondents.

Sampling

One of the truly excellent features of survey research is that a survey's findings can be **representative**: that is, the results collected from a survey can be confidently used to infer something of fact for the greater population from which the sample was taken. There is a very important proviso associated with this truly excellent feature, however, and that is all to do with who you ask to fill out your survey. Researchers who are interested in a larger dispersed population such as a nation, a city, or a diaspora of people with certain attributes of interest – and not, say, members of an organization like a company or a client database – invariably do not have the resources to ask the whole population, so they rely on a sample of the population from which they can generalize to the broader population and make confident scientific statements of **inference** and generalizability.

Representative sampling makes a census of a population unnecessary to some extent, so researchers often do not need everyone relevant to the research participating in it. Sampling is a complex practice and takes many forms, but it can be usefully distinguished along two broad lines: probabilistic and non-probabilistic (or what is also called 'random' and 'non-random' sampling). Probabilistic sampling, as the name implies, relates to the mathematical laws of probability. Non-probabilistic sampling does not. In a population of interest, the researcher needs a way of allowing each member of the population to have an equal chance – or probability – of being chosen in the sample. For non-probabilistic samples it is a matter of simply finding anyone to answer your questions, as those research workers who stand on street corners and in shopping centres do, or when a company or organization asks you to fill out a survey that pops up on a webpage you might be browsing.

Ethics

Any research on humans conducted by university, government, or community-based researchers is usually required to satisfy the demands of an ethics committee. Ethical standards in research exist to attempt to ensure that the research is conducted in an environment that is voluntary, non-exploitative, non-harmful, and informed. In survey research, the risks of harm are usually not high, but there can be questions that are asked about sensitive issues, that are invasive, and that can illicit answers that may be perceived as socially unacceptable, making respondents feel uncomfortable. A key ethical concern for survey design is that the data respondents provide are confidential and anonymous; indeed, personal details beyond a range of demographic measures are not necessary in most cases.

Beyond these immediate ethical concerns associated with respondents there are more philosophically and politically based ethical issues that survey researchers need to be aware of. Data are often given to researchers through surveys for free (some research projects do offer very small financial or material incentives) and projects run through government or a university are often publicly funded, so there is an argument to say that the data should be publicly available to all, as well as details on how data were collected and what they will be used for made fully transparent. Surveys administered through the internet are a revolutionary advance for survey design; however, what is currently emerging is the darker side of the phenomenal reach of analytic techniques that can glean data from various personal networks throughout the internet without permission and used to manipulate the flow of public information. This has a range of pernicious consequences, given the sheer number of people who are connected to social media, as recent commentary alleges on certain national elections. Survey research must take these issues into account now and into the future. As stated at the beginning of the chapter, we are in an age of mass societies, rapid change, and blistering technological reach.

──────────────── YOUR SURVEY ────────────────

Checking ethics requirements

This text encourages readers to develop their own survey in the YOUR SURVEY sections throughout. Different institutions have different ethical requirements for research on people, so please check the requirements for your institution before proceeding.

Limitations

The final section of this introduction to the world of survey design is about limits. I do not use the term 'disadvantage' because any research method is really about context and a disadvantage suggests to me, at least, that there is a disconnect between methodology and aim. Limitation conveys a better sense of what can and cannot be achieved. As we have seen earlier in this chapter, surveys carry certain types of questions that collect particular kinds of data used to answer specific research questions. All research methodologies have advantages and limitations. One of the more important aspects of the research process is the selection of a research method based on the needs of the research, not the ideology of the researcher. As we have seen and will learn more about, surveys are appropriate for certain types of research questions and within particular types of research frameworks. Limitations associated with survey research are of different kinds. Critics of survey research have outlined philosophical, technical, and political limitations and problems with the methodology. While there are certainly limits to what researchers can achieve with surveys, many of these criticisms have already been dealt with comprehensively. De Vaus (2014) and Marsh (1982) in particular address a range of critical limitations concerning the survey method and how they can and have been overcome.

Data type and reliability

A key limitation of surveys was introduced in the previous chapter concerning the type of data that surveys collect: principally quantitative. Of course, these kinds of data are as much an advantage as a limitation, depending on the context or the empirical need. For depth and richness of experience or meaning and deeper appreciation of a context or narrative around human behaviour, quantitative survey data are not particularly well suited. Statistics confer in a unique language stories about rates, levels, strengths, weaknesses, highs, lows, averages, and rankings; they have specific parameters around which limits to what we can learn and know are quite strongly drawn. Essentially what a survey is aiming to achieve through measurement is a series of estimates, that is descriptions or summaries of situations through statistics.

Another limitation is that the data collected are self-reported: that is, survey research projects rely on data that are the opinions of the people who complete the surveys. You are free to state what you want on a survey. Think about that for a moment. Huge studies such as the World Values Survey entailing a sample of nearly 100,000 people could be based on utter lies. That respondents mess with survey design in this way certainly happens. Consider the Jedi phenomenon in the 2001 UK Census (Singler, 2014). When asked about what religion you belong to, nearly 400,000 people recorded 'Jedi' or 'Jedi-Knight' after the fictional religious tradition in the *Star Wars* stories. Census responders in other countries around the world followed suit, and while it is easy to see the funny side, this posed some serious issues for the statistical agencies in the affected countries, to the point that future respondents were threatened with fines and imprisonment for such offences! This has obvious consequences for the quality of data and how representative data can be.

Relatedly, we also know that many behaviours that might be deemed socially unacceptable are under-reported by respondents in surveys. For example, how many people would own up to watching pornography online, or engaging in illicit drug use, claim to have cheated on a partner, or indicate that they have committed an offence? This is understandable; it is not in our nature to open up to strangers about sensitive topics, let alone some researchers from the Department of Deviance or the University of Snoopford. These are subjects that are certainly of interest to scholars with legitimate research interests but it is hard at times to get accurate estimates of these behaviours through surveys. Similarly, we have the scourge of missing data. **Missing data**, depending on the scale, can present significant problems for the research. It is essentially a sampling issue in that if we only have a section of the sample completing the questions, that part of the survey is unrepresentative and the generalizations are then limited. Beyond these limitations which are to a large extent beyond the control of the researcher, there are the more formal limitations that any budding survey designer must come to terms with that impact a project at many different levels.

Total survey error

Limitations such as those above are complemented by a series of complications associated with survey research known as 'error'. Errors relate to all phases of the survey design process and have consequences for data quality and for the inferential capacities of the data collected. Survey design is a complex engagement entailing numerous steps in a process to collect data enabling research of high quality and reliability. Commensurate with each step is the distinct possibility – some would say inevitability – of various kinds of errors. In a research article from the 1940s, W. Edwards Deming cited no less than 13 main forms of error (with a number of subclasses of error) associated with survey design affecting what he termed 'the usefulness of surveys' (Deming, 1944: 359). Survey methodologists are still grappling with many of the 13 forms of errors, and others that have been identified since.

Errors associated with survey research, as Weisburg states, are not mistakes as such but relate to 'differences between obtained values, and the true value for the larger population of interest' (2005: 18). This is a crucial point because as Weisburg further adds 'the ultimate intention [of survey research] is to infer population values from the sample results' (ibid.). Errors therefore are different from mistakes, in that they are not necessarily the result of carelessness but more of a naturally occurring event due to a range of factors that can be beyond the control of the researcher. Survey errors can then be thought of as a series of mismatches resulting in inaccuracies between intended and actual outcomes in measurement, responses, administration, and sampling. Part of the science of survey design methodology is ascertaining ways of properly identifying and reducing various kinds of errors.

Errors are so common throughout the survey design process that a formal framework for identifying and minimizing them has developed under the name 'total survey error'. We will use this framework throughout the text to identify and suggest ways of minimizing errors at each stage of survey design. Given that survey research seems to be plagued by errors, you may be wondering at this point if it is all worth it. It is, and despite errors we still learn an immense amount about people and can use this knowledge to be informed and to improve things, only our knowledge is not entirely perfect. Figure 2.3, taken from Groves and Lyberg (2010), pinpoints the main kinds of error associated with each stage in survey design by demarcating two strands of the survey design process: measurement and representation (which pertains to sampling). For the most part we will focus on the measurement side of error as this is most relevant to survey design.

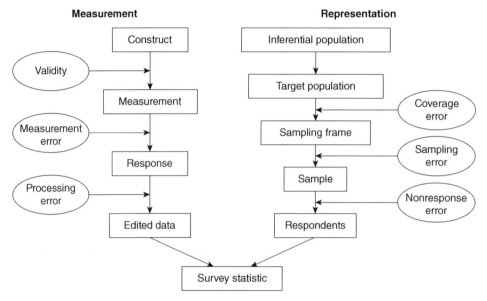

Figure 2.3 Types of error associated with the survey research process

Source: Groves and Lyberg (2010)

—————————————————— YOUR SURVEY ——————————————————

Planning a survey research project

A feature of this text will be this section towards the end of each chapter that encourages you to consider and apply the material in each chapter to your own survey design. The aim here is to apply the various components of the survey design process so you may be able to design your own survey.

Beginning a survey research project requires discussion and planning of a range of preliminary steps associated with the research process and the survey design process.

The first aspect of a project you should plan is what kind of project will you embark upon. There are many interesting projects that you can do associated with a class or course, an industry, business, or service, or special interest group. These projects can be hypothetical, or if your class has ethical clearance and a willing partner such as a business, service, or special interest group then why not embark on a real survey design project? I would recommend that community organizations be local and relatively small so a project is manageable. Firstly, decide on the options from the list below:

- Design a survey for a student-based class project (with permissions, why not engage students across your institution for a larger sample?).
- Design a general social survey for a large population (hypothetical).
- Design a survey for a special interest group (such as a community group, a leisure/sports club, a religious organization, or a gallery).
- Design a survey for a small business or service (for example, a community health clinic, a local welfare service, a co-op, or a small business), other group or community of interest to you, preferably a smaller local group so the project is manageable.
- Design a survey as an individual or a team. I think a team of at least two members is preferable given the work involved.

In thinking about a survey research project as an individual or as a team, consider the following, broadly noting that many of these considerations will be dealt with specifically in the following chapters so you can refine appropriately:

Research process:

- What topic am I or are we interested in? What is needed to be known that a survey can assist with for a business, service, group, or students that you are designing the survey for? This will require some consultation with your potential respondents, certainly if you are designing a survey for a local organization. Approach a group for whom you think a survey would be useful and discuss with them.
- How do I/we refine a topic and what might be some more specific research questions based on the topic? From a general topic you can begin to consider some key specific research questions. You can refine this to be more precise after future chapters.
- What literature exists on this topic? Begin broadly and refine the literature later. What theories relevant to your topic can you identify in your discipline? What other survey research has been done on your topic, related to your field or interdisciplinary work? Begin to compile a relevant body of topic literature.
- Should we use a survey for this research? Yes, but is our topic and are our research questions suitable for a survey? What kinds of research questions are suited to surveys?

Survey Design Process considerations (preliminary discussions here):

- Purpose, context, and measurement? What is your survey aiming to measure? Which concepts? What estimates or statistics does your research need? This will be based on your questions which you can refine in a later chapter.
- Theory? Does your survey aim to test a theory? Is the research deductive, or is it inductive?
- Sample? Who might the sample of interest be? Who is relevant to the research? How many potential respondents will you seek to survey? If working with an organization, service, or business, discuss this with them. If your sample is a student/faculty population, how many student/faculty respondents will you need?
- Mode? How would the survey be administered most effectively? What is available to you as students or beginning survey designers? Do you have access to adequate

(Continued)

printing, postage, and/or web-based survey design programs such as Qualtrics and Survey Monkey?

- Constraints? What practical constraints do you think you would encounter? Consider time. Also cost. The survey project should not incur any personal expense but perhaps some small costs for your institution, perhaps some printing, but if for a small organization or group a web-based survey might be adequate. Most universities and colleges have survey design software such as Qualtrics or Survey Monkey.
- Ethics? How might you assure an ethics committee that your project would cause no harm and that the data would be anonymous and confidential?

Key knowledge and skills

This chapter has built on the material introduced to you in the previous chapter through a presentation of the key components and types of surveys researchers use. The key knowledge and skills presented in the chapter are as follows:

- Survey design is a component within the broader scope of the research process.
- Survey design involves a process of planning and executing a survey entailing numerous sequential steps I have called the 'survey design process'.
- These sequential steps are made up of various components of survey planning and administration.
- Survey design is subject to various limits, constraints, and ethical concerns.

Further reading

Most texts on social research methods in general and survey research provide overview chapters that introduce surveys and survey research. Two texts I have found especially useful for situating surveys in social research are:

Chapter 1 'The Nature of Surveys' from de Vaus' *Surveys in Social Research* is a brief but very clear summary of the uses of surveys for social research.

For an excellent discussion of the most appropriate use and a defence of surveys in social research, Cathie Marsh's *The Survey Method* is also well worth consulting.

It is also advantageous to consult a range of detailed reference works in survey methodology. These texts provide useful and concise overviews of the various components of survey design and survey research; some also include a brief history of the development of survey research.

Good titles include *The SAGE Handbook of Survey Methodology* and *The International Handbook of Survey Methodology*.

Full text references:

De Leeuw, E., Hox, J., and Dillman, D. (2008) *International Handbook of Survey Methodology.* New York: Taylor & Francis

De Vaus, D. A. (2014) *Surveys in Social Research* (6th edn). St Leonards: Allen & Unwin

Marsh, C. (1982) *The Survey Method: The Contribution of Surveys to Sociological Explanation.* London: Allen & Unwin

Wolf, C., Joye, D., Smith, T., and Fu, Y.-c. (2016) *The SAGE Handbook of Survey Methodology.* London: Sage

 Discover the digital resources for this chapter, including reflective questions, case studies, and templates, at https://study.sagepub.com/aarons

Three

Survey Design and the Research Process

Survey design is embedded within the research process. As a result, survey design must reflect the key contexts and drivers of the overreaching research if the data it collects are going to be useful. This chapter will cover the following key areas:

- How survey research is subject to the research process
- Refining broad topics into research questions
- The role of theoretical frameworks in survey research
- Types of research questions most appropriate for surveys
- The logic of relationships between quantitative variables from survey data
- How previous literature informs survey research
- The role of research design in survey research

So, where do you start when embarking upon some research using a survey? Many research projects begin with hunches, gut feelings, and intuitions, as well as less mystical forms of thought. No matter where an idea for a research project comes from, all research in the behavioural or social sciences proceeds formally through what is known as *the research process* (Figure 3.1). This is a multi-staged series of steps that guides our thinking and contextualizes how to progress the research we want to undertake. Survey design has its own tributary research process that is connected to the general one which I have called the *survey design process* (Figure 3.2). In this chapter then we will consider, in depth, the research process relevant to survey design. I want to do this partially with the aid of a personal example. My example may well resonate with you if you are starting out in research, having to design a survey without having done so before, or you just want to understand how survey design and research are conducted from start to finish. My example relates the experiences of my honours-year thesis project in sociology for which I used a survey, and from which my supervisor and I worked up a couple of respectable publications. The example is instructive also in the sense that if this whole business of survey design appears daunting, then if the likes of me can plan, design, and execute a successful survey research project, then there should be nothing stopping you!

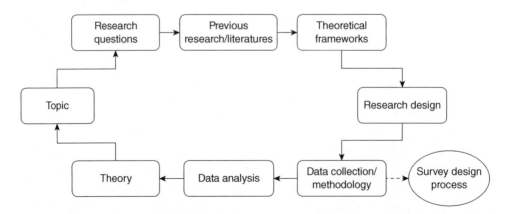

Figure 3.1　The research process

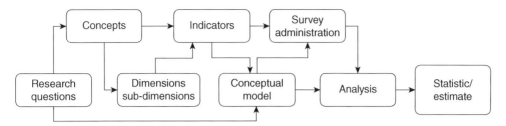

Figure 3.2 The survey design process

Let's take a closer look at the research process in a way that is relevant to survey design. Survey research is constrained and limited by a series of factors and conditions as we saw in the last chapter, but its initial derivation can be inspired from different points and perspectives within a field of enquiry. We do not need to concern ourselves too much with the latter stages, such as data analysis and discussion, for the present, as these stages of research come after survey design. What is important for our immediate purposes, given the emphasis on the 'front end' of survey research, are the first six steps: topic, previous research, theoretical framework, questions, design, and data collection. These six key stages of the research process guide the research primarily through a process of clarification, refinement, and structure, then on to how to answer questions so as to allow the researchers to focus on what they really want to find out and ensure that the project is ultimately doable. Further, getting these stages right will assist you greatly when it really counts – the collection of valid and reliable data.

Topic or focus area

A topic is a broad area of enquiry that is in need of refinement and focus; it stands before the researcher much like a block of stone does the sculptor before the creation of a work of art. Some topics are easier to refine than others. At other times, however, you may not know what you want or need to research. Let me share with you my own example of having to do this as an honours student in sociology some years back. After I signed up for an honours year, I had to formulate a research project for a thesis component of about 15,000 words. I had little idea of what I would do for my thesis when I enrolled. My supervisor/advisor said, 'Ask yourself: What are you interested in?' My answer was, 'Ummm, something to do with religion and society, maybe.' 'OK fine, what about it? Which religions? Which societies? What aspects of religion: belief, practice, history, philosophy? What aspects of society: the economy, education, health, the family, employment, politics, sport?' 'Ahh, s**t, I'm not really sure' was my exact answer. So I began the process of refinement by thinking through the topic as he suggested. What did I have at this point that might assist me in a topic? I had interests: I was interested in religion in western societies, such as my own, where religious beliefs and religious identities were changing – this much I knew from my previous reading in sociology. I was also interested in religions from non-western societies in general, and in the sense that they were becoming more and more noticeable in my own society as Australia became increasingly ethnically and culturally diverse. I also knew that many people in the west were not specifically irreligious, but what the sociologist of religion, Wade Roof (1999), called 'seekers', meaning they are interested in alternatives and seeking other forms of religious experience, for whatever reason.

Ah! A light came on for me and the first (metaphoric) chips of stone started to fly off the block. Westerners interested in 'non-western' religions? So I got reading. Actors such as Richard Gere and his Hollywood ilk who were known for their interest in religions such as Buddhism were a starting point; needless to say I moved on from there quite quickly. I sent actress Uma Thurman's dad, Robert (a Professor of Indo-Tibetan Buddhist studies at Columbia University), a vague email about Buddhism in the west, to which he returned a nice short reply. The Dalai Lama (whom I also wrote to, but never got a reply!) and others were like rock stars whenever they toured the world. Religions like Buddhism and forms and techniques from Hinduism such as yoga seemed to be increasingly popular and were even in the news. There were feature articles written in the big weekend papers about 'eastern' religions (for which I did an interview once!), as well as lots of groups that had sprung up teaching Buddhist philosophy and meditation for seekers in the west. Also seminars, workshops, an ever-burgeoning internet presence, even feature films directed by Martin Scorsese no less (check out *Kundun*). OK: Buddhism, westerners, and western interest in Buddhism. Here then was my topic – the bold outline of my sculpture had taken shape.

Most research does not start from this far back, and most researchers will not be as clueless as me before starting. Even as an undergraduate, and definitely as a graduate or postgraduate student, you will be reading about topics within a discipline and get a sense of their components, perspectives, and frameworks enough to formulate topical interests. The same is true for those of you who are practitioners who work in and know a professional field about which you may need to design survey research. Yet when it comes to doing your own research project you will still need to be thinking about refinement.

Previous research

It is almost guaranteed that whatever topic you think of has been written on before, perhaps not in the exact same way as you might eventually write about it, or precisely the same topic as you are interested in, but be confident that there is something out there that will inform your project at this stage and assist in the refinement of your topic. So, what had been written before about Buddhism? There should be a wealth of literature from which to draw on to assess what is happening in a field such as that. There wasn't, not for me, zilch pretty much. Bits and pieces, here and there, lots of books on Buddhism itself, but not much about Buddhism from a sociological perspective that directly related to my topic, nothing on Buddhism and westerners as a sociological phenomenon, though quite a lot on personal reflections of western converts, some comparative religious studies, and quite a bit in the self-help section of a number of bookshops, and quite a number of journalistic accounts too.

Yet there were of course numerous works on related topics, certainly 'eastern' religions, the 'New Age', western religious change, religious identities, and the like, that all contributed to how I might contextualize my study theoretically and methodologically, and what themes might be important in explaining any patterns that I might have found. And there were empirical studies in the sociology of religion that assisted in thinking about the methodological aspects of my study – measuring concepts such as religious practice and belief, and measuring attributes of the self, such as identity. I therefore did have plenty of literature to go on, even if it was not directly related to my topic – which in hindsight was actually good news, because it meant that I had struck upon something perhaps new and original, while being able to draw on established and relevant theoretical and methodological platforms.

Types of previous research

There are three important aspects to previous research, I contend, that have relevance to survey design: perspective, theory, and method. Whatever your topic there will be a range of different methodological and theoretical approaches to it that previous research demonstrates or illustrates. For some projects, perspectives are relatively easy to identify and fall under the type of discipline expertise that the researcher has. In others, perspectives have to be thought out more carefully. For example, I have taught students in health sciences who are interested in some social or cultural aspect of health, but social science and cultural studies are not their area of expertise. How a research project progresses is dependent on what perspective is used to frame the research, including how survey methods contribute to it. This will also have a profound effect on survey design later on in the survey design process.

Some literature will be purely theoretical, other literature will be mostly empirical, and others still a good balance of the two, and all of it should be within a perspective in your field of study or interest. It is important, and rewarding, that you read all kinds, even those that are not strictly survey research related. You should also make a clear distinction between scholarly literature and more popular literature. I certainly read some popular literature around western interest and experience of Buddhism, but only to get a feel for this as a social phenomenon I was interested in, not as a means of studying it to measure it. The popular literature such as personal accounts, some journalism, and fiction, can be great reading, but they are written for different purposes than scholarship and social science.

How is this relevant to survey design? Through your reading you may find that the majority of research on your topic has a particular emphasis or been written from a particular theoretical or methodological perspective, leaving wide-open spaces for you to explore with survey design. In my own project there was a lot of qualitative and theoretical sociological work about westerners who had identified with different forms of religion and spirituality (nothing on Buddhism specifically) – that is, a number of studies that drew on textual interview data to describe meanings and deeper social contexts, but really nothing in the form of how many people, what levels of engagement, and which forms of religion and spirituality. I could make an assessment then of the work, how it was done, what its focus was, and how it could be used to assist my own, and how my own could complement the extant work in the field.

Previous research, once you have waded through it, will inform you about the gaps in knowledge about a topic or pique your interest in **replication**. It will also provide insight into how research is interpreted and what theoretical perspective the research is couched in, leading to possibilities for replication or to test the theory. Findings from survey data are not simply neutral, they often reflect a theoretical perspective that is inherent in the design of the survey.

──────────── Theory and perspective in survey research ────────────

In my field of sociology, the famous French sociologist Pierre Bourdieu's great work *La Distinction: Critique Sociale du Judgement* (*Distinction: A Social Critique of the Judgement of Taste* in English, but of course like most things it sounds far better in French!) was evidenced by a survey that asked respondents about their cultural tastes and practices such as tastes in music, film, art, and sport. However, Bourdieu had a very clearly defined theoretical platform in mind when he designed the survey. He was interested in the role of cultural consumption in the class composition and class relationships characterizing French society of the latter twentieth century and theorized a specific mechanism through which cultural consumption operated, meaning that tastes in music for example were not theorized to be simply neutral individual choices but part of a broader, complex social and economic process. Theoretically he positioned the research within a conflict and interactionist perspective, and thus the survey aimed to measure the theorized class differences. This perspective was evident in the types of questions and response categories his survey employed.

Theoretical framework

Any survey research project in any field will need to be associated with and incorporate the theoretical perspectives of that field. Theories are crucial to the research process and to survey research in two ways. Firstly they give us a range of explanations for why things happen and how they happen, such as why there are differences in income, health, or consumer patterns, and what causes them. Secondly, they are tested, can be revised, and/or are built by the data the survey collects.

In this sense they help justify and frame research that seeks to answer descriptive and relational or explanatory research questions. If we hypothesise about a relationship between two variables in a survey, we are suggesting via a theoretical basis that the relationship is plausible: that is, it can be imagined or thought to be true. It is often the role of theory to assist us in interpreting and structuring relational questions and correlations as plausible because of the way theory logically outlines how events occur and why they occur. So, theories frame our analyses, and provide context and explanation for any relationships we see in our data. We want to avoid at all costs what is known as bland empiricism. Indeed, quantitative research has gained a bad reputation in some quarters due to the reporting of statistics that just hang in the air, not meaning anything or taken out of context. What does a 10.5% increase, or a difference of 16.3%, mean if not couched in some form of explanatory context such as a theory?

Theories and plausibility

Theories can be tested with survey data, or they can be built with survey data, but any relationship that is examined and suggests some form of relationship using survey data must make sense and be plausible. To get a feel for this point, check out the website http://tylervigen.com/spurious-correlations for a bunch of absurd relationships that a guy named Tyler Vigen has created. Despite the many correlations Vigen has found in the data he analyses, none of the relationships are plausible; that is, there is no theory that can remotely explain some of the relationships he poses. In the language of quantitative research, it means 'correlation does not imply causation'! There are lots of relationships that can be spurious – that is, relationships that appear to be correlated or causal but bare no relation to reality; in effect they are unrelated despite being so statistically. Dependent variables, such as why people die

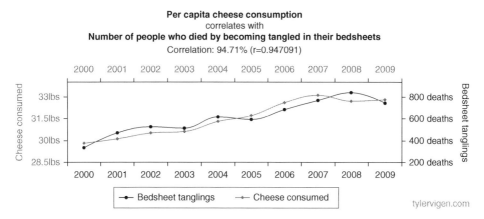

Figure 3.3 Spurious relationship between cheese consumption and dying from bedsheets

by becoming tangled in their bedsheets, can be explained by a number of independent factors, or they are purely correlated coincidently with random variables such as rates of cheese consumption as indicated in Figure 3.3. Theories also guide how a survey should be constructed because they mostly contain plausible sets of concepts or constructs about a topic that represent relationships in the data.

For my project, there were a range of theories within the sociological perspective that were available to explain the situation I was interested in, or frame how my research might proceed. Certainly, there was the work done by Paul Heelas and others (1998) who considered religious change through ideas about the transition of society and culture from modernity to post-modernity. I considered Wade Roof's theories (1999) about religious traditions as consumer items that in the west had been uprooted from a particular form of social and economic organization through something called 'late' or 'post-modernity' and were up for sale like any other consumer item. I was also drawn to ideas about western societies such as their particular forms of change described as late, post-, and neo-modernity and how they were also connected to more fractious identities and increases in individualism described as a set of what Zigmund Bauman calls 'fluid identities' (2000) which I thought sounded kind of interesting and relevant. There were also the theories of Max Weber, the great German sociologist, whose work on the sociology of religion and rationalization (see Gerth and Mills, 1958) discussed how, as rationality, science, predictability, and modernity advanced, we became more and more disenchanted with life – as magic and mystery were emptied out of the world (as religious belief was replaced by science and rational processes) we became more and more dull, basically. This idea in particular got me thinking pretty seriously! So, I had a range of theories to frame my study, and to think about how to attempt to explain why westerners were becoming interested in religions such as Buddhism from a sociological perspective.

Research questions

From there the research needs to be refined further into a manageable form with specific foci that reflect its position within the literature and your discipline's perspective. From the broad topic and a literature search you carve out a space for your own work that is different yet related to previous work, or indeed a replication of previous work in a different setting or context. Here you need to work out the actual questions that your research will attempt to answer. Research questions can take a number of different forms generally. In research using survey design, however, we tend to focus on two or three kinds: descriptive questions, relational or explanatory questions, and hypotheses (predictions). These kinds of questions are asked with estimates or statistics in mind.

Descriptive and relational/explanatory questions

Descriptive questions are just that – enquiries that seek descriptions of the state of play concerning a particular issue or phenomenon, for which we desire an **estimate** or **statistic**. For example, if we are interested in the broader topics of wealth and inequality, we may want to know what the income levels are within a given population. Who or what proportion of a population are high-, middle-, or low-income earners, and has this changed for better or for worse over a defined period of time? For example:

What proportion of Canadians are high-, middle-, and low-income earners?

Also common to survey research projects are relational questions that seek to assess the influence of one or more 'factors' on a particular state, position, or phenomenon. Sticking with wealth as our example, we may wish to refine this interest and build on the descriptive findings with a set of questions exploring why it is that some people earn more income than others, for a population or sample of individuals or households. What accounts for the various levels of income distributed throughout a society such as Canada's that our descriptive question sought an answer to? Now, there may be many different factors that produce variation in the level of income that people report, such as type of job they do, how many hours a week they work, and the type of qualifications they possess, and these may well be distributed through demographic factors such as age, gender, and geography. When we ask these types of questions we are stating clearly that we are interested in sets of relationships, relationships that we can measure with survey questions, and then empirically examine with survey data. Often these types of questions are exploratory in nature and are posed like this:

Do the hours worked, type of job, and level of education influence/effect income levels for Canadians?

Further, these questions are often refined into what we call specificities that reflect more nuanced or *specific* investigations concerning the particular demographic groups or attributive factors we mentioned above and that may be of interest to the researchers:

Do the hours worked, type of job, and educational levels influence/effect income levels for younger Canadian males and females in rural and metropolitan areas?

So, here we have added some more context to our original question and we can pursue a range of specificities to delve deeper and deeper ('drilling down' as it is known) into more and more specific areas of investigation to explore whether specific sites of human experience, social background, and identity have meaning. This allows us to carry out more sophisticated analyses and to be more precise in identifying and determining patterns. These questions are different from the types of questions qualitative research projects ask. For example, qualitative researchers may be interested in the same topic and have refined it into similar conceptual areas such as income, but the questions driving a project for which qualitative data would be more suitable might read something more like this:

> *What is the experience and meaning of job type and hours worked for younger male and female, low-income earners in rural Canada?*

So, the emphasis or focus is not necessarily on what has caused or produced this particular situation or pattern, but what the lived experience of it looks and feels like related through text from methods such as rich description, interview, and image. In many instances qualitative work based on questions such as this nicely complements any survey-derived quantitative patterns to produce mixed methods research or triangulation – this qualitative complementation is colloquially called 'putting meat on the bones'.

Hypotheses (predictions)

In addition to posing relational or explanatory questions, researchers can also pursue hypotheses. Hypotheses are questions that are in the form of predictive statements. There is essentially no difference in how the research will proceed, but hypotheses are more formally wedded to and seek to test specific theories, or aspects of specific theories within a given field. Hypotheses are often written thus:

> *H1: Income levels for Canadians will vary as a result of different job types, hours worked, and levels of education attained.*

Or:

> *H1: The more prestigious a job held, the longer the number of hours worked, and the higher the level of educational attainment, the greater the level of personal income earned will be for Canadians.*
>
> *H2: Income levels for Canadians will also vary as a result of age and gender differences, such that if you are younger and if you are male, the greater your income will be.*
>
> *H3: Income levels for Canadians will further vary as a result of living and working in either a rural or metropolitan area, such that the further away from a large metropolitan centre one lives, the lower their wage will be.*

What hypotheses relate also, you may have noticed, is a strong sense of proportion and direction. They are characterized by sets of levels or rates – commensurate with quantitative survey data – that then produce or influence different levels or rates in whatever they are used to explain, such as levels of income in our example. This type of question is firmly and unambiguously set within a quantitative framework. Consider also how these types of questions meet the criteria for survey research set out in the previous chapter of requiring quantitative data to answer them, are social in nature (that is, they aim at a group with particular attributes), and are for a population rather than an individual.

Irrespective of how the questions are asked, theories will help produce them, or will help explain the descriptions the data give about them. Again, it will be useful to consider the direction of the research with regard to theory and data: deductive or inductive. Also, irrespective of the question type, we are aiming for an estimate, a statistic, and/or research objective that our survey instrument is designed to produce, only that statistic or estimate needs clarification or specification.

In terms of my project, I was interested in basic information in the first instance, given the previous literature did not have much. I could ask some descriptive questions about western Buddhists or westerners interested in Buddhism that could be based on the sociological theories of interest. How many of these western Buddhists were there? I mean, so much for the popular noise in the media and Hollywood, but what about the patterns in everyday life in ordinary communities? Were these people (whoever they were) just Buddhist, or were they Buddhist and something else, were they shopping and seeking, or were they more settled in their Buddhism? Had they formally converted to Buddhism? Who were they? Which people seemed to be attracted to Buddhism in the west? Younger or older, male or female, educated, middle class, previously religious, or atheist? How did they practise Buddhism? How often did they practise Buddhism? What did they believe and how strongly did they believe it? I had a series of these kinds of descriptive questions for which I figured a survey would be an appropriate methodology of data collection to provide some of the key empirical contours of the phenomenon, which to that point did not exist. I also was not necessarily interested in the meanings and deeper experiences of the engagement people in the west had with Buddhism, so I did not need to pursue a bunch of interviews that would give me qualitative data about the experience of Buddhism (as interesting as that may have been).

I could also begin to think about relational or explanatory questions, such as was involvement in Buddhism attributed to certain aspects of life experience and social background? Was involvement in Buddhism related to specific aspects of western identity and forms of social change in western societies? Following Max Weber's theories, was involvement in Buddhism related to a form of social or cultural disenchantment or something like it? From there I was able to refine the topic into a series of research questions that would allow me to design and construct a survey that sought to collect enough data to answer these questions.

Refining topics into research questions

Our research questions can be any one of the three presented above. The three types of questions are also related. We can ask a number of descriptive questions about topics as well as relational/explanatory-type questions within the one project.

What are descriptive-type questions?

Here I want to present a guide for thinking about the different types of questions that your survey research project should consider as part of the planning stage before you launch a survey into the field. Let's look at some descriptive-type research questions in more detail than the ones I posed above. Again, whatever questions we ask in survey research we are interested in the survey producing an estimate or statistic relevant to our research interests. Descriptive-type questions are not necessarily interested in gathering data to assess or determine relationships between factors that suggest association, correlation, or cause. Descriptive questions allow us to get a basic idea of the lay of the land in terms of the empirical contours of a phenomenon, a benchmark estimate, or statistic for example. This is especially important if the topic you are interested in is relatively new or understudied – as mine was. In survey research that collects quantitative data we are interested in describing a situation empirically, without, at this stage, necessarily wanting to know what produces or causes it. Our survey questions will generate such data quite easily, but we have to plan for it. So, what kinds of questions should we ask to get descriptive-type data?

Extent-type questions:

- How often does something occur?
- How many or what proportion of something?
- What level of something?
- What rate of something?

Distribution-type questions:

- Who/what is affected/effected?
- Who/what is relevant?
- Who/what is meaningful?

Phenomenon-type questions:

- What do people do?
- What does it entail?
- How is it done?

In research question terms we can ask such questions to assess the empirical range and shape of a phenomenon. If we were to conduct a survey on the topic of gaming for a sample population for instance, we could ask the following descriptive questions:

Extent: What is the extent of gaming in (a population)? Of the people who play video games, how often do they play? Are gamers long-time gamers (say many years) or short-time (only a few years or less)?

Distribution: Who plays video games in a population? Do more males than females play video games? Are gamers mostly younger or older? Are gamers more likely to be urban rather than rural? Are gamers more likely to be wealthy than poor?

Qualities: Which genre of video games do most people play? How do people play video games – alone or with others? Do gamers use different consoles or just one?

In my study of Buddhists, I asked questions like these to ascertain empirical patterns and get a sense of how Buddhism for a sample of people in a modern western context looked and was experienced:

Extent: How many people in a population identify as a Buddhist? How often do Buddhists meditate? How often do Buddhists read sacred texts? How long have those who identify as Buddhist been Buddhist? What proportion of Buddhists have undertaken a pilgrimage or have been ordained?

Distribution: Who is a Buddhist? Are more females than males Buddhist? Are Buddhists older or younger? Are Buddhists more or less educated? Are Buddhists more or less economically advantaged?

Qualities: What kind of Buddhism do westerners favour? How do people practise Buddhism in western contexts?

And so on. A number of survey research projects are interested in these types of questions, at one point in time, or over the course of a number of years, and in a variety of contexts. You can pose these questions for a range of topics or themes such as those I discussed in the previous chapter: health, consumer habits, politics, athletic performance, and migration, for example.

Relational or explanatory questions

In addition to wanting to know about the descriptive aspects of a research problem, survey design will also be deeply concerned with what causes, affects, or influences the descriptive patterns we plan to find in our data. We are interested in explaining particular patterns with reference to theories through either theory testing or theory construction. Here I identify three key kinds of relational or explanatory questions:

Why:

- Why does something occur?
- Why do people with particular attributes have particular experiences?

Predictive/hypothetical:

- This will/could occur.

- As a result of this attribute, this experience will also occur.
- People who are like this will experience that.

Causal/(e)affective/associative/correlative:

- Does this attribute cause that experience?
- Is this attribute associated or correlated with that experience?
- What is the effect/affect of this attribute on that experience?

Why: Why do women generally earn less than men? Why do people who live in rural areas on average experience poorer health than those who live in urban areas?

Predictive/hypothetical: On average, men will earn more than women regardless of industry worked in. People who live in rural areas will, on average, experience poorer health than those who live in urban areas.

Cause/association/correlation: Is the income gap between men and women mostly caused by child-bearing and primary care of children? Is poor health correlated with living in a rural area? What is the effect of living in a rural area on one's health?

Again, in my project I was interested in what influenced people to become Buddhists, or to be associated with a Buddhist group. I was also interested in what factors led to some people being more dedicated to Buddhism than others, and whether having a western background was at all correlated with a higher interest in and practice of Buddhism. As my study was more exploratory, I did not structure my questions as hypotheses, but I did have associative and correlative questions:

Why: Why are westerners interested in becoming Buddhist? Why are westerners who are interested in Buddhism interested in particular forms of Buddhism, such as Tibetan Buddhism?

Cause/association/correlation: Is western interest in Buddhism correlated with dissatisfaction with western identity? Is western interest in Buddhism correlated with particular social background identities such as gender, level of education, occupation, and social class? Is the type of Buddhist practice and the level of Buddhist practice patterned by particular social background identities such as gender, level of education, occupation, and social class?

Summarizing topics and research questions for survey design

OK, let's take stock. Summarizing thus far, we select a topic, then refine that topic into a series of manageable research questions. From the broad topic we refine to the more precise dimensions of that topic and proffer research questions of interest that survey data can help us answer. This process is assisted ably by a review of the literature and a building of our knowledge to focus our research on identifying research gaps or to lead us into attempting to replicate previous research in different contexts. Our topics

and questions are forged also within a scholarly discipline and perspective and therefore set to test or frame the research within a particular theoretical framework in that
discipline (Table 3.1).

At this point in the research process we turn to research design – that is, how we are
going to collect the data that will answer our questions, which for our purposes means
how are we going to construct a survey, who for, when, and where?

Table 3.1 Summary of topic and research question, western Buddhist example

Topic	Research questions for survey design	Discipline	Perspective
Westerners involved in eastern religions	Descriptive: • Extent • Distribution • Quality	Sociology Psychology	Weberian New Age
Refined		**Sub-discipline or area**	**Theory**
Australians involved in Buddhism	Relational/explanatory: • Why • Predictive/hypothetical • Causal/associative/ correlational	Sociology of religion Psychology of religion	Disenchantment Spiritual supermarket

Research design

The questions you pursue in your research determine the type of method or form of
data collection you use to answer them. The questions lead the dance, so to speak.
This is crucial because it safeguards the researcher against confusion and ambiguity,
as well as ideology. Recall at this point the various advantages and purposes of survey
research. Your research questions, styled like those above, will fit nicely with the pur-
ported advantages that survey research has. It is not a case of better or worse, but more
or less appropriate when it comes to methods and data type. Who you ask, how you
ask them, how often you ask them, and how you plan to analyse the data that you
have collected are crucial concerns that relate to what we call research design.

Research design, as an element of the research process, can entail a range of different components within a limited or more expansive notion of how to proceed.
Some survey methodologists such as de Vaus consider research design to be a focus on
what he terms 'the structure of the data' (2014: 30) by which he means specific relationships between concepts in particular contexts that allow for specific types of data
analysis, while others maintain that research design is more comprehensive, entailing such elements as survey design, sampling, and mode of administration. In this
chapter I follow de Vaus and others such as Salkind (2010) and will focus on the more
concentrated notion of research design that structures the data. The other aspects that
are included in more expansive versions of research design I consider in later chapters.

Let's consider the more specific notion of research design that centres on how analysis might proceed. This step is concerned with how you will go about structuring your study and answering your questions. Principally, for our purposes, you will propose to answer your questions with a survey – no brainer. Research design is important, in much the same way the research process is, because it suggests a particular logic and orientation to how we progress our project. Research design is also fundamental to research projects in all academic fields and professional practices that require research on human behaviour and populations. Its coverage is almost commensurate with the extensiveness of the applications of survey design, so whichever academic discipline or professional industry you are in that uses a survey, the various research designs discussed below will be relevant to your needs.

The logic of research design: Cause, association, correlation, and direction

Essentially what we are trying to do in survey research is to arrive at an estimate or statistic through an assessment of the impact of one variable on another, or many variables on many other variables. We ask what is happening, and how it happens to be that way, with the aid of some or many influencing factors that we have theorized or hypothesized will have some influence. Following our research questions, we look to see how a variable such as attitude, opinion, value, or attribute is distributed throughout a population, and then what accounts for that distribution, through the data the survey collects. So, with my Buddhists for example I was interested in finding out how the practice of Buddhism measured through a variable such as how often one meditated was then influenced, caused by, associated, or correlated with a range of social background factors such as age, gender, social class, or education. In other words, Buddhists practise Buddhism through meditation, and Buddhists meditate a lot, sometimes, and not very often. Males mediated more than females, the more educated meditated more than the less educated, older Buddhists more than younger Buddhists, and so on. Survey research proceeds thus and when it does it enacts the relational logic of cause and effect.

This notion of cause or relationship (association or correlation) in survey data is indicated by the relationship between an **independent variable** and a **dependent variable**. Some particular state, attitude, opinion, or attribute that we measure in a survey we therefore test or consider to be influencing or affecting another. So, one variable (the independent variable X) influences another variable (the dependent variable Y). What we are really aiming for is how we might explain the types of variation we witness in a behaviour, attitude, experience, or feeling that we measure and observe with survey questions and survey data that are reflective of real life.

Consider going out and having a few drinks and how things such as your mood change with each drink you consume (up to a point). With each drink you either feel happier, chattier, and more sociable, or, conversely, become moody, argumentative, and cantankerous. Your mood is the dependent variable caused, associated, or correlated with such a thing as the number of drinks you consume. A more orthodox example was presented earlier. For example, we know that many people earn different incomes, but why do they earn different incomes? What causes or explains the variation in income levels? The variation in income can be explained by a range of causal factors such as the type of job, the level of education, and hours worked, among other explanations. These are all plausible theoretical or previously empirically proven possibilities that might explain differences in income levels.

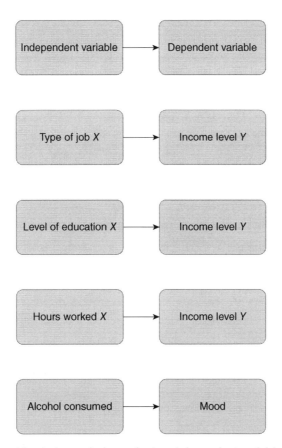

Figure 3.4 Relationships between independent and dependent variables

Figure 3.4 graphically represents this essential relationship between the independent and the dependent variable. In our models here we are theorizing and stating that income levels will be influenced by the type of job, the level of education, and the number of hours worked. In quantitative analyses that use data from surveys we mostly aim to witness what is called covariation – that is, as the independent variable changes (increases or decreases) so too does the dependent variable. What we are in fact stating here with the aid of survey design is that human behaviour and various attributes are dynamic – they rise and fall as a result of different influences – and these influences or causes assist with mapping the reality of differences between people, as a result of the multitude of factors that impact on them and produce specific patterns of action.

The relationships between independent and dependent variables are at the heart of the various types of research design using surveys, some simply stated, others more elaborate and complex. Research designs reflect what researchers want to know and in which contexts they want to know, but consistent to them is the relationship between independent and dependent variables.

There are four key types of research design I will cover here that are common to survey research: experimental/evaluation, cross-sectional, case study, and longitudinal; some have further variations such as quasi-experimental. In the previous chapter I made a point about appropriate methodological techniques, that is data collection methods, and types of questions. I made the point because there has been some discussion and wider reflection on social science perspectives about the uses of quantitative and qualitative research that tend to assume that particular perspectives use particular methodologies. This can all get tediously myopic at times, with quantitative researchers claiming that they can measure anything and everything with surveys and qualitative researchers completely dismissing any claims to knowledge that quantitative methods can bring to a problem. Indeed, one review in response to an article I had submitted to a journal using my western Buddhist data stated emphatically (that is, in bold type) that the article should be rejected outright on the basis of the research method alone. Ouch! Was it something I said? No (not sure the reviewer had read that far), only the way I wanted to say it.

A similar inflexible pattern is at times associated with research design. For our purposes, experimental, cross-sectional, case study and longitudinal design can all be performed with the use of surveys. You may well read or hear stated occasionally that case studies must always be performed with qualitative methods, experiments with laboratory observations, and cross-sectional and longitudinal studies strictly performed with surveys. A vast range of research methods can be employed to conduct any of the research designs discussed here. What might differentiate a survey-based experiment, cross-section, case study, or longitudinal research design from the others? You guessed it: the types of questions asked, the nature of the group(s) specified for study, the context (social, about humans and not animals), and the concern with attitudes, opinions, attributes, and behaviour that can be measured with a survey.

Experimental design/evaluation

Experimental design and evaluation is a form of research design that compares two or more groups at two points in time on a dependent variable or dependent variables before and after some form(s) of 'intervention' or 'treatment'. The two groups involved are called the 'experimental group' and the 'control group'. The experimental group is given, treated with, or exposed to an intervention and the control group is not. Both groups are pre-tested; then the researchers 'upload', inject, expose, or somehow or other convince ingestion of the intervention to the experimental group only, and then post-test both groups. If the intervention has 'worked' there should be variation of some sort regarding the dependent variable between the experimental group(s) and the control group. From reading this description it should be obvious that surveys can be adequate and appropriate data collection tools for such a research design. Indeed they are, but of course, as stated, it depends on the context of the study and the nature of the questions we want to answer.

Let's consider a couple of examples that use surveys in a classic experimental design or evaluation. A few conditions, however, must be considered first when using surveys in experimental designs. The experiment must, again, concern people and not animals, it will have two or more groups, and it should aim to measure, among other things, a dependent variable using a survey, such as attitudes, opinions, values, behaviour, or attributes.

A range of disciplines that take on a social science perspective such as social work, economics, education, public health, and psychology all make effective use of surveys to conduct experimental designs and evaluations. Surveys incorporated into this form of research design are often highly effective means of conducting evaluation research also, given the direct and practical nature of policies, programmes, and campaigns. What might an experimental design using a survey from a social science perspective look like (Table 3.2)?

Table 3.2 Experimental design template

Group A (experimental)	Intervention	Group B (control)
Time 1		Time 1
Intervention applied		Intervention not applied
Time 2	Change? Variation? Increase or decrease?	Time 2

Social work is a discipline that often seeks through its academic and practical efforts to produce and study interventions through experimental design to improve conditions of personal and communal disadvantage and/or disparity. Such experimental designs are common in studies of youth empowerment programmes (YEPs) for example (Morton and Montgomery, 2013) wherein experimental and control groups of young people are pre-tested before and post-tested after the adoption and completion of a YEP (Table 3.3). Many YEPs aim to increase self-efficacy and self-esteem in young people through various forms of intervention such as workshops and other activities. Survey research is a key methodology used in the experimental designs concerning YEPs and evaluation of such programmes to collect data concerning the dependent variables self-esteem and self-efficacy. These concepts are measured through valid and reliable scaled survey questions developed over time. The surveys designed and employed in an experimental design produce the data that indicate whether self-esteem and self-efficacy have changed or remained the same post-intervention for the experimental group. The data collected at different time points, pre- and post-intervention application, allow the researchers to assess whether or not the interventions or treatments such as YEPs have any effects on the young people studied. Experiments also have an evaluative quality in that an intervention such as a YEP can be assessed or evaluated as successful or unsuccessful (Figure 3.5). In a policy framework this lends evidence to the effectiveness of the intervention or programme.

Table 3.3 Experimental research design example: self-esteem and self-efficacy

Group A (experimental)	Intervention YEP	Group B (control)
Time 1 pre-test	Measure of dependent variable(s): levels of self-esteem, self-efficacy	Time 1 pre-test
Intervention applied		Intervention not applied
Time 2 post-test	Change, variation, increase or decrease in dependent variable(s): self-esteem and self-efficacy evidenced by survey data	Time 2 post-test

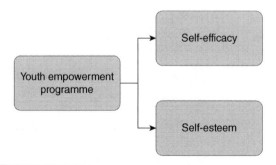

Figure 3.5 Relationship between youth empowerment programmes and self-esteem and self-efficacy

In economics, household surveys are vital forms of data collection that measure and track household expenditure over time for a variety of socio-economic groups. In many ways, according to economists such as Angus Deaton, household surveys are an excellent means of assessing the impact of an 'intervention' (1997) such as a change in economic policy. How does a change in policy, or a tax on a good such as grain, impact household purchasing power, nutrition, health, and poverty levels in developing, transitioning, or low-income countries if it is introduced in one region or country and not in another, for example? For Deaton, these surveys are not necessarily 'experiments' in the classical sense[1] but these situations have all the hallmarks of experimental design nonetheless and adhere strongly to an evaluative logic. Surveys are perhaps the best empirical source of learning about the effects of economic change for large populations which are impacted, sometimes severely, by changes in economic policy.

Evaluating or modelling such change is a key aspect of economic and social policy practice. The advantage of surveys such as these is the coverage of a range of important measures for large groups of people. This coverage allows researchers and policy specialists in a range of fields to gather empirical evidence to make the best estimates of how institutional impacts such as policy change affect great numbers within a population. It is not just in developing or low-income countries that these surveys are of value to researchers interested in evaluating policy, as many wealthier countries have established long-running household surveys enabling the same kind of analysis and empirical feedback to government. Aside from the example highlighting a research design (Table 3.4), there is also, on reflection, an ethical dimension concerning empowerment in experiments such as this. Survey design, through measuring the effects of policies (Figure 3.6), can enable the establishment of data-driven problems and produce evidence leading to change.

Table 3.4 Experiment research design example: policy change and health, nutrition, purchasing power, and poverty

Group A (experimental)	'Intervention' Policy change, tax	Group B (control)
Time 1 pre-test	Measure of dependent variables: purchasing power, health, nutrition, and poverty	Time 1 pre-test
Intervention applied		Intervention not applied
Time 2 post-test	Change, variation, increase, or decrease in dependent variable(s): purchasing power, health, nutrition, and poverty evidenced by survey data	Time 2 post-test

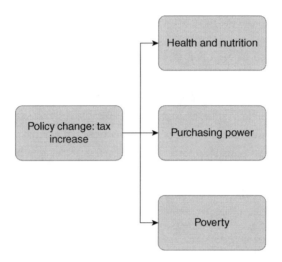

Figure 3.6 Relationship between policy change and health and nutrition, purchasing power, and poverty

Cross-sectional design

A cross-sectional design is a research design that is a one-off study into a phenomenon that considers comparisons between groups on dependent variables of interest. There are a few fundamental differences between a cross-sectional research design and the experimental design that we have just considered. The main difference is there is no intervention or treatment to impose on a group and assess effects, therefore cross-sectional research design does not seek to pre- and post-test across different time frames. It differs from an experimental design also in the sense that the researcher does not control an intervention or the experimental and control groups, but relies on groups that exist in the population of interest and what differences these groups display through attributes and other aspects of identity. The logic of relational effects between independent and dependent variables and covariance is still a feature of a cross-sectional design, however. The nature of such logic in cross-sectional research design seeks to measure extant variation between groups on dependent variables and not assess the contrast between groups as a result of some imposed condition such as an intervention.

A number of survey research projects use cross-sectional research design to capture data at a point in time about a phenomenon that may be of interest to academic questions, or current public or policy debate at the time of the study. Natural constraints such as money, people, and time may compel researchers to pursue a cross-sectional research design rather than, say, a longitudinal project, otherwise a one-off study may well simply satisfy the needs of the researchers. Cross-sectional studies can be repeated, however, giving them a longitudinal scope, yet with a new sample each time. According to authors such as de Vaus (2014), this has some consequences for the nature and assuredness of causality when highlighting change.

Many of the large survey projects such as the Afrobarometer, the General Social Survey, and the European Social Survey, mentioned in the first chapter, are excellent examples of cross-sectional research designs. These studies are also longitudinal, or repeated every few years, but use different samples each time.

Table 3.5 highlights the key causal/correlative relationship associated with cross-sectional research design using surveys. The model is designed to reveal variation and difference between the different categories of attributes on the values, opinions, and attitudes that the survey questions measure. These are mostly presented as percentages.

Table 3.5 Cross-sectional template

Extant groups/values, attitudes, opinions, behaviours	Attribute 1 (%)	Attribute 2 (%)	Attribute 3 (%)
Value 1			
Value 2			
Value 3			

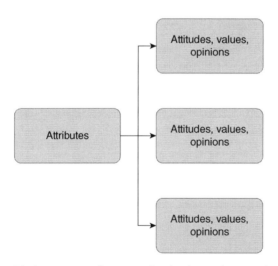

Figure 3.7 Relationship between attributes and attitudes, values, and opinions

Let's look at a couple of examples to highlight surveys using cross-sectional research design to illustrate how the logic of relational/causal explanation is used in cross-sectional surveys to address issues and answer questions. In the Afrobarometer surveys, respondents from a variety of African nations are asked a number of questions about attitudes regarding social, economic, and political issues. The Afrobarometer, like many other large cross-sectional surveys, allows easy access to the data sets through its online analysis functions, so you can follow along with the example and undertake your own analysis (the website is listed on the companion website). Taking Figure 3.7 as the model of how the research logic proceeds, we can see from Table 3.6, called a **cross-tabulation**, that we are able to assess the attitudes towards satisfaction with democracy for a selection of different countries. Cross-sectional design here seeks to assess the differences of opinions towards an issue based on the group differences. In this instance the different groups or the independent variables are nationalities and the dependent variable is satisfaction towards democracy (Figure 3.8). We read across the columns to discover that variation in the attitudes is produced or caused by national differences.

Table 3.6 Cross-sectional example: nationalities and satisfaction with democracy

Category	Total (%)	Country (%)							
		Benin	Côte d' Ivoire	Kenya	Malawi	Mali	Uganda	Zambia	Zimbabwe
The country is not a democracy	2.2	0.1	1.3	1.1	0.7	0.8	1.7	1.1	10.8
Not at all satisfied	19.7	17.0	18.1	11.7	31.8	32.7	14.5	16.1	18.5
Not very satisfied	28.0	30.6	34.4	21.8	27.0	28.6	29.4	31.4	23.2
Fairly satisfied	32.3	36.2	29.9	43.5	26.0	26.4	35.8	31.9	24.6
Very satisfied	12.5	14.3	10.7	12.3	10.9	10.5	10.8	16.8	13.8
Don't know	5.3	1.7	5.6	9.5	3.6	1.1	7.8	2.6	9.1
(N)	9,957 (100%)	1,199 (100%)	1,191 (100%)	1,597 (100%)	1,199 (100%)	1,200 (100%)	1,197 (100%)	1,192 (100%)	1,182 (100%)

Afrobarometer R7 2016/2018 (Benin, Côte d'Ivoire, Kenya, Malawi, Mali, Uganda, Zambia, Zimbabwe) Correlation r = −0.026

Source: Afrobarometer

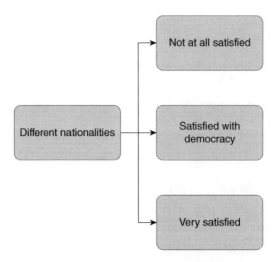

Figure 3.8 Relationship between nationality and satisfaction with democracy

Cross-sectional surveys such as the General Social Survey in the United States (another large-scale survey project that has an excellent online analysis tool) conduct repeated surveys to assess the relationship between independent variables and dependent variables over time. This allows us to chart the differences between extant groups on various attitudes, opinions, and values, and to do so across a number of different points in time. Consider the next chart in Figure 3.9 with reference to our model above. We can see that again (Figure 3.10) there is a structure of enquiry that seeks to account for variation and difference between groups on an attitude or a value that the independent variable – 'level of education' – is associated with, correlated with, causes difference, or produces variation on the dependent variable – 'racial differences due to inborn disability (those who answered "No")'. The same pattern of enquiry is repeated at different time points and the data reveal a pattern of increase or decrease in the dependent variable for the different groups, and for the different groups over time.

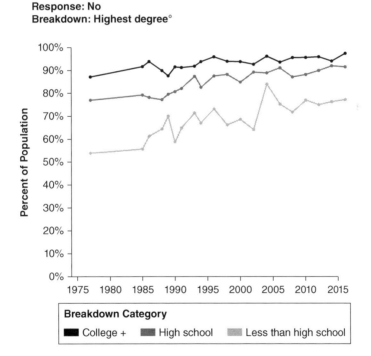

Figure 3.9   Relationship between education and racial differences, 1975–2015

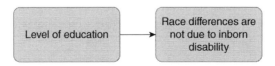

Figure 3.10   Relationship between level of education and attitudes towards racial differences

Longitudinal design

Longitudinal research design is, as the term implies, a research design that sees the research carried out over time in preference to a once-off approach. A range of events and changes can take place over time that longitudinal research design studies aim to measure and explain. Longitudinal research designs can be used for experiments and cross-sectional studies also. As we have seen, experiments and cross-sectional studies can be repeated numerous times to gauge change across different time points. In terms of survey research, a key difference between a longitudinal research design and a cross-sectional research design is the sample. For a survey project with a longitudinal design, the sample should ideally be a panel of respondents that take part in the study each time it is run; that is, the same respondents in each wave of the study, compared with a new sample of respondents each time as happens in cross-sectional design. Panels can be made up of cohorts, groups within the sample who are different ages, or an entire panel of people the same age. Think of the long-running *7 Up* television series in the UK that began in the 1960s to assess the impact of social class on upbringing (at the time of writing, the documentary makers were up to *63 Up*). Every seven years interviews were conducted with panel members, namely the same participants who were a part of the study from the beginning, and a new documentary was made.

With a panel sample as part of a longitudinal research design using a survey, the research can follow or track a series of individuals and groups across their life course or important sections of it, and according to some commentators this enables a more scientifically valid set of causal relationships and patterns because it deals with the same people each time (Bryman, 2015). Following a panel and/or a cohort within a survey allows the researcher also to probe deeper and reflect more personally on the specifics of the group or individual cases within the group over important phases of the study. For example, the specifics of schooling for a group of young people over the course of their school years, or the working and home life of a group that entails specific types of change.

There exist a wonderful range of longitudinal survey projects that use panels and cohorts, which you can investigate. Longitudinal panel and cohort studies tend to be favoured for particular topics such as socio-economic issues for households, specific age or year cohorts, and people or groups with specific qualities or attributes. Survey research on twins, for example, is a fascinating area of study internationally for which longitudinal panels are appropriate. Some examples of longitudinal household surveys are the Household Income and Labour Dynamics in Australia (HILDA), Understanding Society (UK (incorporating The British Household Panel Survey)), US Panel Study of Income Dynamics, and the German Socio-Economic Panel. These surveys track – among other things – a range of patterns concerning family expenditure, participation in the labour market, and the impacts on family life due to social and economic change. A recent example of a cohort survey project is the UK's Millennium Cohort Study which was launched in the year 2000 to measure continuously and assess child development for those born at the turn of the Millennium. Other cohort studies include surveys on youth and people through their life course. A census that seeks to take the whole population as the sample, as is done in smaller countries such as Australia, could also be seen as a panel study, since the whole population participates with each round of the census. Many countries, however, settle for a cross-sectional design with the census drawing on a different sample for each census.

Longitudinal research design employing surveys uses the same kind of relational or causal logic between independent and dependent variables to assess difference between groups and also change over time between groups and within groups (Table 3.7).

Table 3.7 Longitudinal template

		Cohort/wave 1			Cohort/wave 2			Cohort/wave 3		
Cohort, panel, groups	Values, opinions, behaviours	Group 1 (%)	Group 2 (%)	Group 3 (%)	Group 1 (%)	Group 2 (%)	Group 3 (%)	Group 1 (%)	Group 2 (%)	Group 3 (%)
Value										
Opinion										
Behaviour/experience										

Figure 3.11 is an example of a longitudinal pattern of change in childhood poverty rates from the Household Income and Labour Dynamics in Australia Survey. You can clearly make out the relationship between family types (single-parent and couple-parent) as a panel of cohorts or groups and the dependent variable of childhood poverty between 2001 and 2017 (Wilkins et al., 2019).

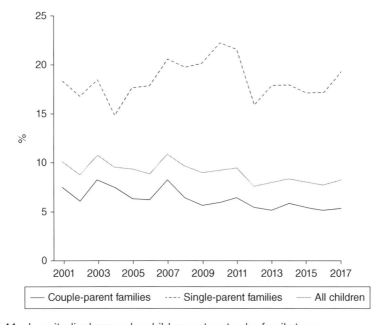

Figure 3.11 Longitudinal example: child poverty rates by family type

Source: HILDA Report 2019

Case study

Case studies are research designs that typically have a narrower focus on a specific activity, situation, individual, or group. For the purposes of survey design wherein we collect and analyse quantitative data, they are mostly confined to groups, which can be small, but not too small. A key question about case studies is of course: what is a case? The definition of a case is a useful criterion against which we can differentiate this form of research design from the others. De Vaus (2001: 220) provides a useful outline of the varieties of cases as units of analysis. In addition to studying an individual

> we can select many other types.... A marriage, a family, or a household may serve as a case. *Places* such as a block of houses, a residential community, a region or a country can all serve as cases; as can *organisations* such as a business, a school, a government department or a union. (emphases in the original)

In the social sciences, case studies are synonymous with disciplines such as psychology and anthropology, wherein an individual, group of individuals, or a smaller group/community is the focus. These types of studies can be conducted with quantitative data but are mostly reliant on qualitative data due to the nature of the questions to be answered. A number of the types of cases de Vaus identifies are appropriate for survey research because they are groups, about whom we can ask questions relevant to the collection of quantitative data. Indeed, some groups are quite large, such as a nation.

My study of western Buddhists can be classified as a case study. They were a group of around 400 people associated with a Buddhist centre at the time I was conducting my research. What also differentiates case study design using a survey from other research designs is that there is a trade-off between an in-depth empirical examination of a group and the extensive data that you may receive and any inference and generalizability to the broader population. So sampling is a key issue in case study designs. The Buddhists that took part in my study are not representative of the wider population of Buddhists, because my sample did not include Buddhists from a wider range, only those who belonged to the group. The same holds for organizations, schools, or other groups that are the subject of a case study design.

The nature of the case study as a focused research project will to some extent structure the types of research questions asked. Descriptive questions and relational or explanatory questions will certainly be part of a survey used in a case study, but they will only be pertinent to the group, and may not have wider relevance. For example, the Buddhist group that my study centred on practised a particular kind of Buddhism, so some items on the survey I used are only valid and relevant measures to that group. It would be the same if you were to survey members of a specific organization that provides a unique or specialized service or product. Case studies using survey research also have the problem of access to a group (so too do the other research designs, arguably). As a study design that is more or less focused on a specific or specialized group, you may need to negotiate access to the group and work with them throughout the research process. Case study design projects can be excellent sites of mixed methods research also. A number of case studies that use survey research data can combine quantitative data with qualitative data allowing for deeper contextual descriptions of the broader relational patterns that the survey data provide (Table 3.8).

Table 3.8 Case study template

Specialized/specific groups/ values, attitudes, opinions, behaviours specific to the group or context	Specific attribute 1	Specific attribute 2	Specific attribute 3
Attitude/behaviour 1			
Attitude/behaviour 2			
Attitude/behaviour 3			

Table 3.9 Case study example: commitment to Buddhism by affiliation and devotion

	Q1. How important is Buddhism in describing how you see yourself?			Q2. What is your religious preference?		
	Important (%)	Not important (%)	Total (%)	Buddhist (%)	Other (%)	Total
All respondents	59	41	100	1	39	100
Pattern of commitment: eight-category measure						
2–3 practices/3–4 beliefs	81	19	100	93	7	100
1 practice/3–4 beliefs	76	24	100	80	20	100
0 practices/3–4 beliefs	75	25	100	69	31	100
2–3 practices/1–2 beliefs	77	23	100	82	18	100
Cut-off point						
1 practice/1–2 beliefs	52	48	100	44	56	100
0 practice/1–2 beliefs	23	77	100	23	77	100
1 practice/0 beliefs	50	50	100	50	50	100
0 practice/0 beliefs	10	90	100	10	90	100
Gamma		0.61			0.72	
N		169			169	
Pattern of commitment: collapsed two-category measure						
(i–iv) The strongly committed	78	22	100	84	16	100
(v–viii) The weakly committed	31	69	100	29	71	100
Gamma		0.77			0.86	
N		169			169	

Source: Aarons and Phillips (1997); $N = 169$

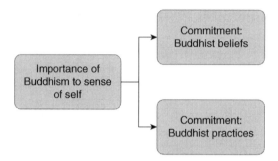

Figure 3.12 Relationship between importance of Buddhism to sense of self and Buddhist beliefs and Buddhist practices

Table 3.9 is an example of the type of analysis my honours supervisor and I were able to perform with the data I collected through the survey about the group and its practices and beliefs that conform to the logic and structure of the relationship between independent and dependent variables. One of my research questions was concerned with whether the level of commitment to Buddhism (dependent variable) was correlated or associated with a strong or weak identity as a Buddhist (independent variable). In other words, if you strongly identified as a Buddhist, had been initiated as Buddhist, and were nothing but a Buddhist in terms of religious identity, then you might be more committed in terms of practice and belief. The data answer a range of descriptive and explanatory questions such as this and lead to some interesting discussion, yet a limitation of this study, due to its case study design, was that we could not claim that the data were representative of the broader population of western Buddhists due to the focus on that group and its members.

Research designs structure and contextualize your study and the analyses that you will perform once you have collected your data, but they also give you a sense of who should be involved and how a study should be structured depending on what your research needs to find out, in line with your topic and research questions. It is time now to turn to how surveys are actually built to collect the data we need to perform the study we are interested in. In the next chapter we consider the first key step in survey construction, namely operationalization of concepts.

───────────────── YOUR SURVEY ─────────────────

Refining a topic, developing research questions, and selecting a research design

Taking your own survey design into account and building on the YOUR SURVEY section from the previous chapter, specify using the template in Table 3.10 provided as a guide:

- The topic/refined topic.
- Specific research questions.

- Discipline and/or sub-discipline.
- Potentially relevant perspectives within the discipline relevant to the research.
- Potentially relevant theories. (If your project is with a community group or organization, they may not be particularly interested in theories, but working within an academic discipline you will be. Survey data can serve both practical and theoretical ends, so consider theories even if the research might be very practical in orientation.)

Table 3.10 YOUR SURVEY: Refining a topic, developing research questions, and selecting a research design

Topic	Research questions for survey design	Discipline	Perspective
	Descriptive: • Extent • Distribution • Quality		
Refined		Sub-discipline or area	Theory
	Relational/explanatory: • Why • Predictive/hypothetical • Causal/associative/correlational		

Further, consider, plan, and outline in detail:

Previous research: What has been written on your topic previously, taking into account different forms of literature – theory, perspective, empirical (especially previous research that has used survey methodology), and specific to your topic and questions?

Research design: What research design should you employ to best carry out your research and answer your questions? For most projects a case study would suffice and be the most practical. If an evaluation or experiment is of interest and relevant to the research questions, then time will be a crucial factor and will need to be planned for. As a class project a longitudinal design is not practical; however, there is nothing stopping you from proposing that your survey could be used again, especially if your project is for a local community organization, service, or business.

Key knowledge and skills

This chapter has considered how a survey research project is subject to the research process incorporating the various stages in refining a project associated with designing a survey and embarking on survey research. The key knowledge and skills for this chapter are as follows:

- The commencement of a survey research project involves the first steps of the research process: deciding on a topic and refining the topic through various sources of the literature.
- Once a topic has been refined through perspectives, theoretical frameworks, and empirical literatures, then the project should entail the development of research questions that are answerable with survey data.
- Research questions generally appropriate for survey data are descriptive, relational/explanatory, and causal/associative/correlative.
- Survey design and research questions and aims are contextualized through an appropriate research design such as experimental/evaluation, cross-sectional, longitudinal, and/or case study.
- Consistent with research design employing surveys is the logic of relationships between independent and dependent variables.

Note

1   There are a number of technical conditions that must be met to ensure a proper experimental design such as random samples constructed by the researcher, interventions and treatments controlled by the researcher, and other conditions that space does not allow me to elaborate on. See the further reading section for sources that have as their subject a more advanced discussion of research design.

Further reading

Of interest is the insightful and instructive discussion on the relationship between theory and empirical research by Robert Merton in his *Social Theory and Social Structure*. Merton's discussion is comprehensive and situates well the relationship between abstract theory and empirical evidence. A text that describes the sometimes difficult-to-grasp process of developing research questions from topics in clear language is Bouma and Carland's *The Research Process*. Research design is a topic well covered in the research methods literature, but not all texts on this topic specify research design as it relates to survey research. Recommended is de Vaus' *Research Design in Social Research* which is a clear, comprehensive, and practical text on research design of value to survey research.

Full text references:
Bouma, G. and Carland, S. (2016) *The Research Process* (6th edn). Melbourne: Oxford University Press

De Vaus, D. A. (2001) *Research Design in Social Research*. London: Sage

Merton, R. (1968) *Social Theory and Social Structure* (2nd edn). New York: Free Press

Discover the digital resources for this chapter, including reflective questions, case studies, and templates, at https://study.sagepub.com/aarons

Four

Concepts: What's the Big Idea?

In this chapter we begin the specific practical process of survey design by learning about the role of concepts in survey research, and working with these concepts in the development of a survey (Figure 4.1). This chapter will cover:

- What a concept is
- Why concepts are so important to survey design
- The process of how to begin the operationalization of a concept
- Real-world examples of concept operationalization
- Concepts and measurement error

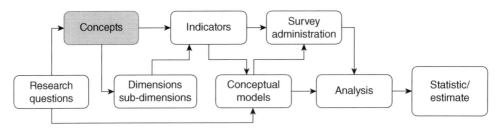

Figure 4.1 Survey design process – concepts

From the previous chapter let's reconsider briefly the topic and question aspects of the research process. Topics give us a general orientation towards a research problem, and research questions are more refined channels of enquiry that clarify our research and make what we want to know more precise. We collect data using surveys in an attempt to answer them, but embedded within them are some key components for surveys that we need to pay very careful attention to. Consider these topics and questions. Education and schools: 'What are the effects of school type on educational success?' Or social media and identity: 'Does social media use affect self-esteem?' Religion and social life: 'Is religion a positive social force in community life?' Work/life balance: 'What are the impacts of contemporary employment patterns on family life?'

These are a set of standard social-science-type questions that researchers from various disciplines attempt to answer with survey data. What you can also see is that these questions contain key components that are crucial to the survey design process. Within these questions are sets of concepts that relate to each other, such as 'social media use' and 'self-esteem', 'religion' and 'community', and 'employment' and 'family life'. A very important component of survey design, greatly impacting survey data quality and the end results of our research, is to make these concepts clear and then measurable so as to answer our questions. Accurate measurement of concepts, however, is a lot more difficult to achieve than it may appear.

This chapter considers the importance of concepts as central to survey design and how useful a survey is to the research that employs it. Concepts, I contend, have been overlooked and neglected in favour of other aspects of survey design such as sampling and modes of survey administration. Concepts are at the heart of what we call '**measurement error**' within the total survey error framework, and many examples of flawed or inaccurate survey research, when examined carefully, are found to have conceptual problems in their survey designs. What is crucial to survey design is to overcome, or limit as much as possible, measurement error, by trying to achieve **concept validity** through a process of concept clarification.

The great sixteenth-century Florentine polymath Galileo Galilei observed that 'all scientific research is based on measurement'. Measurement of course is the key purpose and function of a survey. Many of us can readily appreciate this. What is less easily grasped, however, and what a guy such as Galileo cannot tell us, is precisely what is to be measured and how to measure it. This is a crucial point because what may appear at first thought to be deceptively simple is actually complex, detailed, elusive, and at times mistaken. What we think is a straightforward process of asking questions and presenting answers can end as a nonsensical watery soup of vague and ambiguous data that do not have any relationship to what you wanted to know. What we want or need to measure revolves around the notion of the concept (or construct as some may prefer). Concepts require careful thought, contextualizing, clarifying, and defining. A systematic discussion of concepts in survey research, entailing what they are, how they are defined, and what statistics their measurement generates, is crucial. By association, how those statistics are applied to various public, policy, and commercial debate and decision making is always based on how key concepts are defined. By discussing the role of concepts in survey research this chapter also introduces the opening stages in the technical process of measurement associated with survey research which we term operationalization.

Concepts and measurement

Measurement is at the heart of survey design and research, and indeed is what the notion of mapping experience is all about. Any empirical evidence, be it qualitative or quantitative, bearing on a research problem is a form of measurement because it has been derived from some means of trying to illustrate, communicate, or indicate a concept or idea that is embedded in our research questions. Concepts, however, are at the heart of measurement in the survey design process. Measurement is at once a creative and artful process, as well as a scientific one: a creative and artful process in the sense that the researcher has to imagine how to represent the concept in a series of measures requiring an accurate connection between abstract thinking and concrete representation – not unlike a song or a visual composition – but certainly different in its manifestation; and scientific in the sense that how we measure must be valid – that is, actually measure what we want it to – and reliable, and can be used again and again to tap accurately whatever concept we are interested in.

As we saw in the previous chapter a key stage in the research and survey design process is the formulation of research questions. Research questions focus our research from broad topic areas to more precise and manageable parcels of enquiry. The 'front end', as I call it, of the research and survey design process is very much a process of refinement. A further key part of that refinement is to define accurately the concepts embedded in research questions. You can think of this refinement metaphorically by relating to what some have called '**descending the ladder of abstraction**', entailing stages of refining abstract ideas into survey questions from concepts, dimensions, sub-dimensions, and indicators as Figure 4.2 display.

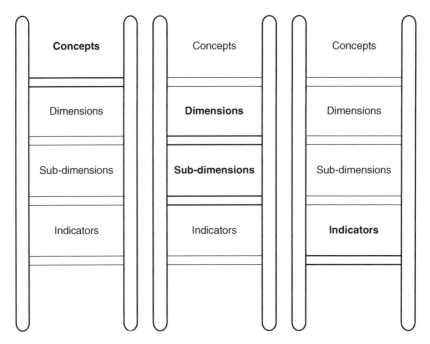

Figure 4.2   Descending the ladder of abstraction – concepts

What is a concept?

A **concept** is a big, amorphous, inchoate idea. Familiar and intuitive, at times, yet strange and confusing at others, especially when we try to define and measure one, whatever it may be. Concepts – also sometimes known as constructs – are the building blocks of any theories we have about the world, the people in it, and their behaviour. Concepts are relevant to all academic and scientific disciplines and have to be measured in order to relate ideas or theories to some form of reality so as to be of use or to be applicable to some setting.

Most of us are aware of many key concepts associated with important debates and we engage with them when we think about or discuss issues, such as one's health, social problems, or the economy. It is in this way that they are familiar, irrespective of whether you know anything about them or not. Indeed, when we discuss an issue, say informally between friends, or more formally through public or political debate, what and how we are discussing or debating is often through our understanding of relevant concepts. Let's look at some examples to illustrate how concepts can be familiar yet also vague and strange. These will help us think about what we want and need to measure, and how descending the ladder of abstraction is a crucial task in beginning survey design. This will also bring the research process alive, and alert us to the specific kind of survey error associated with measurement. Get a pen and paper, or open your laptop and get comfortable – this will hopefully be interesting, but it could drive you a little crazy also!

Well-being

Take 'well-being' as our first example. No doubt you've heard of this term, perhaps you've even tried to attain it, or perhaps you have attained it, once and briefly, or you're a walking, talking testament to it. What is it, though? How do you attain it? How do you know you've attained it, and then how do you measure it: the way the Bhutanese government does with happiness (however that is defined!) through its Gross National Happiness Index? Go on, take a moment and write down what you think well-being means. Don't google it, just try and define it with what you currently know, or don't know, about it! Actually, go on and google it if you like – it won't help you much and will prove just as vague as your general knowledge (providing you are not some kind of expert) given that when I googled it, the search engine gave me 'About 250,000,000 results'! Once you've written down a few ideas about what you think well-being is, reflect on what you've written and now think about how you'd translate that into a survey through a series of measures. But let me speculate a little, if you'll indulge me in illustrating the complexity of concepts.

It sounds as though it relates to our health, and/or our emotions, perhaps some kind of state relevant to how we as individuals feel, or something about the whole person, not just the body, and it could be.... This all might be true but it is still very vague. 'Well' is a state of being surely, and one that is somehow positive, or effective, or 'good', but what aspect of being? Let's say health. But what is health? If bodily health or mental health then why do we need to say well-being, why not just say health or good health? You see that there are layers here and as we dig deeper we come across more and more concepts and are no nearer to a clear definition. What is health? Again, yes, we might have some strong but vague intuition of a definition of health. Let's take a look at a dictionary definition, which might help. The *Oxford Dictionary of English* is a reputable publication – what does it say? 'Well-being: noun the state of being comfortable, healthy, or happy: an improvement in the patient's well-being.' This does not really help. Now we have to define 'comfortable', 'healthy', and 'happy'.

Let's say we do define it and are happy with that definition. Does our definition accord with different contexts? One person's 'well-being' may well be another's misery. Is a health retreat where you are not allowed gadgets, music, alcohol, comfort food, cat videos, reading, or visual material, in order to sit and meditate or do yoga for a week, well-being? Is a strict diet of brown rice, quinoa, broccoli, and green tea well-being? For some this will be a blissful means of re-energizing and casting off the accumulated dross of the world to recalibrate mentally and physically, a means of attaining what we may assume to be well-being, but for others something tantamount to prison. Well-being for others will be their team winning the English Premier League title after years of languishing mid-table or recently being promoted from a lower division – just like Leicester City did in 2016. Supporting sports such as football and well-being are strongly related (Wann and James, 2019). I cannot really say what well-being is with any accuracy.

Religion

Religion, like football (very much like football in some respects!), is a thing that elicits strong opinion and reaction irrespective of belief or experience. Religion is an important aspect of identity, family and cultural life, and also a key topic of recent debate and public policy, but what is religion? Again, take a moment or two, then again grab a pen and paper, or start typing. Again, there is a lot that might be familiar to us concerning religion, despite our imperfect knowledge or our lack of need to be concerned with defining it. You may be religious, or been raised in a religious tradition and know something about the religion to which you belong or belonged, but is that the same as other religions? We know that there are religions that people identify with, practise, and proclaim, and the evidence for their lived existence is both seen and felt through buildings, art, books, behaviour, and religious actors. We could probably name the key religions themselves, but this is not defining it to measure it. Sociologists and psychologists of religion, theologians, and other scholars have tried with tremendous difficulty to define religion precisely.

Indeed, there are numerous definitions of religion, some helpful, some interesting, some baffling. For example, the famous French sociologist Emile Durkheim defined religion as: 'a unified system of beliefs and practices relative to sacred things, i.e., things set apart and forbidden – beliefs and practices that unite in one single moral community called a church, all those who adhere to them' (1996: 65). Fine, *merci* Professor Durkheim. This sounds interesting and certainly plausible from what I know, but I have few questions about your definition. What exactly do you mean by sacred? My old jeans are sacred – are they a religious artefact? And what's this about set apart and forbidden – some religions actively recruit members? Also, what is a moral community? Actually, what is moral, and what is a community? Does one need to be religious to be moral or communal? Um, 'church' you say – they are forms of association and actual buildings particular to Christianity, but what if I am not a Christian, and identify as a Muslim, Jew, Hindu, or Buddhist, am I still religious? The English term 'religion' is derived from the Latin *religare*, which means to bind, similar to the Sanskrit term yoga! So, it is something that binds us? To what? To each other, to a God, or gods? Perhaps I will leave religion and focus on spirituality instead. Great, but what is spirituality? Again, familiar but difficult; again a concept explained by other concepts!

Community

We all live in or are members of communities, communities within communities, within other communities. Research on communities is a central and direct concern for many social scientists, especially in times such as ours when lots of political, economic, and social patterns are about how divided some of our communities are, be they nations, regions, neighbourhoods, or interest groups. Two of the most influential books about society ever written in the social sciences take community as their topic. Benedict Andersons' *Imagined Communities* is number 49 in *TIME* magazine's all-time most influential books written in English, and Robert Putnam's *Bowling Alone* is a modern classic in social science, yet neither of these two great works give particularly satisfactory definitions of community! Community is another concept that is spoken of a lot, intuitively familiar, immediately apparent, but again, like well-being and religion, also notoriously hard to define precisely. Delanty (2009) has stated that there are around 100 working definitions of the concept community (absolving Anderson and Putnam to some extent), which does not sound like much help at all, does it? Despite the odds, and the experts, let's have a go, shall we? Community is a group of people living together, yeah? Community is a group of people with a common interest? A community is a collection of people with similar attributes? Sure, something about connection, commonality, togetherness…? That also sounds a bit like a network. How are networks and communities different, if at all? Now, how do we define connection, commonality, and togetherness? Community is a positive thing conjuring up ideals of warmth, positive connection, and support and…. But there are also negative or less socially acceptable communities such as gangs – who perhaps also provide each other with warmth, connection, and support. Like religion there are definitions of community, but there are always lots of 'yeah buts' and 'what ifs' that attend them.

Concepts and assumptions: Challenging what we know

So how did you go about trying to define these concepts? Better than I did for sure. Did you experience that sense of thinking, yes I know what that is, and then begin to question your definition as the layers of 'what abouts', 'what ifs', and the compounding impacts of other concepts were brought to bear on your thinking? This is fine, and indeed an important step in operationalizing your concepts. You no doubt found that as ambiguous as concepts are, when you tried to define them, you found other concepts that they relate to or are associated with them in some way, all depending on how we think about them and what we know about them, from our limited knowledge.

Another interesting aspect of this exercise, apart from perhaps leaping from vague idea to vague idea and realizing how difficult concepts are to define, is that you are probably relying on a set of assumptions to try and define concepts like well-being or religion. This is perfectly natural but something ideally you want to unlearn for the purposes of survey design. Recall my statement earlier about mapping reality and the purpose of research – we can only see into the lives of others imperfectly when we research, and assumptions about life experiences, groups, attributes, and other stuff we aim to measure in surveys are part of this. Assumptions are exactly what we want to challenge with the attempt at any knowledge building (Charmaz, 2006): it is a key aim in research and a key aspect of learning about a field as well as designing a successful survey.

Despite the confusion and ambiguity surrounding concepts, we have to cut something if our research is ever to progress. We have to define a concept somehow to make it amenable to measurement in a survey and for it to contribute meaningfully to our research questions through the data it will be represented by – we simply cannot do that if a concept is vague and without refinement. Galileo is also famous for saying 'make measurable that which cannot be measured', a paradox to be sure, but I think there is a level of practical wisdom here for survey research. The guy is saying to us, get on with it and measure something, we can always improve it – and this improvement and refinement of definition and measurement are exactly what happens in the real world of survey design and research. In approaching survey design, we need to get our concepts into some kind of defined shape that will allow them to be measured – or made operational, despite the difficulties. The more precise, the better, however. Precision in measurement mostly comes with refinement through thought and application, practice and repetition. The more our concepts are revised and thought about in relation to previous research, the more useful they will be in an operational sense.

The examples above partly describe and highlight the importance of thinking through the concepts that we seek to measure because concepts are central to our research questions, and measurement is central to our concepts. The relationship between concepts, research, and real-life events ensure that concepts are crucial considerations for any survey project. Conceptual development is an imaginative intellectual development wedded to theory. You will notice from the case studies later in the chapter that precise definitions of concepts are far from settled even for professional researchers whose working lives involve trying to measure phenomena such as poverty, homelessness, health, and employment. Yet survey design still proceeds and builds on earlier research with the continued aim of improvement in clarifying and operationalizing concepts. It is a science, but not always an exact one.

You will be relieved to know that definitions for concepts are eventually arrived at in survey design. From here let's consider the ways in which survey researchers go about clarifying concepts, with the aim of arriving at definitions in readiness for measurement. The rest of this chapter will be devoted to the formal process of clarifying concepts on the way to arriving at a definition, from which we can further clarify and take the next rung down on the ladder of abstraction. Some concepts will be easy to define and, as a consequence, easier to measure; some, however, as we have seen, are not so easily defined and measured.

Clarifying concepts

You may be wondering by now how on earth do researchers come to clarify a concept like well-being, health, or community so as to measure it effectively? Beyond attempting to reinvent the wheel, how do researchers begin to clarify a concept? Where to start given how confusing and complex concepts turn out to be, after we thought we knew them, or realized that we actually were reliant on a bunch of assumptions that simply reflected our own values or lack of knowledge? This is where previous research is of tremendous value. We do not have to reinvent wheels when it comes to the concepts that drive our questions in survey research but we do have to lubricate them so they start turning to our advantage.

Most, if not all, concepts relevant to human behaviour, but certainly the ones we have been discussing in this chapter, have been written about before. In all kinds of scholarly fields, researchers have, in their attempts at interpreting human societies and behaviour, invariably attempted to define and in many cases measured in a survey the concept you are interested in. However, despite whatever conceptual development and measurement have transpired before, society and people change, and so must concepts. Conceptual development and survey design as reflections of society and behaviour also need revision from time to time. Further, we have to ask who are the developers and definers of concepts? What are their experiences? How well do they know about whatever it is they seek to define and measure?

––––––––––– Cross-cultural concepts: Contexts and experience –––––––––––

As difficult as it may be to define concepts ourselves, how are concepts such as well-being, poverty, health, and community defined and measured in different societies? Given these concepts are important to researchers the world over, we cannot assume that what one group of people in a particular place or circumstance feel or think about what well-being or

(Continued)

community is the same for people in other places. Comparative international survey projects often face this problem of translating concepts for equivalence. This equivalence is crucial to any notion of comparison and must reflect the social context of the place where the concept is being measured.

Poverty is an excellent example. How poverty is defined and measured in a place such as the EU or the United States is very different from how it might be defined and measured in some parts of Asia or Africa, for example, although some qualities of the concept may be similar or the same.

Most survey research has been developed in European or American contexts usually by men of certain social and economic status. Concept development and measurement often reflect these kinds of experiences. How do researchers go about developing concepts in other parts of the world where cultures and social contexts are different from Europe or North America? The more the participation in survey design by researchers from around the world builds our knowledge of accurate definition and measurement, the more the increase in concept validity and reduction in measurement error.

Searching the literature

How does one enter this maelstrom of ideas with a modicum of confidence? As the research process suggests, a great place to start is with a literature review. Researching the literature as we have seen will assist with refining a topic for your research project, but it will also ably assist you in clarifying concepts. Your given concept or concepts will require some context, however. While there are many sorts of literature that you should consult when building your knowledge about a concept, I recommend beginning with the theories associated with your discipline, related to your topics and research questions, which you will have some knowledge of already – without them there is no academic discipline.

Theories

Recall from Chapter 1 the role of theory in the orientation of pursuing research. Theories are forms of explanation which are composed of concepts or have concepts as their main concern (Merton, 1968). They are abstract systems of thought made up of conceptual propositions that are used to explain why and how things such as health, education, employment, and community 'happen' or are experienced differently. They are also a kind of ethereal intellectual laboratory in which we can think through experiments and map out ideas that we think define and explain human action. Given that we humans have been speculating on all aspects of life for ages, most contemporary theories in a field are often related to previous theories which have been debated, tested with empirical evidence, and refined within an intellectual field. When we enter into research, we encounter such theories and the studies that have tested, discredited, or supported them, so we have to map the ebb and flow, direction, and purpose of the forms of research to learn more about concepts to suit our own research needs.

Development of theory and measurement

There is an iterative process that occurs through theory and empirical observation that is fundamental to the business of knowledge building. For the purpose of survey design and concept clarification, theories represent the creative manifestations of ideas and process that often classify and define human or organizational behaviour, give it shape and form, and explain how it works and why. Below is a broad-staged progression of theoretical knowledge to measurement that can help us think about how concepts can be clarified and operationalized:

- Theoretical discourses identify concepts through engagement with historical, critical, and empirical phenomena.
- Concepts are abstract but defined through theoretical delineation and reflection identifying qualities, dimensions, and natures, and possible real-world applications to explain phenomena.
- Theories also define concepts in formal terms often through a series of related propositions.
- A clearly formulated theory contains concepts that can be measured.
- Theories can be applied and tested in empirical studies.
- Attempts are made at consensus and the establishment of common standards in theory and measurement.
- Theories are revised after empirical evidence through time.

Theories in a given field are many and varied and are like family trees in that there are numerous branches representing the transmission of various ideas and concepts, and like some families there are theories that do not talk to each other, that get along fine, that meet up on special occasions, and that have members that are a little crazy and offbeat, sometimes in a good way, sometimes not. Theories are organized into branches, lineages, and schools on account of original insight and orientation, application, and later developments. They reflect various perspectives on the world and various perspectives on a problem within a discipline. Theories are also imaginative mechanisms, in that they explain, usually through a process or set of procedures, how systems, institutions, and patterns emerge and work. Theories take on all kinds of shapes and are configured in many ways; however, importantly for our purposes we are aiming for theories or concepts within them that are testable through measurement. Not all theories are testable and therefore potentially falsifiable, however; their value therefore as theories can be questioned – this is a debate in the philosophy of science that we do not have time or space to consider more deeply, but important to signal (if you are interested in this debate look at https://plato.stanford.edu/entries/scientific-method/#StaMetForHypTes).

Refining contexts

Beyond theoretical debates and formal theoretical knowledge in a discipline there are a number of different literatures you will need to draw on to better enable you to learn about and begin to clarify a concept. Databases are very powerful tools for researching and if you plug in a term like 'poverty' or 'well-being' they will return hundreds of thousands, if not millions, of hits (recall my Google search above), which is a good sign, but not a very efficient one. You will need to contextualize your search to conform to the research domain that you are most interested in. This is another step in the refinement process. You may be interested in poverty, community, religion, or well-being only in a certain discipline or domain, such as sociology, medicine, economics, politics, or social work, and within a particular setting, such as the United States, Bangladesh, China, Great Britain, or rural or inner city, or within a community setting. You may only be interested in poverty for example in recent times, say the last 10 years or under a certain government or administration with a particular policy agenda. Or you may be interested in how a concept has been treated within a theoretical tradition within your discipline. Your literature searches should reflect these domains and contexts; your results will then narrow down and become more relevant to your current needs.

Finally, you can pursue previous studies that are theoretical, empirical, or methodological in orientation. Many scholars not only devote time and reflection to how to define a concept like well-being so as to theorize and measure it, but also are reflexive about how others have defined and measured it, usually with the view of critiquing how successful, problematic, or efficient various attempts and methods have been across different domains and how to improve them. So, the scope of your reading should be wide but focused and encompass the domain or perspective that you are interested in, theoretical approaches within that domain and perspective, and methodological appraisals of survey research associated with the concept of interest.

Assorted literatures

Any good piece of research whose focus is theoretical, empirical, methodological, or some combination of the three, will provide definitions of a concept or the concepts their research is concerned with, and some will go to great lengths, especially if the research is attempting to break new ground or reconceptualize an existing idea due to a theoretical or empirical innovation. Other research papers will give only brief definitions or allude to a broader definition of a concept that they have explicated at length elsewhere, or they are writing within a perspective or sub-discipline where the concept is well known in the scholarly community that the author is writing for. Check the reference list of papers like this – they will often have listed the studies that contain the more dedicated efforts of conceptual definition and measurement.

In many disciplines there appear from time to time summative studies that aim at gathering together the various strands of conceptual definition and operationalization of key topics and concepts, especially if the field or sub-discipline is emerging. These studies are tremendously helpful for the survey researcher for a number of reasons. Here are two. Firstly, they allow a researcher an efficient entry point into the main conceptual and operationalization debates, rather than having to leg it around the various literatures attempting to source the disparate research. Secondly, they focus directly on what a survey researcher wants, that is concepts and measurement. An example of this kind of literature that I have found helpful in my own research sought to collate and critique various definitions of religion and spirituality, which as we are aware from my example above can be very confusing. The aptly titled *Religion and Spirituality: Unfuzzing the Fuzzy* (Zinnbauer et al., 1997) listed and organized the various definitions that a sample of people gave the researchers, drawing on the lived experience of those identifying as religious and/or spiritual.

Consultation, participation, and qualitative data

Often another excellent source of preparation for conceptual development and operationalization of concepts in social science is qualitative research. Qualitative researchers test and build theories and concepts through the collection of textual data. Interviews, focus groups, and documents that produce textual data enable qualitative researchers to specify concepts and to relate how people have experienced them through whatever aspects of their lives are relevant to the aims of the research. A strength of qualitative research, and an indirect ally of survey design then, is the deep description of meanings, experiences, and feelings associated with an area of behaviour that identify particular themes associated with a concept, or how a concept is related by a respondent, that we may use for the clarification of a concept and its eventual measurement using a survey. It has long been known and accepted that mixed methods and triangulation are powerful approaches to empirical enquiry, giving greater perspective and dimensionality to a research problem, and qualitative data that deal with a concept of interest can be a crucial aspect of combined efforts.

Qualitative data towards the clarification of a concept for survey design are often collected by researchers in a consultation phase. Given the complexity of some concepts and the desired use of them for industry, policy, or basic research, what currently exists by way of definition may not be sufficient for measurement, so there is a need to consult and gather testimony from relevant people (participants) who can inform the research about how they experience whatever it is the research is trying to measure.

This form of concept clarification is synonymous with what is called in the social sciences 'grounded theory' (Glaser and Strauss, 1967) or 'action research' (Bryman, 2015) and relies on inductive and reflective forms of developing concepts proceeding from data to theory. Different definitions and measures of concepts such as poverty are developed in just this way through coding various responses into themes that then stand as criteria for the concept in question. Psychological research often uses such a process of concept development. Often in cross-cultural contexts researchers listen to how people in specific situations describe the lived experience and the informal definition of certain concepts like poverty, from which researchers develop an operationalized concept. Operationalized concepts such as the Individual Deprivation Measure (Bessell, 2015) – a refined measure of poverty – have successfully used this process. Consultation can also involve researchers from outside a specific context with specific expertise and experience associated with a concept of interest. Concepts for measurement in development by government for example often consult academics and industry researchers or practitioners also.

Replications

Sometimes, the best or the most useful and relevant studies for the purposes of concept clarification are the ones that use survey research methods and quantitative data concerning the concept that you are interested in. Often researchers will attempt to replicate the work of others and rely on the definitions and measures used in the original research. In my own discipline of sociology Pierre Bourdieu's work on cultural consumption has been replicated in a number of places since his book *Distinction: A Social Critique of the Judgement of Taste* appeared in English in 1984. Sociologists interested in the role cultural consumption plays in class relations and social structure sought to discover if what Bourdieu found in France concerning cultural consumption was apparent in the UK, Europe, North America, and Australia. The researchers aimed to measure concepts specific to Bourdieu's theories of culture and society such as 'cultural capital' through questionnaires that used similar indicators and formats.

Numerous papers reported on these attempts with commentary on the concepts, their definitions, and contexts, many also including reflections on the specifics of the survey approach (see Bennett et al., 1999; 2008). Indeed, what has emerged as a result is a dynamic sub-discipline of sociology devoted to this research inclusive of the roles of surveys, from which key concepts can be identified, various definitions critiqued, and the measurement of them considered. Replication is also another key plank in a scientific approach to research, and a form of revising critique for some disciplines to gauge methodological appropriateness. In psychology for example a number of scholars are currently debating the notion of a 'crisis of reproducibility' wherein results under similar if not the same conditions are not reproduced (Stanley et al., 2018). This 'crisis' is not unique to psychology but an ongoing challenge for scientific enquiry in general; to some extent these crises relate to concepts and their measurement.

Research outside of academia

Research aimed at public policy, community programmes, planning, and governance beyond academia will have established literatures that cover many domains and perspectives with methodological critiques of the roles of surveys and the clarification of concepts. These types of studies, usually reports on a specific issue, evaluations, and/or position papers, will share some aspects of theory and conceptualization with academic studies for a given topic. Many studies using surveys in public policy for example have been replicated, adding to the corpus of knowledge, and represent a wealth of information for any new research project involving a survey methodology.

If your research project is within a government agency or department, NGO, community group, or in an academic context as well, you may well benefit from such publications through the methodological information they contain pertaining to concepts of interest. Often this kind of research draws on what is known as a 'concept dictionary' created to benefit policy or industry research and make it more standardized. These sources of conceptual definition are produced by numerous research and statistical branches within agencies such as the United Nations or World Bank, and more local community groups and government statistical agencies. Always beware, however, that the concepts published in the various research outlets that rely on concepts from academic theories and/or government may not meet your needs.

As a part of the front end of your survey research project, therefore, you should have assembled a vast but focused amount of literature that you can draw from. Consider how well it may work with respect to your own needs. Do the concepts they discuss match your concepts and survey research needs? How are they the same? How are they different? Are they unique to the context or setting the research is placed within? Bourdieu's work mentioned earlier contains an interesting disclaimer that the author inserted in the introduction to *Distinction*: 'This is a very French book...' Bourdieu (1984: 23) warns, and the warning is wise and appropriate for what culture such as art, music, and literature means to the French of the late 1960s and early 1970s is very different for the Americans, Australians, Germans, and Chinese of today. As did happen, the results of replicative studies failed to provide evidence for some of his theoretical positions, which is not a problem in and of itself necessarily; indeed we only know this because researchers tried to replicate the work, but it does highlight the importance of contexts and uses of concepts.

Contexts and purposes of concepts

Following this point then, another important consideration when seeking clarification and settling on an **operational definition** is the context of a concept, that is the different intellectual locations and ultimate purposes of measurement. Often concepts that are employed in survey design have different definitions due to their different contexts and purposes in research. This might be to do with political or ideological processes or, less cynically, a function of practicality and stated need. Here I identify three key contexts in which conceptual definitions are found to differ, often producing different estimates and statistics when concepts are measured in a survey. Firstly, as we have already discussed, is the theoretical: any scholarly field has a body of theoretical work from which concepts are usually born. A key aspect of these theories is purpose. What is the theory trying to explain? Concepts, measures, and statistics from surveys will then be aimed at testing the theory. Secondly, a concept may be set within research relating to industry. The rendering of a concept may or may not be the same or similar in an industrial context than it is to a purely academic theoretical context and be defined and measured to solve a particular industry problem. Thirdly, concepts are employed in governmental and policy settings; these settings may also require different or alternative definitions of concepts measured in surveys depending on their specific purpose relating to political philosophy.

Now, as different as these three contexts are, they are also related, and it is by no means uncommon for industry and policy to borrow or adapt concepts from a purely theoretical realm such as academia and vice versa. As abstractions, concepts will have to relate to the real world in some way and are suited to different types of research problems based on what the researcher needs, and how they think the concepts relate to the varieties of reality that each perspective may want to advance. In terms of survey research then, there will be a range of competing and alternative definitions of concepts that reflect these different purposes that we will have to deliberate over. Also, within these three contexts there will be a variety of definitions that reflect research differentiation from within. For theorists in a field, debate over concepts is at the heart of how a theoretical perspective is formed. It is not unusual at all to find a range of competing conceptual definitions of key ideas. The same is true for industry and policy research contexts.

Towards a process of concept development and clarification

From the preceding discussion I would like to tie the various strands of conceptual thinking together and develop a more strategic process through which clarification of concepts can proceed. There are three key elements to the clarification of concepts in readiness for operationalization in surveys: (1) theory/perspective; (2) previous research/existing definitions; (3) consultation and qualitative data. These elements can be thought of as representing a matrix of top-down and bottom-up conceptualizing (Figure 4.3) and entail specific contexts of concept validity: basic research, policy, and industry. Each context may require different conceptual definitions for different purposes (and produce different estimates and statistics), but often conceptual definitions will overlap and be useful for different contexts as Figure 4.4 indicates.

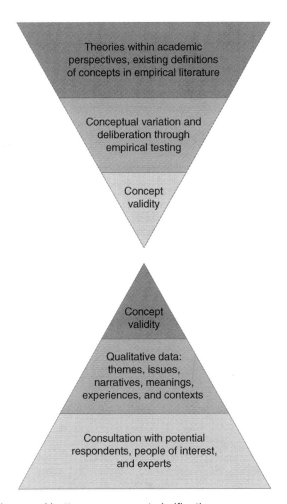

Figure 4.3 Top-down and bottom-up concept clarification

Top-down conceptual development consists of an intellectual exercise in which researchers and experts will seek to clarify a concept from theories and existing definitions and then apply it to a survey and test it on respondents. Bottom-up conceptual development is more inclusive, involving mostly consultation with potential respondents from which qualitative data are gathered and themes are extracted from which operationalization is then developed. A combination of theory and existing definitions as well as consultation and qualitative work is also an effective and well-practised means of clarifying concepts. Further, I contend that many conceptual definitions are either *outcome* definitions, in that they are derived as an outcome of a calculated threshold within the definition, or *process* definitions aimed at measuring an outcome with the aid of more complex relationships within the concept.

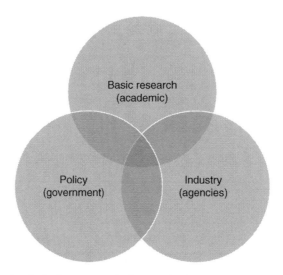

Figure 4.4   Concept validity for survey design contexts

Figure 4.5 shows a model of the staged process of concept clarification that entails the various relevant considerations associated with concepts discussed in the chapter thus far. This model assumes the variety of research contexts that use surveys to collect

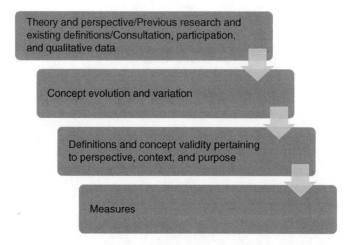

Figure 4.5   Model of concept clarification and operationalization

data, and their shared concerns. In the next section I present a series of case studies that apply the model of concept clarification to outline how some of the most important and complex concepts are operationally defined for measurement in a survey. The real-world case studies highlight different aspects of conceptualization. The case studies also should help you appreciate the role of surveys in addressing key social problems and how the role of clarifying concepts in their design is a complex process of debate and development within overlapping contexts.

Case studies

To better illustrate this process of concept clarification, I present four case studies below. They all involve highly complex concepts that have been measured in many surveys in the contexts of basic research, government policy, and industry. The case studies highlight the relationships between theories/perspectives, previous research, and consultation.

Case study 1: Poverty

Firstly, let's consider poverty. The phenomenon of poverty represents a fundamental challenge for governments, agencies, and researchers the world over, but what is it? Again, if asked for a definition you may have a confident intuition about how it should be defined, but it may also be ambiguous and vague once you think about it a little more. Intuitive in the sense that you could quite easily discern that it is a lack of resources for living, such as money. Ambiguous and vague in the sense of what is a lack? How much money do we need, and for what exactly? A comfortable life? What is comfortable? The 'basics', having shelter, clothes, and food? Sure, but what quality of shelter, clothes, and food? How many bedrooms? And what about furniture, gadgets, heating, and air-conditioning? How satisfactory should these things be? What is a need and a want, as the economists say? Who is in poverty? An individual, a household, a community? Does a unit of analysis have any bearing on a definition? Is it different from, say, being poor? What is poverty across different societies?

Poverty represents an overt form of human difference and suffering whose perverse consequences often last a lifetime and are reproduced generation after generation. As our model of concept clarification suggests, there are many ways to approach a definition of poverty for the sake of measurement and for the purposes of understanding and addressing it through policy response. Governments are reliant on social surveys such as a census and other large-scale surveys to estimate empirically who is experiencing poverty, as it defines it, for the express purposes of however a government wants to deal with it, usually through some form of income redistribution or support benefit from the state.

With respect to policy response, governments will model and then evaluate programmes or policy initiatives designed to reduce the level of poverty as government has defined and measured it. Governments do not act alone in this endeavour; indeed there are a number of non-governmental actors such as university and/or industry researchers who are also involved for their own purposes and also sometimes to advise government. The success of larger welfare or social security policy programmes worth billions of dollars is therefore based on operational definitions of poverty. What is often contentious and indeed controversial at times, however, is how a government or government agency defined poverty in the first instance to produce an estimate or statistic and then a response.

How do governments estimate poverty levels in a society? Very often most governments rely on a definition of poverty that is focused on monetary income. The World Bank – reflecting an economic and financial perspective – has developed a poverty line to estimate the level of poverty in a given country, and many countries have established their own versions of a poverty line.

In the United States, for example, an official definition of poverty was derived in 1964 as part of President Johnson's 'war on poverty', where the US Census Bureau (https://www.census.gov/programs-surveys/cps/technical-documentation/subject-definitions.html#footnote1) defines poverty as:

> a set of money income thresholds that vary by family size and composition. If a family's total income is less than that family's threshold, then that family, and every individual in it, is considered poor…. The official poverty definition counts money income before taxes and excludes capital gains and noncash benefits (such as public housing, medicaid, and food stamps).

Poverty thresholds that abide by this definition do account for inflation and are adjusted. This definition is operationalized through sets of measures in surveys such as the Current Population Survey, and in other data collection instruments. Currently in the United States there is a Federal Poverty Level which is an income threshold that relates to this definition. Notwithstanding the merits or failings of the concept's operational definition, the level is used in a particular context (policy) and is derived from a certain perspective (economic) for a specific purpose (to determine welfare qualification). The definition of poverty here is practical and outcome based and attempts to solve a problem of estimation in a particular way.

Is this definition of poverty, fashioned in the 1960s, still relevant or accurate? Indeed, the conceptual definition of poverty in the United States has received a lot of attention since being introduced. A major revision of the operational definition of poverty was suggested in the mid 1990s through the National Academy of Sciences (NAS) and further experimental definitions such as the Supplemental Poverty Measure (SPM) were developed to reflect life in the twenty-first century (not yet adopted by the US federal government). The official definition of poverty provides unreliable estimates according to some, because it does not take into account specific forms of difference and change for a national population. For example, Blank (2008) cites three key problems with the current definition of poverty. This definition does not take into account variation in the cost of living in different regions in the United States, nor does it consider any changes in household budgets and expenditure patterns to keep pace with consumer changes such as the proportion of a household budget spent on food (less since 1960s) and housing (more since the 1960s). Further, the official definition does not include non-cash income such as certain welfare provisions. Differences in how to define income and therefore poverty have led to startling statistical differences. Blank (2008) highlights that poverty levels for single-parent households range from between 9.8% compared with other measures that estimate 47%.

Other recent conceptualizations of poverty have aimed to revise the narrow focus of established definitions on income and the household and sought to develop a more comprehensive conceptual and process definition of poverty with a focus on developing or low-income countries. Income is still important, but income is in some perspectives related to other forms of deprivation or lack, such as health, education, and wealth, that all contribute or are related to income. For example, Alkire and Santos (2014) have devised a Multidimensional Poverty Index (MPI) that broadens the conceptual definition of poverty to include health, education, and standard of living, in addition to income. Similarly, Bessell (2015) and colleagues have aimed to reconceptualize poverty through what they term the Individual Deprivation Measure (IDM), again with a more expansive definition including a focus on the individual and gender distinctions, leading to a more extensive concept that will produce different estimates and statistics.

How a household experiences poverty, through lack of income, is different to how individuals, especially individual men and individual women, might experience it. Perspective and context are important here and reflect how the researchers see current definitions as deficient from a particular point of view with a particular purpose. The more expansive definitions reflect the researcher's interest in gender, education, individualism, health, and other concerns in relation to mere income. Of interest here is whether these more expansive definitions are considered and recognized by governments and agencies with an interest in poverty to change how an estimate of it is produced. If governments were to accept these broader definitions, then what would the level of poverty estimate be, compared with an income-based definition? What would welfare support look like? Would this measure succeed in eventually reducing poverty? How practical for a population is a revised conception of poverty of this kind? Can it be validly and reliably measured through a major survey such as a census?

What is also important to discern here is how concepts evolve from certain perspectives, contexts, and purposes and from narrow or established definitions to broader and more inclusive ones. The income operational definition of poverty is an example of a top-down definition, defined by economists and other experts in income distribution and income needs in a specific economic context. The revised definitions of poverty on the other hand are more bottom up in that they include consultation with people who are thought to be experiencing poverty. Qualitative data collected through interviews have given the researchers a grounded concept of poverty as it is lived. The revised definitions are also to some extent top down, in that they will rely on academic theories, expert input, and industry perspectives in addition to qualitative data, as well as an acceptance that income is important. We can also detect a distinction here between what I have called outcome and process definitions of the concept of poverty.

Poverty is a complex concept and there is an extensive conceptual literature in which researchers and theorists promote and defend various conceptualizations with the aim of operationalization. Conceptualizations of poverty are, as our model suggests, reflective of perspectives and theories, contexts, and purposes. What data are ultimately sought depends on the aims of the research, and the various contexts where the data are used. Let's summarize the discussion of poverty by applying the model of concept clarification to it (Table 4.1).

Table 4.1   Competing definitions of poverty

Conceptualizing poverty	Money/Income:	Wealth/Social scientific:
	Outcome	Process
	Established	Revised
	Narrow	Extended
Top-down/bottom-up conceptualization	Top-down	Bottom up
Perspectives/theories	Economics	Economics
	Income	Health
	Monetary policy	Education
		Standard of living
		Gender
		Development
Previous research/existing definitions	Builds on and refines income measures and redistribution theories without significant change	Accepts previous/existing conceptualizations but broadens the concept considerably; seeks to address deficiencies with narrow conceptualization
Consultation/participation/ qualitative data	Consultation with experts	Extensive consultation and collection of qualitative data from participants and potential survey respondents

Concept validity context (basic research, policy, industry)		
Main context	Economic policy Social policy Income distribution	Basic research
Related contexts (applications)		Economic and development policy Industry: NGOs, Welfare agencies
Purpose (estimate or statistic)	Extent of the population under a specific income level or line to qualify for welfare benefits	Level of deprivations for individuals with specific attributes through a scale measure

Case study 2: Homelessness

Homelessness is another serious social issue that has deeply occupied social researchers and welfare agencies in recent times across many societies. While homelessness is certainly on the current policy radar of many governments, one problem in developing policy around homelessness, much the same as poverty, is the lack of reliable estimates of the extent and demographic nature of homelessness in a given population. The lack of reliable statistics is due mostly to a lack of consensus concerning what homelessness means and how to best operationalize it (Chamberlain and Mackenzie, 2014). As governments in many countries began to focus on homelessness, especially for young people, as a policy area of increasing importance from the 1970s and 1980s, there was a strong need for accurate estimates for given populations. Accurate statistics on homelessness were, and to some extent still are, quite difficult to come by as a result of different definitions reflective of competing contexts and purposes, process, and outcome definitions.

So, what does it mean to be homeless? Again, homelessness is a concept we can intuitively define as non-experts. On the surface homelessness sounds like an uncomplicated concept to define and operationalize. A basic definition might be the lack of shelter. Yet a shelter can be any structure which is not what most of us might think of as constituting a home, such as under a bridge. Lack of a dwelling? What is a dwelling? Whose dwelling? Does a definition need to include a building? What about a place? Cultural distinctions and lived experience of, say, many indigenous peoples might consider a region or geographic place home more than a specified structure. Can you camp at your friend's place and not be considered homeless? What about people who are institutionalized, such as prisoners? The notion of home has an emotional connotation, as in the sense of belonging. Again, is this a place or a building, or a connection to a group? Can home be thought of as commercial, as in owning a home or land? Legal also in the sense of owning property? What if you are a renter, are you homeless? If you have a lease, are you homeless at a certain time? Is homelessness relative? That is, are there different notions of what the concept of home means to different social groups? Can we assume an objective standard about the concept, or should we accept more personalized and subjective notions? Questions such as these are asked by the theorists of homelessness and are worked into policy and industry settings, and account for how the concept is contemplated for definition and measurement.

As it turns out, homelessness can be a very complex concept to define and has accrued many different conceptual definitions that reflect various contexts relating to theory, policy, industry, and service provision. The complexity of clarifying homelessness has led some researchers to suggest that it simply cannot be defined (Field, 1988; Watson, 1984), yet as a social problem in need of estimation largely assisted through survey data, a definition is needed and has been attempted repeatedly. Cue Galileo!

Chamberlain and Mackenzie (1992; 2014) provide a succinct history of the development of the concept of homelessness for survey design that entails four key definitions, reflecting the framework of perspective, context, and purpose reflecting outcome and process definitions. They cite 'skid row' or conventional, conservative, radical, and cultural definitions of homelessness that have been used for various purposes at different times operationally to define and measure homelessness and produce various estimates and statistics for large populations.

'Skid row' definitions of homelessness were a product of the 1960s and include a population of mostly middle-aged and older men, often with alcohol problems, living in single rooms in boarding houses and cheap hotels in the inner-city precincts of US cities. Studies that are based on a 'skid row' definition of homelessness according to Chamberlain and Mackenzie (1992) differ in the estimates of the homeless, yet there appears to be very few who lived on the streets. The majority of this group lived in boarding houses, so have some form of shelter. A criticism of this definition is that homelessness was mostly based on attributes such as 'disaffiliation' and a 'lack of integration' with family, friends, and other social networks, but does this mean that these people are actually homeless? In other words, is this definition conceptually valid? Again, it depends on what you think 'home' means.

What Chamberlain and Mackenzie call a 'conservative' definition of homelessness has been used as a practical definition to attempt to gain a national estimate of homeless persons. The conservative definition is also known as 'rooflessness' (Chamberlain and Johnson, 2001) and pertains to a literal or outcome definition of homelessness. Chamberlain and Mackenzie cite the United States Department of Housing and Urban Development's (US HUD, 1984) definition of homelessness as:

1. Public or private emergency shelters which take a variety of forms – armories, schools, church basements, government buildings, former firehouses, and where temporary vouchers are provided by public and private agencies, even hotels, apartments and boarding homes.

2. In the streets, parks, subways, bus terminals, railroad stations, airports, under bridges, or aqueducts, in abandoned buildings without utilities, cars, trucks, or any other public or private space that is not designed for shelter.

One problem here is that some people may self-fund temporary accommodation, and move constantly to various forms of accommodation. The definition therefore could be missing potentially large swathes of the homeless in any estimate.

Radical definitions extend the definition of homelessness to include the perceptions of people thought to be affected by homelessness. The radical definition of homelessness builds on conventional and conservative definitions to include subjective states of individuals about what a home is and how adequate it is through consultation and qualitative research. In Australia this definition became the official definition of homelessness enshrined in an Act of Parliament (Supported Accommodation Assistance Act (SAAA)):

> For the purposes of this Act, a person is taken to have inadequate access to safe and secure housing if the only housing to which the person has access:
>
> (a) damages, or is likely to damage, the person's health; or
> (b) threatens the person's safety; or
> (c) marginalises the person through failing to provide access to:
>
> > (i) adequate personal amenities; or
> > (ii) the economic and social supports that a home normally affords; or
>
> (d) places the person in circumstances which threaten or adversely affect the adequacy, safety, security, and affordability of that housing. (1994: 5)

This definition, Chamberlain and Mackenzie (1992: 280) claim is related to a previous industry definition developed by agencies advocating for the homeless, such as the National Youth Coalition for Housing (NYCH). The NYCH definition included provisions such as 'existing accommodation considered inadequate by the resident for such reasons as overcrowding, the physical state of the residence, lack of security of occupancy, lack of emotional support and stability in the place of residence' (NYCH, 1985). These definitions have been criticized for containing problematic and vague statements that are difficult to operationalize. For example, what exactly are 'adequate personal amenities'? These definitions reflect the industry and advocacy contexts in which various agencies and professionals have worked with homeless persons but are problematic to operationalize.

Finally, Chamberlain and Mackenzie offer their own definition which they termed a 'cultural definition'. Drawing on sociological theory and social constructivist perspectives, the researchers conceptualize homelessness as relative and benchmarked against 'minimum community standards' based on 'housing conventions of a particular culture' (1992: 290). According to Chamberlain and Mackenzie, 'the problem of defining homelessness must involve the central task of identifying the community standards about the minimum housing that people have the right to expect in order to live according to the conventions and expectations of a particular culture' (ibid.). This means that:

> In Australia [and many other countries], the vast majority of the population live in suburban houses or self-contained flats.... It follows...that an independent person (or couple) should be able to expect at least a room to sleep in, a room to live in, kitchen and bathroom facilities of their own and an element of security of tenure – because that is the minimum accommodation that most people achieve who rent in the private market. (Ibid.)

The cultural definition was influential for a number of years in Australia and internationally, yet it too has been problematic with respect to operationalization according to some commentary. The Australian Bureau of Statistics (2012) for example has sought a new conceptual definition of homelessness after citing the cultural definition as inadequate.

The various definitions, reflecting the different perspectives and contexts, have naturally given researchers at times very different estimates of the homeless whenever the concept has been operationalized in surveys and censuses. For example, Chamberlain and Mackenzie (1992) report that estimates for homelessness in the United States in the 1980s based on the radical definition were around 3 million people, compared with around 250,000 estimated using the conservative definition. Such discrepancies result in confusion over which estimate is most accurate, especially given the margin, and naturally complicates efforts to alleviate homelessness.

Top down/bottom up?

The various definitions of homelessness have been developed with both a top-down and bottom-up approach (Table 4.2), yet there is a core consensus among them about a lack of shelter or dwelling. Conservative definitions have often relied on government departmental needs and are very top down for the purposes of large population estimates; these definitions centre on outcomes relating to specific tight formulae. Radical definitions reflect industry experience of homeless people and involve consultative and participatory forms of concept development to meet the needs of the homeless through service provision and are more process defined, citing relational components of the person and their circumstances in relation to homelessness. Chamberlain and Mackenzie's definition as both top down and bottom up is a further evolution of extant definitions with some refinements. It is based on both sociological theory and qualitative data produced through case studies with an attempt to overcome subjective problems in definition and benchmark minimum standards with reference to the prevailing expectations of a broader community.

Table 4.2 Competing definitions of homelessness

Conceptualizing homelessness	Skid row/ conventional: Process Narrow	Conservative: Outcome Narrow	Radical: Process Revised Extended	Cultural: Process Revised Extended
Top-down/ bottom-up conceptualization	Top-down	Top-down	Top-down and bottom up	Top-down and bottom up
Perspectives/ theories	Academic literature	Government department	Subjective perceptions	Sociological theory/social constructivist
Previous research/ existing definitions	Development of literalist definitions such as a lack of shelter. Extended to disaffiliation and a lack of ties with social networks	Narrow definition, based on the literalist conceptions	Accepts elements of conventional and conservative definitions. Extends definitions to include the subjective opinions of the homeless as to what is adequate	Accepts elements of conventional and conservative definitions. Refines definitions of subjective standards to objective standards relative to the community of interest
Consultation/ participation/ qualitative data	Observation and qualitative data		Long-term work with homeless population. Case studies, observations, industry feedback	Case studies of 3,000 clients of a homeless agency
Concept validity context (basic research, policy, industry)				
Main context	Basic research	Government Housing research	Industry Housing and welfare agencies Advocacy groups	Basic research
Related contexts (applications)	Policy	Basic research Industry	Policy Australian government housing legislation	Policy National statistical benchmarking
Purpose (estimate or statistic)	Extent of the population that is homeless	Extent of the population that is homeless	Extent of the population that is homeless	Extent of the population that is homeless

Case study 3: Who are the middle class?

Of particular interest to researchers in the social sciences is the fate of various class groups as a result of economic change. Socio-economic status or social class is a crucial concept for social scientists that attempts to gain clarity around levels of economic and social advantage and disadvantage. One's social class often predicts how future generations will fare economically and in a host of other ways, and how forms of material advantage and disadvantage are reproduced. For the purposes of trying to understand social and economic differences, social classes were often divided into at least three – upper, middle, and working class – reflecting the economic or material structure of a society. Broadly, the upper classes were either nobility or the very wealthy, the middle classes were those with university or specialist qualifications and worked in one of the professions such as business, law, or medicine, and the working classes were those that performed manual or service work. There are many other variations on this basic taxonomy but essentially they serve to classify groups in society based principally on economic resources of an individual or household.

Classes were once thought of as somewhat easy to define, yet over the last 30 years or so, what constitutes the various class groups has increasingly come into question. For example, there are serious doubts about whether a working class exists today as it once did throughout most of the twentieth century, and in its place has emerged a 'mass middle class' (Abramowitz and Teixeira, 2009). Social class is a key concept measured by many social surveys. Most respondents consider themselves as middle class when asked where they see themselves in the class structure, yet not everyone or almost everyone is middle class (depending on the definition of course), so who is? How would you identify yourself or your family background within the class scheme of your society? Upper, middle, or working? If you think you would report yourself as middle class, what does this mean to you?

The importance of class as an operational concept is relevant to the three key contexts that we have used in our scheme. Academic researchers associated with various perspectives are interested in how concepts such as class relate theoretically and empirically to an economic structure and how as a result various class groups are economically and socially advantaged and/or disadvantaged in a society. Governments and policy developers are interested in the precise levels of socio-economic inequality and how various class groups as households might fare under specific tax regimes, cost of living increases, and welfare initiatives; industries such as welfare and social security need statistical or estimate thresholds to make practical the limits and boundaries of their work, much like they do with concepts such as poverty. Different definitions of class groups therefore proliferate and consequently so too do estimates and statistics of who is middle class.

Economic change is a constant, especially in our modern world. How economic changes impact on individuals and households has a lot to do with how conceptualizations of class should also change. Social class measured by longitudinal household surveys is an excellent means of tracing such change. Related to social class is the idea of social mobility: that is, if class groups move up or down in status or wealth over time as a result of economic and other social change. In many societies since the end of the 1960s there has been a large shift in the economic and social status of many households and individuals from working-class origins to a middle class. More recently, however, as a result of further economic change, there has been a lot of attention paid to a perceived threat to the middle class and decline of the middle class in western societies. The middle class is important because it is often seen as a barometer for how an economy is performing overall due to its consumption practices (Easterly, 2001). Thus, a flourishing middle class, then a flourishing economy, and its opposite. Outside of Europe and North America, a rising middle class in Asia and Africa is seen as a positive sign of economic and social development. In addition to the economic importance of a thriving and attainable middle class, being middle class has cultural status and political consequences.

Part of the enquiry into the fortunes of the middle class is a review of how to define middle class and gain valid and reliable estimates to assess threat, rise, or decline. There are numerous ways in which middle class has been defined. A prevailing and practical measure of being middle class is income. Economists in particular, whose scholarly and practical perspectives are associated with the distribution of money, use income levels or income brackets to define who is included and excluded from the middle class. Typically, this definition is based on an established income range or bracket benchmarked against an income marker such as the median wage for a population, which households or individuals fall within or beyond. This measure can be relative to how much income on average an individual or household earns per capita. There are many different ways in which an income-based definition of the middle class can be benchmarked in addition to pinning it to a median income, however. Much like a literal definition of homelessness, middle classness defined by income aims to produce readily collectable statistics that can be used for policy. Such definitions are narrow and outcome focused also.

Income definitions are at times themselves remarkably complex and differentiated, however. In *A Dozen Ways to be Middle Class*, Reeves and colleagues (2018) present a summary of 12 different income-based definitions of the concept of middle class (Figure 4.6). All 12 are based on defined income brackets or a relationship to median income. When operationalized in surveys, all 12 definitions produce different estimates of who is middle class, as Reeves et al. (2018) note: 'Taken together, the twelve definitions could mean that nearly nine out of ten US households – with incomes ranging from $13,000 to $230,000 – are middle class.' These definitions suggest that the proportion of households that are middle class ranges from 10% to 73%.

With numerous definitions some researchers have steered clear of calling particular groups classes at all, and refer to 'income groups', 'wealth sectors', and simply 'high-, middle-, and low-income households'. Income, however, can be quite a complex concept as well, as we have just seen. Which incomes are middle, for example? Should income be measured before or after tax? Should income be household income or personal income?

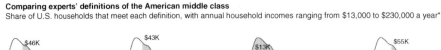

Comparing experts' definitions of the American middle class
Share of U.S. households that meet each definition, with annual household incomes ranging from $13,000 to $230,000 a year*

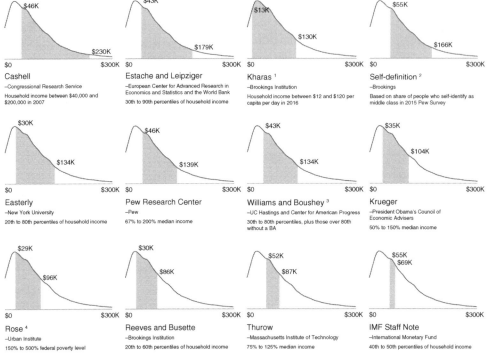

Cashell
–Congressional Research Service
Household income between $40,000 and $200,000 in 2007

Estache and Leipziger
–European Center for Advanced Research in Economics and Statistics and the World Bank
30th to 90th percentiles of household income

Kharas [1]
–Brookings Institution
Household income between $12 and $120 per capita per day in 2016

Self-definition [2]
–Brookings
Based on share of people who self-identify as middle class in 2015 Pew Survey

Easterly
–New York University
20th to 80th percentiles of household income

Pew Research Center
–Pew
67% to 200% median income

Williams and Boushey [3]
–UC Hastings and Center for American Progress
30th to 80th percentiles, plus those over 80th without a BA

Krueger
–President Obama's Council of Economic Advisers
50% to 150% median income

Rose [4]
–Urban Institute
150% to 500% federal poverty level

Reeves and Busette
–Brookings Institution
20th to 60th percentiles of household income

Thurow
–Massachusetts Institute of Technology
75% to 125% median income

IMF Staff Note
–International Monetary Fund
40th to 50th percentiles of household income

Income share: Share of total U.S. pre-tax, pre-transfer income in 2016. Income Growth: Growth in average household income since 1980, adjusted for inflation using the PCE deflator. Share of Households: Share of U.S. households in 2016.

[1] Kharas' original global definition of the middle class includes all those in households with per capita daily incomes of $10 to $100 in 2005 purchasing power parity dollars, updated to 2016 to account for inflation.

[2] We make the strong assumption that individuals rank themselves in order--that is, that the 47% who identify as middle class are located between the 39% who identify as lower or lower-middle and the 12% who identify as upper or upper-middle.

[3] Visually, we represent only the income range of the 30th to 80th percentiles. Estimates of the share of households, share of income, and growth in average income include households in the top income quintile in which no household member has a four-year college degree (about 5% of all households in 2016).

[4] We combine Rose's definitions of the lower-middle and middle class. He separates the two at $50,000.

Figure 4.6 A dozen ways to be middle class

Source: Reeves et al. (2018)

Beyond income, however, some economic definitions combine income with wealth. Wealth is different to income because it is mostly assets, such as property or shares, some of which may derive income, but often do not, unless sold. The importance of the difference here is that some people could be defined as middle class by their assets, which might be substantial, but not by their income, which may not be. For example, farmers can be in this category where a farm may be a valuable asset in and of itself, but due to market prices, weather, or other circumstances may not make much income in a given year.

Economic perspectives and contexts are also important to other social scientific definitions of middle class. For example, sociology and political science extend economic definitions of middle class by including individual attributes such as occupation type (such as a professional) and education level (such as a university degree).

The rationale for inclusions such as these is that income is derived from the work one does in an occupation, which in turn is related to the qualifications one holds as a result of education. Middle-class income (however defined) might not be related to these attributes in every case, but for the greater majority of individuals in a population these factors are often strongly correlated with income categories that indicate class groups as survey research constantly confirms.

Extended, revised, and process definitions reflect the theories and perspectives of economists, sociologists, and political scientists who are interested in the causes of class differences within an economy consistent with theories about social class and economic life. Within these extended economic conceptualizations there is further variation on definitions of middle class such as different schemes to classify occupational structures (Connelly et al., 2016; Goldthorpe et al., 1987; Wright, 1985).

Further, more elaborate definitions of middle class also include cultural criteria such as taste, consumption habits, and personal style such as clothes preferences and speech (Aarons, 2012; 2018). This is what is typically meant when someone is said to 'have class' or 'be classy'. Cultural criteria similarly reflect a concern with how class is theorized for specific purposes. For example, the French sociologist Pierre Bourdieu (1984), introduced earlier, theorized that cultural taste such as preferring classical music to pop music is a key form of belonging to the middle class through its relationship to education, and that cultural taste in turn has an impact on occupations and consequently income. To complicate things further, sociology and related disciplines also conceptualize middle class often by denoting middle *classes*, that is various fractions within the larger middle-class group. For example, sociologists of different theoretical backgrounds refer to the 'bourgeoisie', 'petite bourgeoisie', or 'managerial', 'professional', and 'administrative' middle classes that broadly correspond to upper, middle, and lower middle classes. Clearly Bourdieu and other social scientists have different purposes for their definitions and measurements of concepts such as middle class than do some economists, and definitions of the concept are operationalized in different ways as a result, producing different survey statistics.

As logical as these definitions sound, more comprehensive definitions of middle class can sometimes produce confusing estimates and statistics when operationalized in a survey, however. There may be many in a population that are not middle class as defined by income but qualify as such because of educational and cultural attributes, such as university students, recent graduates still looking for employment, or retirees. Similarly, there may be sections of a population that qualify as middle class based on their income but whose cultural and educational attributes do not meet the extended definition, such as some successful small-business owners. Again, which definition is valid and for what purpose, as each of these definitions will produce different estimates of who is middle class (Table 4.3)? Is it as Reeves et al. (2018) have stated, 'cash, credentials, or culture'?

Top down or bottom up: theory, context, and purpose

Income-derived definitions of middle class tend to be top down and are derived from economic and policy perspectives that suit contexts of economic policy for large populations. Extended economic definitions that include occupation and education are also mostly top-down definitions derived from basic research, but are also investigated in qualitative projects through consultation that feeds back into these kinds of definitions. These definitions are sometimes used in policy such as tax reform but are mainly used in academia. Economic and cultural definitions are derived from and mostly relevant to basic research and specific perspectives and theories. They are derived and revised through a combination of top-down and bottom-up theorizing and empirical testing including qualitative data and consultation.

Table 4.3 Competing definitions of middle class

Conceptualizing middle class	Income: Narrow Outcome Established	Economic and Social Scientific: Extended Process Revised	Economic and Cultural: Extended Process Revised
Top-down/bottom-up conceptualization	Top-down	Top-down	Top-down
Perspectives/theories	Economic Policy research Academic research	Economic policy research Academic research: • Economics • Sociology • Political science	Academic research: • Sociology • Political science
Previous research/ existing definitions	Economic policy	Accepts definitions derived from economic policy and extends definition through academic research	Accepts definition derived from economic policy and extends definitions through basic research and qualitative data Extends definition through academic theory and survey data and qualitative data
Consultation/ participation/ qualitative data		Some observation and qualitative data	Some observation and qualitative data
Concept validity context (basic research, policy, industry)			
Main context	Economic policy	Economic policy Basic research	Basic research

Related contexts (applications)	Social policy	Social policy	Economic policy
			Social policy
Purpose (estimate or statistic)	Extent of the population that is middle class at a specific time or over time	Extent of the population that is middle class at a specific time or over time	How social class determines and reproduces advantage and disadvantage within a society
		How social class determines and reproduces advantage and disadvantage within society	

From the case studies we can discern the key components and challenges of concept clarification. We have concepts that are common to a range of survey design contexts that produce different definitions for a variety of purposes associated with those contexts. Consequently, these differences produce different – sometimes wildly different – statistics and estimates of the concept in question. The case studies highlight also the complex nature of common concepts that are often measured by surveys and so remind us that statistics are the end product of a much more involved process at the front end of survey design and the refinement of abstraction. As a result of these case studies and the identification of the components of concept clarification, you will be in a position to begin to refine literatures and thought so as to begin to clarify a concept.

Concepts and the total survey error approach

The clarification of concepts should also be seen as a key part of the total survey error approach to survey design and survey research as more broadly conceived. Authors such as Weisberg (2005) and Groves and Lyberg (2010) only briefly mention concepts within their discussion of the framework of total survey error in terms of validity error. That is, how valid is the concept to the research? More consideration is given to measurement error in terms of question wording and question arrangement within a survey that relates to a communicative discrepancy between researcher and researched. This is a very important consideration, and one we will deal with in a later chapter. But I would advocate for conceptual clarification to be considered as an important dimension of the total survey error approach. Most certainly, questions that act as indicators for concepts are important, but prior to the development of indicators are the problems of clarifying concepts. A lot can go wrong at this stage and if a concept is vague and imprecise then the questions are not going to indicate much that we would recognize or want to use, nor will the data they collect contribute much to the field of research or the intellectual or practical problem we want to solve. The current disputes surrounding false memory research, examined below, are an important case in point. Given what we know about the importance of concepts, errors can begin at this stage and compound progressively. Avoiding error associated with concepts contains a number of steps associated with immersing yourself in the theoretical knowledge of a scholarly field, as we have seen.

Case study 4: Concept validity error, false memories, and beliefs

The seventeenth-century Dutch philosopher Baruch Spinoza stated that 'many errors, in truth, consist merely in the application of the wrong names of things'. In this case study I wish to highlight an example of concept validity error. The case studies presented above differ considerably in definition yet contain common elements that are then built upon to attempt to clarify the concept further, or contribute to an overarching concept, though researchers may argue that various definitions are erroneous in some ways. For example, poverty and homelessness may be considered as dimensions of a greater concept, 'deprivation'. At times, however, measurement and research proceed from concepts that are quite different, even though they are thought to be the same. Concept validity error can be subtle but consequential.

False memories, memories that are suggested to people through a process of manipulation and then imagined, particularly for young people, are a phenomenon that is particularly egregious in a range of contexts, such as the criminal justice system. The notion of the forced confession through false memory persuasion is a heinous miscarriage of justice, yet many of us are susceptible to such manipulation according to research. False memory suggestion is a dynamic area of research in psychology. One purpose of the research into false memory is to attempt to learn the proportion of a population that is vulnerable to such a phenomenon and in which contexts. You might be alarmed to learn that nearly one in five and in some cases one in four people are susceptible to false memory suggestion (Scoboria et al., 2017). If somewhere between a fifth and a quarter of a population can be manipulated into confessing to things they have not done, such as crimes, you can intuit how important the concept of false memory is, and how crucial is its measurement. Well, if you are alarmed at one in four or five, how would you feel if I told you that there is research out there claiming a figure of more like seven in ten people potentially susceptible to false memory persuasion (Shaw and Porter, 2015)?

In recent times false memory research has been the subject of intense public interest after researcher Julia Shaw and her colleague Stephen Porter reported findings from a series of studies to be well above the rate of incidence that many in the field have reported through numerous previous studies. Shaw and Porter's estimate of the proportion of those susceptible to false memory suggestion, and that of others, is in dispute, however (Wade et al., 2018) and the key problem is the definition of the concept 'false memory' and the criteria associated with the concept that are used in measuring it. This is a very complex field with numerous ways of defining the concept of false memory.

One of the main problems contributing to the vast range of reported incidences from a number of studies of false memory is, according to Scoboria et al., that there exists a wide 'variation across studies in how false memories were operationalized' (2017: 147). That is, how the concept of false memory is defined and then how it is measured is inconsistent. The contention in studies such as Shaw and Porter's is that some scholars in the field suggest that what the Shaw and Porter study actually measures is 'false beliefs', a closely related but different concept to false memory. To suggest you believe something rather than remember it is different, although the process of suggestion to produce the phenomena may be common. The implications of such differences are substantial, however, for measurement and estimates, and for application in various contexts. It should be noted that conceptual anomalies such as these occur in the social sciences quite regularly and that debates over measurement are not uncommon, and do not represent anything necessarily deceptive. Indeed, they highlight the complexity of theoretical and conceptual thinking within a dynamic field, and again highlight the importance of concepts and measurement, leading to data and knowledge.

―――――――――――――――――― YOUR SURVEY ――――――――――――――――――

Identifying and operationalizing concepts

Proceeding from the work done in Chapters 2 and 3:

- Identify the key concepts in your research questions that will be measured in your survey. Include minor as well as major concepts. Minor concepts will include concepts that are routinely measured in many surveys, such as demographics, or identity attributes, such as education, gender, age, and place.
- If working with a specific theory, how are the concepts you have identified defined within that theory? Can they or have they been measured successfully in a survey before?
- Search the literature for previous empirical research on these concepts, to complement topical and empirical literatures that you explored in the previous YOUR SURVEY sections. Below are some suggestions for good resources to get you started on clarifying your concepts through finding more specific literatures:

  o Discipline-specific databases for books, journal articles, book chapters – check your university or college library.
  o Conceptual dictionaries – statistical agencies, research sections of government departments, technical notes in statistical sections of large national and international surveys.
  o Discipline-specific handbooks: for example, *Reader on the Sociology of Music*, *Handbook of Educational Research*, *Handbook of Law and Economics*.
  o Discipline-specific dictionaries – an excellent source of concept definitions.

(Continued)

- o   Theoretical works and commentaries about them in specific disciplines that deal with the concept of interest.
- o   Qualitative research specifically about or related to your concepts of interest.
- o   Meta studies, reviews, or concept-specific journal articles.
- o   Industry publications, technical reports, and methodological notes about concepts of interest.

- Organize the material and consider the range of definitions of key concepts that you have found. Do they relate to the needs of the research if you are working with a community group, business, or organization? How relevant and practical are they to questions the survey will collect data for?
- Consider the context, purpose, and perspectives associated with your concepts and their potential definitions. Should they be more or less expansive? This will depend on the research question, and to some extent on how the concepts are developed in the next chapter and beyond.
- *Consultation.* If working with an outside organization, you may need to discuss the operational definition of key concepts that your survey will aim to measure so it meets the needs of the organization. Extended definitions of concepts may not be required for organizations that are most probably interested in more practical definitions; however, you should be able to work with an extended definition of a concept that is related to theory and can provide a practical estimate and statistics for more specific needs.

Key knowledge and skills

This chapter has introduced concepts as a vital component in the survey design process. Concepts are crucial to surveys because they are central to measurement and are therefore required to undergo a thorough process of operationalization to assist in valid and reliable measures. Let's recount the key knowledge and skills entailed in this chapter:

- Any research question will have one or more key concepts that will need to be clarified and operationally defined before being validly measured in a survey.
- Concepts are vague and often complex. To commence defining and operationalization of a concept requires a systematic literature search via databases covering theories, empirical studies, replications, and literature outside of academia, relevant to the concept of interest.
- Any concept will have numerous definitions reflecting a variety of perspectives, contexts, and purposes that produce different estimates and statistics in a survey. An appropriate definition will depend on the perspective, context, and the purpose of the study:

    - o   *Theoretical definitions.* Concepts that are embedded in a theoretical perspective of a scholarly field. Often there will be debates about how concepts are defined and understood within a field which can differ.
    - o   *Industry-specific definitions.* These may or may not differ from how a theoretical field in academia defines a concept, but there are certainly interesting comparisons to

be made. At times the definitions between industry and academia may well be very similar, and at other times quite different.

    ○ *Policy or governmental definitions.* Again, these may or may not be aligned with the academic literature and have specific uses for government departments and agencies.

- Concept development will be top down, expert led, and derived, and/or be bottom up, consultative, and participatory, drawing on the lived experience of the concept of interest.

Further reading

Concepts and the process of their clarification, despite being crucial to the survey design process, are given very little dedicated attention in most texts about survey design. For an excellent consideration of the role of concepts in science in general, with many references to the social sciences, a classic paper is Blumer's *Science Without Concepts*. While not discussing concepts generally, Gibbs and Blumer's *Social Measurement Through Social Surveys* is a good source of information concerning a range of key concepts that are often the subjects of measurement in social surveys. I would encourage readers also to consult a range of national statistical agencies that often have concept dictionaries and discussion papers about them. These can be accessed via the internet.

Full text references:

Blumer, H. (1931) 'Science Without Concepts'. *American Journal of Sociology,* 36 (4): 515–533

Gibbs, J. and Blumer, M. (2010) *Social Measurement Through Social Surveys: An Applied Approach.* London: Routledge

 Discover the digital resources for this chapter, including reflective questions, case studies, and templates, at https://study.sagepub.com/aarons

Five

Dimensions, Sub-Dimensions, and Indicators

This chapter sets out the next steps in the survey design process concerning the clarification and operationalization of concepts. This chapter covers:

- Further refinement of concepts
- Identification of dimensions of a concept
- Identification of sub-dimensions of a concept
- Ways in which dimensions and sub-dimensions of concepts are relevant to a research question
- Key considerations for the development of indicators

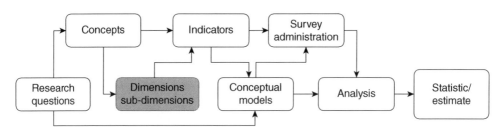

Figure 5.1   Survey design process: dimensions and sub-dimensions

In this chapter we build on the key idea of clarifying concepts introduced in Chapter 4. We considered a number of key examples of concepts to get a feel for what confronts researchers when attempting to design a survey. Despite the differences and definitions that were outlined in the examples in the previous chapter, the journey of concept clarification does not stop there, however. Concepts often need further refining and discernment in order to meet the goal of valid measurement in survey design. You would have noticed that in Chapter 4 despite elaborating on some key concepts that are associated with some of the most common themes of survey research, there were a number of different operational definitions of them. When thinking about the concept case studies from the previous chapter, it is important to realize that the various definitions that were offered for the concepts of interest were not necessarily more or less 'right' or 'wrong', but subject to perspective, context, and purpose.

As such, conceptual definitions are, more or less, appropriate to specific research contexts despite the debates that do ensue about definitions. Perspectives, contexts, and purposes further determine how a definition of a concept might be more concentrated or extensive or focused on outcome or process. This concentration and extensivity of a conceptual definition reflect the inclusion or exclusion of various elements of a concept that go into a final operational definition depending on the requirements of the research. The various elements of a concept are called dimensions and sub-dimensions in the survey design process (Figure 5.1) and represent further steps down the ladder of abstraction to more precise measurement.

In this chapter we build on what we have learned about clarifying concepts by focusing on their more specific components: dimensions and sub-dimensions.

From this more refined version of a concept that includes dimensions and sub-dimensions, survey design then proceeds to the development of indicators. Later in the chapter we will outline some important considerations of indicators, before tackling their more precise development and formation in the next chapter.

Let's start our exploration of dimensions and sub-dimensions with a diagram. As you can see from Figure 5.2, concepts more specifically laid out diagrammatically illustrate their scope as broad ideas and can resemble the structure of a large organization or corporation, with various departments and divisions. The figure illustrates the breakdown of a concept into dimensions, sub-dimensions (and further sub-dimensions, sometimes), and finally indicators, all conveying the complexity of concepts as they relate to measurement in survey design. Coming to terms with this complexity is a key point of understanding and learning associated with the survey design process. These components are all vital in descending the ladder of abstraction and getting our survey instrument to work effectively through specified clarification leading to measurement. You can think of the figure as a template for how survey researchers further proceed in thinking about refinement of a concept and its measurement.

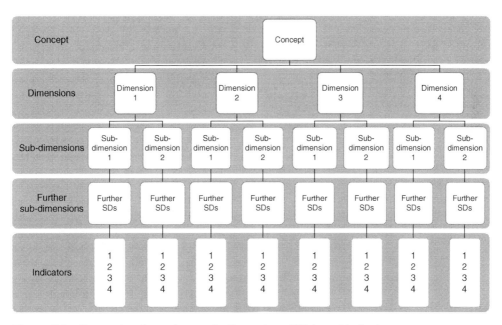

Figure 5.2 Concepts, dimensions, sub-dimensions (SDs), and indicators

What is a dimension?

Dimensions of concepts can be thought of as specific related components of a broader concept. A dimension will have something essential in common with the 'parent' concept, but the accent, emphasis, or focus will be on something more specified.

Many concepts, reflective of their complexity, are what we call 'multidimensional', that is they contain more than one dimension and are therefore in need of further clarification. Indeed, the greater majority of concepts researchers seek to measure through surveys will contain many different dimensions, so this aspect of clarification and operationalization is important to their design but also any clear reading of survey-based research. In addition to further clarifying a concept, identifying a concept's different dimensions will also assist in delimiting and contextualizing the research because not all dimensions of a concept will necessarily be relevant to the research questions.

An example from the last chapter is poverty. Poverty, as we have learned, entails numerous dimensions, irrespective of how it might actually be defined. A number of dimensions of poverty were considered in both concentrated and extensive definitions such as economic, educational, health, and shelter. The same pattern of multidimensionality is noticeable for homelessness and represents different aspects of a common core experience. Further, we might even consider that both poverty and homelessness, themselves complex concepts, are but dimensions of a latent concept such as deprivation. Health, which we also briefly dealt with in a previous chapter, is the same. Many dimensions of health come readily to mind: physical health, mental health, emotional health, even financial health. These dimensions all relate to health in the sense that they represent some form of whatever health is, but with the focus on a particular aspect or segment associated with it. An analogy is a colour chart. If you have ever attempted to paint a wall or a canvas, or decorate a document, you will have to select from among the extensive range of shades of colours available to you – these you can think of as dimensions of a colour, such as those produced by Pantone: 'Moonlight blue', 'Dutch blue'; 'Allure', and so on. Identifying dimensions and sub-dimensions is important to survey design for two main reasons:

- They give a clearer indication of what the overall concept entails. That is, just how broad and complex the concept is.
- They help specify the most relevant aspects of a concept to the research question and to the survey design.

Sub-dimensions

From dimensions of concepts we continue to step down the ladder of abstraction to **sub-dimensions**. A sub-dimension is a further refinement of a dimension of a concept, or another set of shades of blue to continue our colour analogy. Given what we know about the complexity of particular life experiences of people from which we construct concepts such as health, education, employment, and poverty, discerning sub-dimensions for the purposes of measurement in a survey is a necessary and appropriate further step. As with dimensions of concepts, however, sub-dimensions contain the essence of a concept and dimension that it is related to.

Sub-dimensions are quite common in social research, such as the distinctions made between life satisfaction, depression, and anxiety as sub-dimensions of mental health, which in turn is a dimension of health. Sub-dimensions can go deep at times too, with further sub-dimensions. As for dimensions, adhering to and learning to discern sub-dimensions have distinct research and survey design benefits that are more likely to ensure that we are defining and measuring concepts accurately:

- Further refinement enabling greater focus and greater clarity concerning what is to be measured, leading to better operational definitions and data quality.
- More accurate engagement with current/relevant literature in a field, particularly where the field is greatly nuanced.
- Much better odds of developing valid and reliable indicators.

Indicators

From dimensions and sub-dimensions we arrive somewhere near the ground, preparing to step off the ladder with respect to the operationalization of our concepts with the construction of indicators. Indicators are the actual questions that you ask in a survey, grounded in the process of refining the abstract concepts through theoretical reflection, dimensional, and sub-dimensional segmentation in consideration of perspective, context, and purpose. Once we are content with the clarification of our concepts after dividing them into relevant dimensions and sub-dimensions, we can start to develop indicators that will populate our survey and measure our concepts.

The development of indicators is both an art and a science, and beset with its own series of complexities, pitfalls, and errors. Researchers can be creative in the way they design survey questions to measure dimensions and sub-dimensions of concepts (in fact they constantly need to be), but creativity and imagination must partner with and be bound by scientific parameters. There are a number of important considerations accompanying the development of indicators, but of all the important aspects associated with developing indicators, two stand out as absolutely fundamental: (1) validity, and (2) reliability. Validity aims at measuring exactly what was intended to be measured, and reliability is to ensure that the indicator can be used more than once. Here are some key considerations when deciding on indicators:

- *Validity*: Is the indicator you have selected or developed a valid measure of the concept you seek to measure in your survey? In other words, does the question you have used in your survey actually measure what you want it to measure?
- *Reliability*: How reliable is (are) the indicator(s) that you have chosen or designed for your survey? That is, does it (do they) produce the same or similar answers every time it is (they are) used in the same context?

- *Number of indicators?* How many questions does your survey actually need to measure a concept adequately (validly and reliably)? As many concepts are complex, most surveys employ more than one measure, yet how many more are necessary?
- *How the indicators/questions are designed.* Questions on surveys are a minefield of potential problems; how they are worded is a crucial aspect of survey design to avoid confusion and poor and invalid data.
- *How the indicators/questions are set out in the survey.* Beyond how you ask questions is the consideration of how you arrange them in a survey. Indicators need to be carefully and strategically placed in a survey to avoid a range of problems with responses.

These considerations I will only flag here and take up again in much more detail later in the chapter and in Chapter 6. Now I wish to turn to investigating further some of the concepts we met in Chapter 4 to continue to clarify them by delineating their dimensions and sub-dimensions. In the next section I want to reconsider the case studies introduced in the last chapter and illustrate further the process of concept clarification with a consideration of how dimensions and sub-dimensions are discerned for poverty, homelessness, and middle class, with some other examples thrown in.

Case studies

Poverty: Dimensions and sub-dimensions

As we have seen, there are many different ways to conceptualize poverty, with numerous dimensions and sub-dimensions included or excluded. Indeed, as stated in the previous chapter the debates about what constitutes a concept such as poverty and in what perspectives, and contexts, and for what purposes is contested. Beginning with Figure 5.3, we can discern the dimensions and sub-dimensions of an income, financial, or economic threshold-based definition of poverty, which is often favoured by government departments whose core concerns are the economic and financial aspects of a household, region, or nation. Economic and financial perspectives of conceptualizing poverty sometimes include wealth, thereby extending the definition of the concept by making the distinction between two different sub-dimensions of a definition of poverty from an economic perspective: *income*, or what someone or a household earns in a year or a fortnight; and *wealth*, resources of value that can be exchanged for money or that earn money. Further sub-dimensions such as household and personal income can be vitally important and impact the estimate or statistic the measure is designed to collect because an individual may have little personal income, perhaps qualifying them as in poverty yet as part of a wealthy household and therefore not defined as being in poverty. Dependents such as children are relevant to these distinctions.

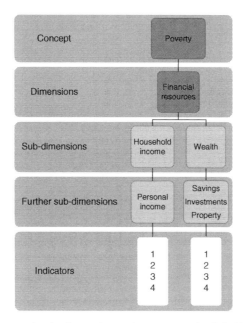

Figure 5.3 Dimensions and sub-dimensions of an economic definition of poverty

A more extensive conceptual definition of poverty such as that represented in Figure 5.4 outlines four dimensions and numerous sub-dimensions of the core concept derived from the literature (I have based this section on Reeves et al., 2016 as an example) that seeks to extend the concept of poverty from a social policy perspective. We reasoned that what is common to poverty is characterized by the idea of 'lack' or 'deprivation'. People in poverty are lacking, not just in the dimensions such as money as the more narrow definitions contended, but also including a lack or being deprived of a range of resources as Reeves et al. contend and that are related to monetary deprivation in a process of being in poverty.

As the previous chapter established, extended definitions often build on previous definitions. While financial and economic dimensions and sub-dimensions are important and meet the needs of certain types of research, a range of other dimensions are also perceived to be important and relevant to poverty, aiming to increase concept validity, reflective of the perspective, context, and purpose. The second dimension of poverty included here is community resources; where individuals live, what communities have, and are like to live in, profoundly influence an individual's experience of lack. Community resources entail two sub-dimensions: neighbourhood conditions and educational resources. Neighbourhood conditions include the level of crime, whether a community has parks, playgrounds, sports fields, and what transport is like in it. Educational resources are the presence and quality of pre-schools, schools, and colleges and universities. A neighbourhood or community is obviously more or less desirable and affordable depending on the inclusion or absence of such resources.

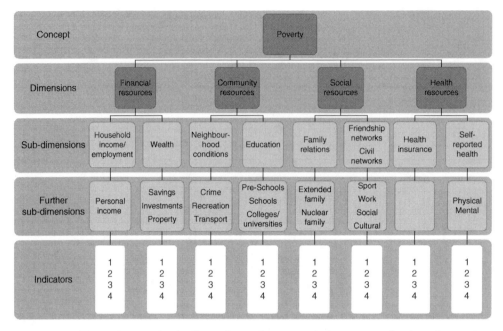

Figure 5.4 Dimensions and sub-dimensions of an extended conceptualization of poverty

There is a choice to be made about the indicators here of course relating to the research question the survey is collecting data for. Recall the types of research questions that are appropriate for survey research. The indicators must adhere to them, so a researcher asking about crime in a community asks about being a victim of crime, perceptions of crime in the community where the respondents live, and if they think crime is a problem. Of interest here is what researchers can do empirically on issues such as crime. Some researchers connect different data sources on issues such as crime so as to get objective and subjective data, and to assess the differences between attitudes, perceptions, and an objective standard such as the number of crimes against a person or property that have been recorded. Survey research can be ably complemented by official statistics; providing accurate geographic information about a respondent is a part of the survey (which for sampling purposes is usually the case).

The third dimension of poverty here that Reeves et al. (2016) have identified is social resources under which are included a few sub-dimensions, but with a list of further sub-dimensions, as you can see in Figure 5.4. You may be able to think of others as your literature search broadens and in line with your perspectives, context, and purpose. Isolation, loneliness, and a lack of social contact are other forms of poverty, leading to a range of negative consequences, some of which directly relate to wealth and income such as trying to find employment, or declining capacity to work due to mental health problems. Lacking in social resources then is marked as being represented by family relations, friendship networks, and civil networks ('civil' here can be understood as various connections people have with groups in what we call 'civil society', such as sporting clubs, leisure groups of all kinds, churches, charity or voluntary groups, and groups associated with social or political causes). These sub-dimensions are categorized into further sub-dimensions such as work, sport, social, and cultural, as well as extended family and nuclear family. Indicators for these are to be thought about also.

A fourth dimension of poverty is health resources, further refined into two sub-dimensions and a couple of further sub-dimensions. Lacking health and the resources aiding good health as Reeves et al. contend is a dimension of poverty. In many countries, having health insurance is an indicator of wealth or relative advantage, and self-reported health, separated into mental and physical dimensions, provides another set of measures for a potential survey research project into poverty.

Let's take a closer look at the Individual Deprivation Measure (IDM), described by Bessell (2015). This definition of poverty is perhaps the most extensive known and entails no less than 15 dimensions of poverty in its operational definition (Figure 5.5). The dimensions can be further divided into sub-dimensions but are discrete and use four indicators for each dimension, so sub-dimensions are not a priority for the way this conceptualization of poverty has been devised. The development of the concept is unique in that it does not consider income directly as a key dimension of poverty, although work is a dimension. Further, the concept as outlined here, grounded in consultative and qualitative work, is hierarchical and suggests dimensions are ranked in terms of importance concerning poverty according to those for whom the concept is directly relevant. These measures are applied to a sample with a unit of analysis that is the individual, unlike many definitions of poverty that are applied to a household. The elaboration of these dimensions also allows us to consider the perspective, context, and purpose of clarifying a concept such as poverty in this way.

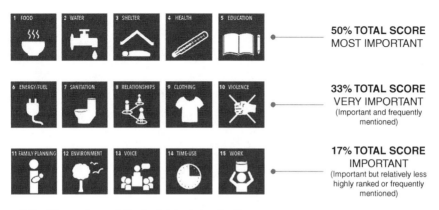

Figure 5.5 Dimensions of the individual deprivation measure

Source: Individual Deprivation Measure 2018

Homelessness: Dimensions and sub-dimensions

Homelessness, much the same as poverty, has been conceptualized in concentrated and extensive styles. Again, the conceptual differences pertain to the kinds of dimensions that different conceptualizations offer in line with their respective perspectives, contexts, and purposes. Consider the 'conservative' or literal conceptual definition of homelessness (Figure 5.6) that we encountered in the previous chapter. We can separate out from the definition only one dimension – shelter. From this one dimension we can also discern two sub-dimensions – emergency and makeshift shelter. A further sub-dimension of emergency shelter is public emergency shelters, or private emergency shelters. Of course, these are important distinctions in terms of an accurate count or estimate of the homeless under these sub-dimensions.

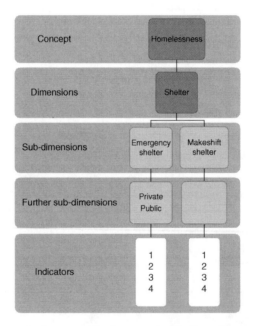

Figure 5.6 Dimensions of a 'conservative' conceptualization of homelessness

Further, we encountered what Chamberlain and Mackenzie (1992) termed 'radical' definitions of homelessness. These built on the literal or conservative definitions but included dimensions and sub-dimensions of homelessness that focused on the perceived needs and experiences of the individual. These definitions derived from academic theories, but also from industry through consultation and qualitative data – from agency workers who also researched homelessness. In Figure 5.7 I have included these dimensions within the literal definitions and earlier skid row definitions as Chamberlain and McKenzie's (1992) article suggests.

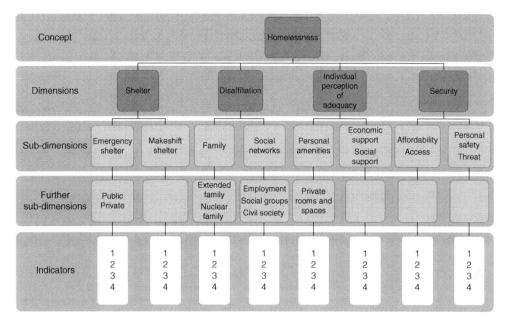

Figure 5.7 Dimensions of a 'radical' conceptualization of homelessness

The cultural definition of homelessness (Figure 5.8) extends and refines both literal and radical definitions of homelessness by incorporating a contextual approach that sought to benchmark and define homelessness through 'minimum community

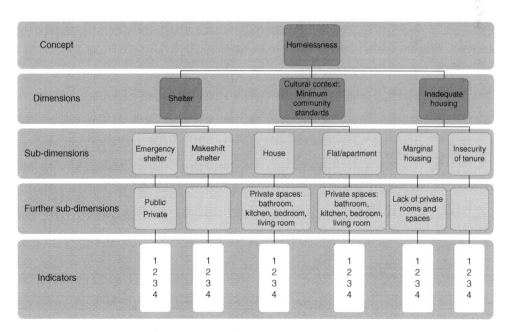

Figure 5.8 Dimensions of a 'cultural' definition of homelessness

standards' (Chamberlain and Mackenzie, 1992). This entails a relative approach to the notion of home grounded in the culture where it will be applied and measured. Highlighting the complexity of this concept is a subtle aside in the cultural approach with the introduction of another possible concept altogether: 'inadequate housing'. However, it can be thought of as a dimension of the parent concept homelessness here. Inadequate or marginal housing is housing that does not meet the minimum cultural standard yet may include people in accommodation that includes most of the criteria that Chamberlain and Mackenzie specify.

Who is middle class? Dimensions and sub-dimensions

Let's apply our model of dimensions, sub-dimensions, and indicators to the concept of middle class. Recall that the previous chapter presented three definitions of middle class: (1) middle class defined by income; (2) middle class defined by income, wealth, education, and occupation; (3) middle class defined economically and also culturally.

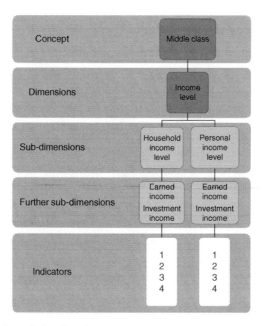

Figure 5.9 Middle class defined as income

Here in Figure 5.9 we can see a conceptual diagram of middle class as narrowly defined as income or as determined by income level. As we have seen, there are many ways in which economists and others have determined to be middle class by income level and its relationship to spending power and distance from the mean income level for a population. Here I have highlighted two important sub-dimensions of an income-determined definition of middle class: household income and personal income. Further sub-dimensions could include, but not necessarily be limited to, earned income and

income from investments. This conceptualization of middle class is a practical operationalization used by governments for the purposes of ease of measurement to denote
who (households mostly) falls between income parameters.

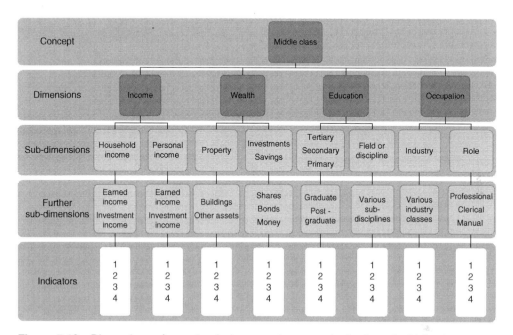

Figure 5.10 Dimensions of an extended economic conceptualization of middle class

Figure 5.10 diagrams the extended economic conceptualization of middle class. I
have outlined four dimensions common to this form of concept clarification. There
are also numerous sub-dimensions and further sub-dimensions in this conceptual definition. This extended economic definition is sometimes used by governments and/
or national statistical agencies for the purposes of measurement for policy, but mostly
it derives from and is used for academic purposes to assess the dynamics between the
various dimensions and sub-dimensions leading to material advantage and disadvantage as numerous theories around class dynamics within the economic system claim.

In Figure 5.11 I have added the cultural dimension and sub-dimensions of the concept middle class. Culture is an extended dimension of being middle class to many
researchers who theorize and seek to measure middle class. Culture is a complex concept in itself, but in the context of defining middle class it is often confined to cultural
tastes and practices. Particular tastes in culture such as music, literature, film, and food
(there are many others) are complemented by cultural practices – usually attendance at
cultural events or participation in cultural activities. Cultural dimensions and definitions of middle class are derived from academic research, not from policy or industry,
and serve various theories about how being middle class is a product of certain forms
of status and privilege that reinforce the economic dimensions of social life.

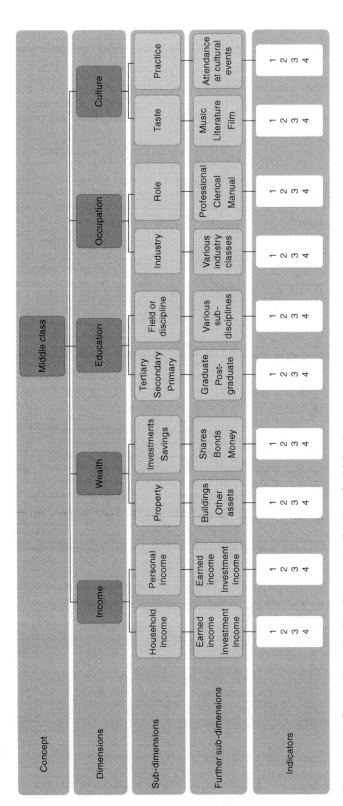

Figure 5.11 Economic and cultural conceptualization of middle class

Building on the clarification process of concepts from the previous chapter, we have sought further, through the survey design process, to clarify concepts through a delineation of dimensions and sub-dimensions. This separating out of the various dimensions and sub-dimensions of a concept is a key part in our 'descending the ladder of abstraction' to operationalize concepts further. I would like to consider briefly some more common examples of key concepts used in social surveys that, conditioned through the survey design process, provide us with more food for thought as to how key ideas in policy, industry, and academic research are debated and measured, leading to various estimates, statistics, and decision making.

Employment: Dimensions and sub-dimensions

Employment is a key concept that measures a broader concept – that of being economically active – as well as a dimension of socio-economic status. Even though we are treating it here as its own concept, it can be reasonably thought of as a dimension of another, as I am sure you may have noticed about some dimensions or sub-dimensions of poverty in the previous example. Nevertheless, employment is a key concept that many researchers are interested in for its own sake. Like most concepts, there are different ways we can go about measuring employment. In the example below, we may only be interested in the descriptive and lived experiences of employment of our respondents, but there are other ways we can measure employment, such as attitudes towards employment policies, opinions about potential employment prospects, employment intentions, employment history, and so on. Let's stick with the personal experiences of employment which will provide us with a series of descriptive data about the work experiences of our respondents.

Again, with the aid of some literature, I have discerned four dimensions of employment: 'type', 'industry', 'occupation', and 'hours'; there may be more that you can think of, or that have been identified in the literature. Employment is a diverse concept and the dimensions in Figure 5.12 are indicative and not comprehensive of the concept.

The first dimension here is 'type' which carries two sub-dimensions 'paid and unpaid'. This might sound a little strange, but there is a theoretical argument to include unpaid employment in any definition of being economically active and for the hours put into companies and organizations by those who are not paid through the efforts of volunteers, interns, and trainees. Following paid and unpaid are more 'types' as further sub-dimensions, such as those who work on contracts, who are casually or seasonally employed, and others who have permanent positions.

Another important dimension of employment that researchers are often interested in measuring in a survey is the industry in which individuals work. Apart from the type of work that is done, researchers want to know where (in the economy) it is done. The economies of most countries are incredibly diverse and complex and the range

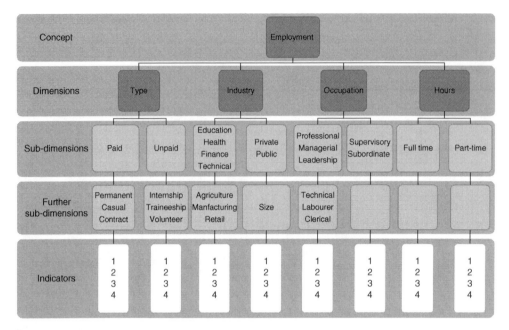

Figure 5.12 Employment dimensions and sub-dimensions

of industries that professions and jobs inhabit is highly differentiated. The industries listed in the sub-dimensions and further sub-dimensions are a mere selection of some of the major industries that individuals work in, yet if we are interested in employment we can discern who works where, if this has changed, and if various industries have increased or declined, as many scholars and observers of employment trends have commented concerning an industry such as manufacturing. Industries are also 'public' and 'private', that is many people work in various organizations that are part of a government department or government-owned enterprise or a private company.

An easily intuited dimension of employment is occupation, that is the profession or job one works in. Surveys that are interested in the employment experiences of their respondents will certainly ask what the respondent's job is as a descriptive title, such as plumber, scientist, or nurse, but there are often other aspects of a job that researchers are also interested in that are latent in occupation titles. There are a couple of key sub-dimensions to occupation that survey researchers often discern that characterize the nature, quality, or status of the occupation an individual indicates in a survey. Many jobs are categorized as 'professional', 'managerial', 'labouring', 'clerical', or other in nature; they also reflect sets of skills and forms of workplace authority and status. In any workplace there are occupations that are supervisory, in that you have a boss or are a boss responsible for what others do, and you also follow instructions as a sub-ordinate.

A common definition of employment that many governments use is that if you are over 15 years of age and have worked for pay for an hour or more you are 'employed'.

The time spent in paid or unpaid work is another important dimension of employment; indeed it is also a dimension of what many consider to be a hidden feature of employment, which is 'underemployment'.

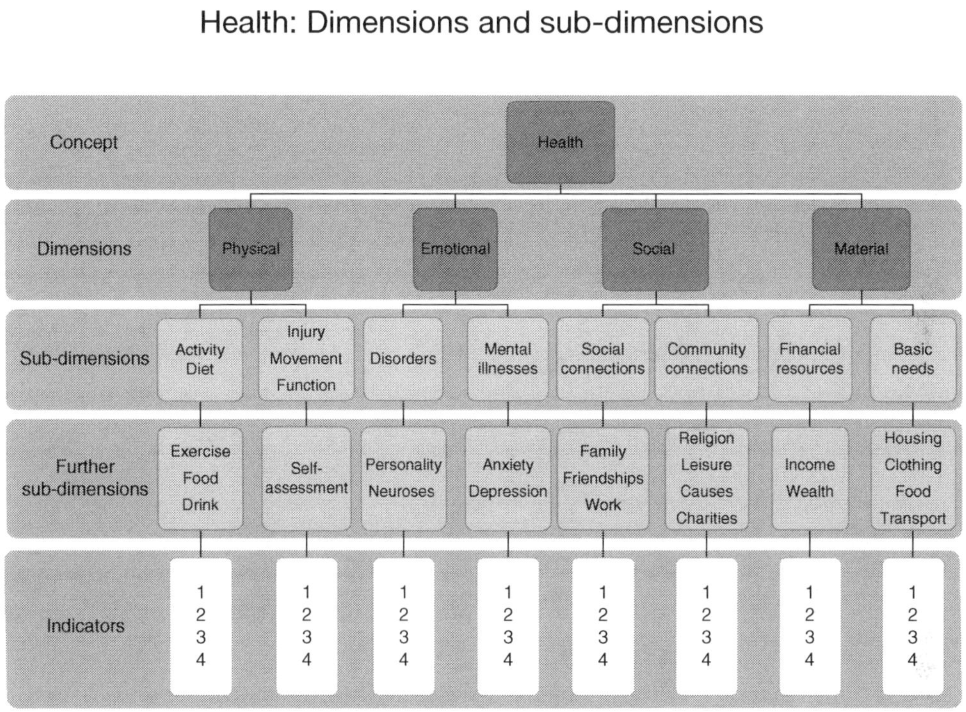

Health: Dimensions and sub-dimensions

Concept			Health				
Dimensions	Physical		Emotional		Social		Material
Sub-dimensions	Activity Diet	Injury Movement Function	Disorders	Mental illnesses	Social connections	Community connections	Financial resources	Basic needs
Further sub-dimensions	Exercise Food Drink	Self-assessment	Personality Neuroses	Anxiety Depression	Family Friendships Work	Religion Leisure Causes Charities	Income Wealth	Housing Clothing Food Transport
Indicators	1 2 3 4	1 2 3 4	1 2 3 4	1 2 3 4	1 2 3 4	1 2 3 4	1 2 3 4	1 2 3 4

Figure 5.13 Dimensions and sub-dimensions of health

Health is a phenomenally complex and layered area of human life. This complexity is reflected in the varieties of models of the concept I could have presented as an example here. There are very many dimensions to a concept like health, but for the purposes of this example, like the others preceding it, I have further attempted to clarify the concept health by identifying four key dimensions in preparation for measurement in a survey (Figure 5.13). Indeed, the limitations on conceptualization are important for concepts such as health if we are to measure them in a survey. Not everything to do with health can be measured in a survey of course. Measures such as blood pressure and other physiological data are not generally collected in social surveys measuring health (although if those data are available they can be added to the survey data), so as previously stated in what kinds of research questions are relevant for survey design, we are limited by our interests and the types of research questions a survey seeks to answer when thinking about clarifying a concept such as health.

Health and its dimensions, however, need the identification of some unifying essence, something that we can say is common to all of the different dimensions that we are interested in for the purposes of measurement. While I stated that poverty might be characterized by the experience of 'lack', health may be characterized by the term 'function'. But those of you who are on your way to being experts will know much more than I and I will leave it with you. Whatever the core of the definition, the dimensions should be commensurate with it and reflect its different components.

Most of us who are not experts in health will of course have some idea about what dimensions of health might be important to measure if health is a concern in our research. Certainly 'physical' health is one dimension most people would easily identify. I would confidently say that, increasingly, many people would also identify 'mental' or 'emotional' health as an important dimension of human functioning. Further, and this is where the roles of theory, scholarship, and reflection are important, conceptualizations of health have changed, to include dimensions such as 'social', 'material', even 'spiritual' (to entail the increasingly diverse number of religious communities in multicultural societies). Health as a concept, like all concepts, needs to be considered in context and also for what purpose. Where researchers once focused only on physical aspects of bodily functioning, research has suggested that health should be broadened to include a range of other dimensions.

On the physical dimension of health, however, we know, expert or not, that there are numerous sub-dimensions and further sub-dimensions of physical health that may be relevant to our research. The human body has numerous systems and components (dimensions in themselves) that could all be counted towards measuring health. Sexual health, brain health, blood health, muscular–skeletal health, etc. We cannot measure the precise nature of their presence in a survey of course, and we may not want to, but we can measure some aspects of the physical dimensions of health such as an individual's experience of health through descriptive questions commensurate with the aims and limits of survey research. I have highlighted a few key sub-dimensions that are common to health researchers who use surveys. How much exercise or how active we are, our diets, whether we have experienced injury, and how well we think our bodies function are some areas of physical health that surveys can measure.

Mental or emotional health is another important dimension of health. It too can be further meaningfully divided into a range of sub-dimensions for the purposes of survey research, far more than the two offered here. Researchers and practitioners whose field is mental health often use surveys effectively to help assess individuals for a range of mental health conditions, disorders, and illnesses, through the clarification of mental health into sets of conditions or illnesses. As with physical health, research on mental health is not just a matter of identifying levels of physiological abnormality or inconsistency in the body or the brain, but attitudinal and attributional measures that researchers have worked out are associated with these conditions or illnesses.

Where once we might have stopped at physical health and perhaps mental health, the theoretical and scholarly debates have widened the field and definition of health to include related dimensions of the concept such as social networks and material resources (you may have joined the dots at this point and be thinking 'any chance health is related to poverty?' Yes it is, according to a lot of research.) These dimensions are related to the first two but are different and reflect again the type of research question a project seeks to answer with a survey. These dimensions are not strictly about health (assuming we have a sound operational definition – which we do not!), they are about the social connections and material resources that one has. Yet they are, after much research, often acknowledged as being strongly associated with physical and mental health (Donkin, 2014). Indeed, public health research over the last 60 or 70 years has strongly identified how the 'social model' of health complements the medical model (chemically treating the physiological causes of illness in isolation) particularly in attempts to prevent illnesses. Here then we can include these dimensions to assess if they are related. These sub-dimensions of health, however, are included or acknowledged and further measured only if they are of interest to the research, but for our example this is how survey researchers think about such concepts.

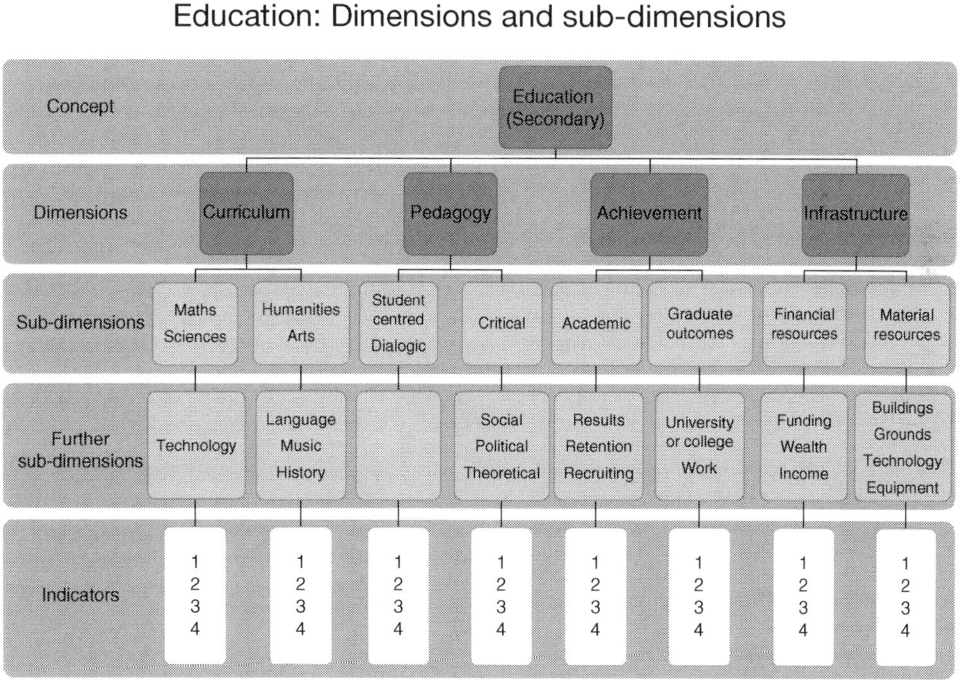

Education: Dimensions and sub-dimensions

Figure 5.14 Dimensions and sub-dimensions of education

Education is another big, hugely important, and often measured concept. Like health it is multidimensional and a fuller treatment of it would comprise its own volume. However, from Figure 5.14 you can get an idea of what conceptualizing and researching education in survey design might entail in terms of dimensions and sub-dimensions, but also context. It is important to acknowledge, with education especially, that we need to distinguish a context. Education is an institution and an industry with many different aspects to it, and, like health, research into education is confined to and appropriate only for certain contexts and questions. Here in the present example I have considered education in terms of secondary education (pre-school, tertiary, or vocational education are other dimensions), research for which might be aimed at a school community entailing respondents such as parents of students, teachers, and school staff, or a general sample of respondents. My present example pertains to high schools and to a specific aspect of them.

What about secondary school, however? Which aspects of a school community might researchers want attitudes, opinions, and experiences from their respondents? Of course, what is taught at a school is crucial, so curriculum is something of a no brainer if we were to seek to measure education in some way. What is taught is often regulated by government authorities and boards, but the quality of what is taught, and how it is taught, is often at variance between schools in a region, state, or area. Pedagogy or how a subject is taught and how learning is facilitated is also of intense interest to a school community and to education scholars. What is the pedagogical orientation(s) of a school? Does it have an impact on achievement? Should it be changed?

Many schools are judged by their achievements across a number of sub-dimensions. Certainly academic achievements are, through results and test scores, but not just these. How many students does a school recruit and retain, for example? Further, schools might measure 'achievement' by how many students are graduates, and where those graduates end up after completing high school. Do they go off to college or university, find employment, volunteer, or what?

The quality of a school could be measured along a series of criteria. Schools carry various types of infrastructure which we can divide as sub-dimensions. Schools, we can easily intuit, rely on their economic circumstances to produce the conditions necessary for some aspects of student success. All over the world schools are richer or poorer than other schools. How is a school funded through government, private legacies, or other sources leading to variation in resources and therefore achievement? Another sub-dimension of infrastructure is material resources, which can be divided into further sub-dimensions such as grounds, buildings, and technology aiding teaching and learning.

Further, all of this dimensional and sub-dimensional deliberation could be complemented with demographic and socio-economic data from the school's student body and/or geographic region.

Religion: Dimensions and sub-dimensions

The last example I would like to include is that of my own research discussed in Chapter 3. Recall that one of my challenges was to clarify what I meant by religion.

Figure 5.15 graphically shows how I did it. There are other dimensions of religion that are discussed in the sociological literature, such as the belief in God and the literalism of beliefs, but they were not relevant to my research questions.

I began by thinking about the context – the society that I live in and where the research was to be undertaken: Australia and for academic research (there are no real policy or industry applications for this kind of research, apart from defining a religion for tax purposes). Buddhism can be considered to be a 'new' religion or a non-traditional religion in the Australian context, say, compared with Thailand where it has been practised for centuries. In Australia Buddhists are mostly recently arrived migrants, as well as local converts, so as I was interested in local converts, I was interested in whether these people saw themselves as Buddhist, or something else, or nothing. There was plenty of literature stating that Buddhism in western contexts was a religious tradition that many people explored or experimented with without calling themselves Buddhist. Was this evident in the Australian context? Religious identity therefore was an important dimension to consider, to begin clarifying what I meant by religion.

Following religious identity, there are two key dimensions of religion that many sociologists have sought to measure – religious practice and religious belief. These two dimensions are quite clear and unambiguous, and 'natural' in the sense that while they are abstract in terms of their being central to theories about religion, they are also at the heart of a personal and communal experience of religion, belief, and practice. While there is a large body of work in sociology on measuring belief and practice in Christian contexts in western societies, there was nothing in sociology on what religious belief and practice might look like and how they might be measured for non-Christian religions such as Buddhism. My knowledge of Buddhist belief and practice was helpful to some degree, but more helpful was what I learned about the Buddhist group themselves, whose practices, events, and forms of teaching guided how I might further clarify the concept through the identification of dimensions and operationalize dimensions such as belief and practice. I was able to draw on my observations of the group, some qualitative data, and other materials such as previous research to assist me in identifying these dimensions for that group. Importantly, anyone who might wish to replicate a study such as mine would have to consider it in relation to the group of Buddhists that they were studying. Not all Buddhists hold the same beliefs (although there are some core beliefs common to all Buddhists) or practise the 'Dharma' (Buddhist teachings) the same way.

Like many of the great religious traditions, Buddhism has a complex and intricate belief system and extensive set of practices that have grown with the centuries and been differentiated in concert with the various branches of the religion. I was not aiming to measure adherence to the entirety of the Buddhist canon, just the basics! Nor was I able to measure the elaborate labyrinth of practices, techniques, and experiences of the religion, but just a few core and relevant practices that the group were involved in.

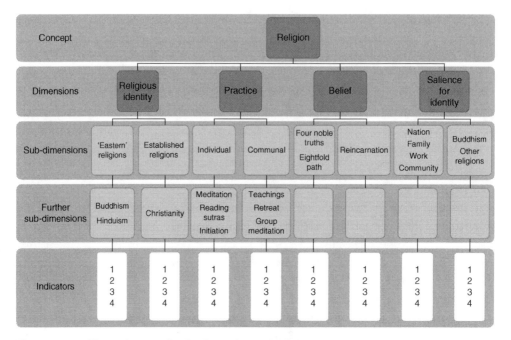

Figure 5.15 Dimensions and sub-dimensions of religion

You can see in the diagram that I settled on some core teachings and some basic practices. I further clarified these in terms of sub-dimensions that specified kinds of teaching and kinds of practice relevant to the group.

Another important dimension of religion is salience. Identifying salience as a dimension of religion aims to measure how important a religion is to a respondent. Many survey designs including religion ask respondents what their religion means to them in comparison with other aspects of their lives such as family, their nationality, and their job. In addition to whether respondents identify as religious, what they believe, and what and how often they practise, the importance of religion to how they see themselves or how individuals identify gives the researcher a measure of how strong this aspect of identity is. In my work, as displayed in Figure 5.15 I considered Buddhism alongside a number of other sub-dimensions of salience relevant to identity.

These were the key dimensions of religion that I sought to measure that I had developed from my topic and needed to refine to answer my research questions. I chose to focus on these as they were relevant to my enquiry grounded in my research questions, and to discard other dimensions of religion that were not relevant. I had clarified the concept of religion in a specific context through descending the ladder of abstraction by delineating the relevant dimensions and sub-dimensions.

Summarizing dimensions and sub-dimensions

Before I begin a discussion on indicators, I would like to summarize the process of further clarifying concepts through the identification of dimensions and sub-dimensions. We have seen through a number of examples that concepts are to be further clarified by identifying dimensions and sub-dimensions of them. This process of further descending the ladder of abstraction can be quite simple in that some dimensions and sub-dimensions are intuitive and commonly known. Others are not. Most concepts are multidimensional and will present the survey researcher with some work to do to identify those dimensions and sub-dimensions that are relevant. How do researchers go about deciding which ones to include and which to ignore? There are no formal rules for deciding which dimensions and sub-dimensions are relevant to your project, but there are some guidelines that you can follow to assist decision making in this process of further clarifying concepts.

Deciding on dimensions and sub-dimensions

Context: What is the context of the research? You will need to be mindful of factors such as geography – where in the world are you conducting this study? Which dimensions apply to specific geographies such as a nation, a region, a city, or a town and which dimensions do not? As we have seen, a cultural definition of homelessness is particularly sensitive to context. Contexts are also institutional, social, political, economic, theoretical, and cultural as well. What is poverty to people in developing or low-income countries, to men and women in developing or low-income countries, compared with those in developed or high-income countries, for example?

Relevance: Are all the possible dimensions of a concept relevant to your research question? You should avoid what are called 'fishing expeditions', that is you should not just throw a line in and hope to catch something, so remove dimensions and sub-dimensions of concepts that you have doubts about or have no logical place in your theoretical or conceptual scheme. Are some dimensions and sub-dimensions ambiguous? Are you doubling them up needlessly? Are there subtle differences in them that you can identify, justify, and differentiate logically? Are these discussed in the literature? Is measuring physical health relevant to attitudes towards mental health? Is culture a necessary inclusion to a study of the middle class of a population?

Necessity: There are practical matters to do with dimensions and sub-dimensions as well. The number that you include in attempting to clarify and operationalize a concept will need indicators to be included in the survey. If you included, say, 18 dimensions and 59 sub-dimensions, then these all need indicators in your survey! You could end up with 3,000 questions! What is necessary and what is surplus or not relevant?

Research question specific: Ultimately the best guide for clarifying and selecting the dimensions and sub-dimensions of a concept are the research questions you are trying to answer. Research questions relate to context not just in terms of where, when, and how, but also in the orientation of the research. Here we again need to be mindful of the kind of research questions that can be answered with surveys and the types of data that surveys collect. As the health example demonstrates, surveys are appropriate and effective for only certain types of research questions about a phenomenon or concept such as health, such as opinions, attitudes, and experiences of health or illness, and those factors we deem associated with them within a context, or specific to a discipline. For health, it is not entirely clear from the example that what we are measuring is actually 'health', rather it is more focused on perceived experiences of, and attitudes towards or about, health as related by an individual. We cannot measure blood pressure, or the presence of a microbe or abnormal cells in a survey, but survey research can measure concepts that are related to health and help predict the specific factors that are associated with the likelihood of contracting disease.

Previous research: The other immensely important guideline to follow in further clarifying concepts through the delineation of dimensions and sub-dimensions is previous research. What has been included or omitted in previous research? While previous research is an excellent guide for the dimensionally and sub-dimensionally perplexed, research is never static and the definition of concepts is debated constantly, so what has been included in previous work may or may not be relevant to the current situation, or indeed the present context of your own research. This was my dilemma when working out which dimensions and sub-dimensions would be relevant to the study of western Buddhists.

Summarizing indicators

So, after we have carefully identified and selected concepts, dimensions, and sub-dimensions we need to develop indicators for them; that is, design or select the actual questions that will populate a survey in order to measure the relevant concepts associated with our research. Indicators, you will note, from reading research that uses survey data, can be called a range of names that all essentially mean the same thing. You will see researchers referring to 'indicators' using a variety of terms such as 'questions', 'variables' (more appropriately referring to the data that are derived from the indicator), 'items', and 'measures'; these terms are used interchangeably by researchers, sometimes in different contexts, but often not. This section outlines some of the key concerns to do with indicators, many of which you may not be aware of but have very important consequences for the outcomes of survey research. In the next chapter we delve quite deeply into the science of question construction.

The development of indicators is another crucial phase in survey design, to the extent that indicators are the mechanisms that collect the data that illuminate our concepts. Many would-be survey designers are unaware of the problems that can occur with poor-quality indicator design or question construction. If indicators are constructed poorly and without care, our data will be flawed, leading to many subsequent problems with analysis and research findings. We should think of indicators in a survey like any other measuring instrument that we use to achieve various ends, such as a timepiece, scales, thermometer, gauge, or compass; if the instrument is poorly constructed, it gives us invalid and unreliable measurements with a raft of unwanted consequences. Within the total survey error framework problems with indicators are known as measurement error.

Validity and reliability

Of all the concerns that occupy the creation and use of indicators, there are two we should emphasize above the others. Overall, indicators should be *valid* and *reliable* (but also comprehendible, unambiguous, and specific). Designing a survey is not the only context in which knowledge about indicator development is important. Researchers who use extant surveys in their research and conduct what we call secondary analysis, also need to be aware of the conditions, problems, and contexts of indicators, perhaps even more so given that they seek to inform their research from survey questions that they have not designed. Another reason to be informed about indicators beyond survey design, much like any other aspect of the survey design process, is to be a critical reader of research and understand what makes a good and effective survey that appropriately contributes to research and knowledge. Let's take a closer look at validity and reliability, as well as some other key issues in indicator development that will prefigure a deeper examination in the next chapter.

Validity is perhaps the most important consideration in developing indicators for a survey or selecting them for secondary analysis. Indicator validity can be defined broadly as *a question's (or indicator's) level of accuracy and precision in measuring a concept or construct of interest.* In other words, does a survey's questions measure accurately and precisely the concept which you seek to measure? This may appear to be an obvious question, but, again, as with concepts that may appear simple and clear cut on the surface, attempting to ensure validity with indicator construction is somewhat complex. Of course, we can appreciate the need for validity, and indeed how it is dependent on a number of aspects associated with the clarification of concepts such as an operational definition, but achieving it is more complex.

The key question here is: how do you know if your indicators are valid? For such an important question, however, there is unfortunately no sure answer. The truth is we have no absolutely sure way of knowing whether our indicators are valid or not. The best we can do is make sophisticated guesses based on previous research and on some pre-testing and consultation with groups we may be interested in surveying if we have to design our own indicators. Below are some of the ways in which survey designers aim to approximate indicator validity.

Content validity

Content validity is validity that is based on the content of the concept to be measured. This logically follows our discussion of concepts, and especially of dimensions.

The content of a measure will to some extent be determined by the specific dimensions of a concept that is of interest. Recall above that not all dimensions may be of interest or relevance to our research questions. Essentially content must 'speak for itself' and not necessarily for the whole concept. For example, indictors may have an emphasis or bias towards only one aspect of a concept of interest, such as measuring religious behaviour and asking respondents how often they attended *church* services. Such a measure is only valid for Christian respondents, and not Muslims, Jews, Hindus, Buddhists, or others. Content is driven by the concepts we aim to measure, how we define them, and how relevant dimensions and sub-dimensions are to our research purposes.

Criterion/expert validity

There are many times when, and various reasons why, researchers try to establish new measures for concepts, such as new theoretical insights. There are two ways in which indicators can be developed and tested for validity. One way is to assess new measures against old established ones (thought to be valid). If similar results from data collected are found for the new measures we can deem the new measures to be valid. However, if there are different results, it does not necessarily mean the new measures are not valid. The established measures may well be invalid. There may be problems or improvements with wording and meaning with both old or new measures. While difficult and to some extent confusing, testing against established measures with set criteria allows researchers to attempt to establish validity for new measures with some logical process.

The other way of trying to establish validity for new indicators, particularly if there are no relevant existing indicators, is to consult individuals who are members of groups whose beliefs, values, attitudes, or experiences are fundamental to the concept in question. For example, as we have seen with homelessness and poverty, if we are interested in developing indicators that measure these concepts, we may choose to consult people who are experiencing these conditions, advocate groups, or agencies that support such people to ascertain their views on questions we have developed or ask about suggestions. In a similar but more general vein we can make some assessment about indicators for concepts with forms of pre-testing, such as focus groups that ask individuals about what they think about certain issues (associated with our concepts). **Criterion validity** allows us to overcome various assumptions, ignorance, and link lived experience to a more valid measurement of concepts of interest.

Construct validity

This form of validity is sought by comparing measures with other measures based on a specific theoretical construct. Let's say we are interested in developing indicators for a concept such as life satisfaction, and a given theory we are interested in proposes that those on lower incomes are far more likely to report lower levels of life satisfaction than those on higher incomes. If the data reveal this to be so after analysis, then we can assume that the new indicators for the concept are valid. However, as de Vaus cautions (2014: 51), if the data based on the new measures do not support the theory, is the theory or the measures the problem? We have to be sure that the theory the indicators are based on is plausible, and that the indicators against which we are testing the new indicators are themselves valid. It may turn out that income was measured poorly or that the theory has been discredited.

Reliability

Reliability is the next most important aspect of indicator design. An indicator is said to be reliable *if it produces the same or very similar results for the same kinds of respondent over time*. There are contexts of course where reliable measures of concepts do not produce the same results. International comparisons can be hampered by reliability issues, and at times there can be discrepancies between how respondents answer the same question at two different times, even though there should be none. There are numerous issues affecting reliability.

Indicator construction

The way that indicators are constructed can be a source of reliability or unreliability. Consistent wording, **coding** (scoring of question response categories), and question meaning should ensure some reliability over time. If indicators, based on the same concepts, are worded differently, coded differently, and interpreted differently from survey to survey, then the possibility they gain reliability is compromised.

Recall

Some indicators rely on respondents being able to recall particular kinds of information to answer questions. Respondents can be vague about specific details of their lives, especially if those details are not particularly interesting to them, even if they are to the researchers. Recall that problems can impact the reliability of indicators through different responses to the same questions at different times. There may be certain aspects of an experience that are forgotten at one time, then recalled at another. For some respondents age and time make it especially difficult to recall certain aspects of their lives so as to respond to questions. The social acceptability of answers at one time and then another may have changed also.

Testing and retesting

A way of trying to ensure reliability is to repeat questions to a sample in a short time period and then correlate the answers with each other; there should be a very strong correlation (de Vaus, 2014: 49) suggests a coefficient of 0.8 or above) that will then represent indicator reliability. There can be practical problems with this method, however, such as accessing the same sample. This method is good for panel surveys. Another form of testing and retesting can be included in the same survey, where very similar questions can be placed in different parts of the survey and then the answers can be assessed against each other. This form of testing indicator reliability is perhaps fine for single measures but not practical for concepts that need multiple indicators.

How many indicators?

An important consideration in the development of indicators is the number needed to measure the concept of interest adequately. The number of indicators necessary will vary with how complex the concept is, how relevant the various dimensions and sub-dimensions are to the research, and how concepts have been measured in previous surveys. Some concepts as we know are simply defined and require few indicators, others the opposite, requiring numerous indicators to measure the concept satisfactorily and accurately. Alongside these conceptual considerations are practical concerns of survey length and analytical strategy; that is, not making the survey overly burdensome to respondents, and making sure that the data are adequate for the intended statistical analysis so as to best answer the research questions.

Concepts may be measured with just one indicator, or with many. It will be up to the researchers to determine exactly how many adequately cover different dimensions of concepts, depending on their relevance to the research. Single items are usually fine for descriptive or demographic indicators such as determining a respondent's age, sex, or level of education. More complex concepts will often require numerous **indicators** which are often set to create **scales** or **indexes** during the analysis phase, as we can see with the Individual Deprivation Measure and its 15 dimensions of poverty.

Another consideration is the length of the survey. There is a trade-off between having as many indicators as possible to ensure extensive coverage of the concepts you need to measure and the amount of voluntary time your respondents are willing to give to completing the survey, before they become annoyed and disinterested. Much like film directors who need to cut scenes from the final version of a film, survey researchers need to restrict or omit questions to make the survey more user friendly and practical.

Issues in indicator construction

Beyond validity and reliability there are a number of construction issues to do with indicators that can make questions invalid and be a source of measurement error. There are numerous ways of asking questions in a survey, from the wording to the structure of the question and the way in which respondents can answer. Before we turn to the specifics of indicator construction in survey design in more detail in Chapter 6 there are some crucial areas of question design that impact the effectiveness of indicators leading to possible measurement error that we need to be aware of:

- Ambiguity/vagueness – questions should be precise and to the point to avoid any confusion causing respondents to think 'it depends' about the question.
- **Double-barrelled questions** – it is best to avoid piling question categories into the one question, so as to avoid confusion.
- Recall and knowledge – that questions can actually be answered drawing on the everyday knowledge of respondents.
- Verbose questions/obscure language – as many of our questions in a survey may/will relate to some possibly complex theoretical frameworks or perspectives we have to work out how to relate this complexity to respondents who are not specialists. We also have to do it without being too wordy (verbose).
- Leading or biased questions – as a science, survey indicator design should aim to avoid value judgements, or create scenarios that may unduly influence how respondents may respond to questions.

Question placement and survey structure

Another key aspect of survey design that involves indicators is where questions are placed in a survey and how they are arranged. If you have ever filled out a larger survey you may not have even considered that the placement of particular questions is strategic, but it is and for some good reasons. Question placement and survey structure are important so as to attempt to avoid response bias and missing data. Often questions are banked together in groups to cover a specific concept, but depending on how they are arranged within a module, results can be more or less skewed. Other concerns about indicator arrangement are associated with sensitive questions and ways of minimizing non-response. For example, there is a consensus among survey researchers to include often sensitive, intrusive, and more mundane demographic data at the end of a survey so as to maximize respondent participation (Dillman et al., 2009). Response bias or what is known as 'question fatigue' can also be a problem if too many indicators (20 or more) are simply listed on a page. Visualization techniques can assist here to make the question set look interesting or break up sections of questions through different colours or shading. If you have a large number of indicators that are necessary to measure a concept properly, for example, and these are all listed on a page one after the other, respondents can simply tick or click the same answer all the way down.

Despite the cautions and constraints around indicators, measurement as I have stated previously can be an art as much as a science. Your imagination can be activated to attempt to find novel and interesting ways of measuring concepts, just as long as they are valid, reliable, and so on. For example, a colleague of mine once developed and used a measure that stated: 'When stuck in a place for a length of time, such as a traffic jam, what do you think about?' What do you think this indicator aims to measure? New and interesting ways of measuring concepts will always be a part of survey design, as our theoretical knowledge progresses, and as social change takes place.

YOUR SURVEY

Dimensions, sub-dimensions, further sub-dimensions

You will now be in a position to clarify your key concepts further in concert with some of the more specific literature that you have collected after reading this chapter.

After identifying the key concepts in your research question(s) from previous chapters, use the template offered on the companion website to work through and refine your concepts into dimensions, sub-dimensions, and further sub-dimensions for your own survey in relation to your research questions:

- What are the key dimensions and sub-dimensions of the concepts your survey is attempting to measure?
- How would you further refine them if needed?
- If working with an organization, group, or business, which dimensions and sub-dimensions are relevant to their needs? You may need to discuss this with your industry partners.
- Here also you may need to make further practical decisions about including which dimensions and sub-dimensions based on perspective, context, and purpose of the research. Again, however, you can attempt to meet industry or client needs as well as discipline specific scholarly needs with extensive definitions that also include concentrated definitions. Homelessness is a good example here.

Iterative planning

Sometimes the survey design process can be iterative: that is, researchers may need to take a step back and refine questions and concepts further in light of new information, practical constraints, or changes in research aims.

- After considering the dimensions and sub-dimensions of your key concepts, do your research questions need refinement also?

- Does the more detailed refinement of concepts still match the research questions or do they perhaps suggest some changes need to be made?
- Despite the dimensions and sub-dimensions you have found, which dimensions and sub-dimensions are relevant and/or not relevant to your research? Again in relation to your research questions, theory, previous empirical work, and the practical aims of the survey design should guide you.

Indicators

While we will attempt to design indicators after the next chapter, consider the key elements of indicator development related to your research questions.

- How many indicators do you think you may need in your survey to this point?

Key knowledge and skills

This chapter has delved deeper into the world of concepts through an analysis of dimensions and sub-dimensions. The chapter's content and examples highlight key knowledge and skills as follows:

- This stage in the survey design process identifies and separates the specific components of concepts so as to refine them further and more precisely discern what needs to be measured in a survey.
- Survey researchers need to specify which dimensions, sub-dimensions, and further sub-dimensions are relevant to the research questions and survey construction.
- This is achieved through clear identification of relevant theoretical perspectives, contexts, and purposes of the research that delimit the definition of key concepts.
- Use of a template can also assist survey design by graphically representing relevant dimensions, sub-dimensions, and further sub-dimensions.
- Indicator development follows from the identification of dimensions, sub-dimensions, and further sub-dimensions.
- Indicator development needs to take into account validity and reliability, various aspects of measurement error, question arrangement, and the number of indicators in a survey.

Further reading

Much like the previous chapter, most texts concerned with survey design do not provide in-depth discussions on dimensions and sub-dimensions of concepts. However, brief but useful accounts are given by de Vaus in *Surveys in Social Research* and Robinson and Leonard's *Designing Quality Survey Questions*.

Full text references:

De Vaus, D. A. (2014) *Surveys in Social Research* (6th edn). St Leonards: Allen & Unwin

Robinson, S. and Leonard, K. (2018) *Designing Quality Survey Questions*. London: Sage

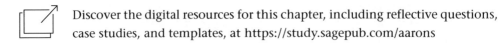 Discover the digital resources for this chapter, including reflective questions, case studies, and templates, at https://study.sagepub.com/aarons

Six

Constructing Survey Questions

The development of indicators is a science, and an art, and requires careful consideration. This aspect of survey design includes a range of potential problems and can directly impact data type and quality. It is crucial that survey questions are constructed clearly and that respondents understand what you are asking. This chapter will cover:

- Knowledge, and appropriate use of different question types
- How answer formats produce data that represent different types of variables
- How variable types are defined by different levels of measurement impacting the kinds of analysis that can be performed with survey data
- Key problems with survey questions and how to improve them
- How to ask survey questions ethically

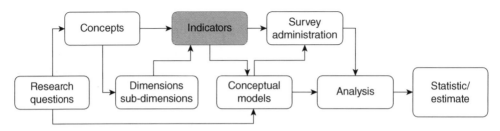

Figure 6.1   Survey design indicators

Indicators, as we learned in Chapter 5, are where we step off the ladder of abstraction and onto solid ground, in the attempt to measure, in concrete terms, the concepts that are of interest to our research (Figure 6.1). While the journey from abstract concept to precise indicator ends here, there is a lot to learn about constructing questions to best measure relevant concepts and ensure data quality. In this chapter we go into depth concerning the construction of survey items that indicate concepts, through an analysis of question formats, answer formats, coding, levels of measurement, and pre-testing of questions.

This phase of survey design is as important as any other given that it is this phase in which survey designers test how well they communicate the ideas of the research through a set of questions to a non-specialist public, namely respondents. This aspect of survey design is often underestimated and dismissed as a mere formality, but many surveys fail to gain valid and reliable data because of measurement error associated with poor question construction leading to missing, ambiguous, and invalid data. Question construction for surveys is first and foremost an exercise in communication usually between experts and non-experts about sometimes complex ideas, entailing considerations about practicality and purpose that determine how questions are constructed, how respondents answer, and what quality of data the questionnaire collects.

Type of question

There are many ways of asking questions in a survey to measure a concept, but we can discern four key question types that recur often in surveys and generally satisfy the overwhelming majority of requirements of a questionnaire for a variety of purposes. Within these question types there is a wide range of formats that survey designers can draw from. In concert with question types there are response types. What many who attempt survey design do not appreciate is that how a question is asked of a respondent and how that respondent is allowed to answer go a long way to the kinds and quality of data the survey can produce and the forms of analysis permitted after data are collected. So, question and answer types do not just measure concepts, they enable various forms of analysis, which should align with the research questions and research design.

I outline four main types of question, other authors may suggest more, but these four are the most important. There are other specialist types of question such as **filter questions**, but these do not actually measure anything and are more concerned with helping respondents to navigate and complete a survey. The four question types are:

1   Rating-type questions
2   Ranking-type questions
3   Knowledge-type questions
4   Descriptive/demographic-type questions

Matching these question types are two response types:

1   Open-ended responses
2   Closed-ended responses

Context and purpose

Following the discussion about definitions of concepts, another consideration that guides the question and response type is the context of the research, or the desired need. The context is dependent on the scholarly discipline or industry. A given question that measures a subjective state or fact can generate valid data in one context and invalid data in another. Depending on the purpose of the question and the context, question type and response category will follow (Fowler, 1995). For example, consider the different contexts of measuring the consumption of alcohol. For marketers the amount of alcohol consumed by different groups in a sample population will relate to sales or the lack thereof with different segments of a population, taking into account brand and type also. For health researchers, however, the level of alcohol consumed will have a different purpose and context. Different questions measuring the same behaviour may be needed as a result.

In addition to these question and response types there is a need to consider the purpose of survey questions. The purpose and context will be determined to a large extent by the nature of your research questions and the discipline or industry that your research is grounded in (Figure 6.2). Fowler (1995) suggests two main purposes of question types: the measurement of *subjective states*, that is the feelings, opinions, experiences, and/or impressions of individuals concerning whatever is aimed to be measured by the survey; and *facts*, that is statements and data about behaviour, attributes, and experiences. These two purposes underpin the greater majority of question types in social surveys. Attitudes, opinions, and experiences are often meaningful and emotional, and there is usually the need to measure particular facts about an individual's life or thoughts that are more neutral. Various modes of question, as we will discover, suit these needs. Properly framing the context and purpose aims at reducing measurement error and maximizing valid and reliable data.

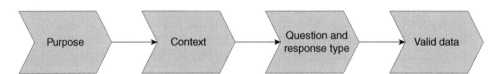

Figure 6.2 Purpose and context of indicator development

Question and response formats

Rating question formats

Rating questions are a very common question format in many social surveys. Rating questions can be applied to many different conceptual concerns seeking to measure the subjective states of respondents on many different issues, from self-rating or internal concerns to external influences on individuals such as impacts of government policy, experiences of various services, or community issues. The common features of rating question formats are that they generally pose to respondents a continuum of states associated with behaviour or experience, that they ask respondents to indicate one state only within that continuum of possible states, and that the various states respondents indicate are made numeric and indicate high to low, strong to weak, and more and less.

Likert scale

Likert (pronounced 'lee curt') scales are one of the most popular forms of question format and appear in just about every social survey you can find. Named after the American social psychologist Rensis Likert who devised the format, they are a versatile psychometric question type designed to attempt to measure the strength of agreement or disagreement with a given statement. A **Likert scale** often assesses emotional or affectual responses through indication of a level of approval or disapproval on a scale between categories such as 'strongly agree' and 'strongly disagree'. Likert scales are often employed to gauge the strength of feeling on social issues, political opinions, policy positions, impact of events, and various scenarios that can often be divisive, sensitive, or controversial. Opinions and attitudes on such topics and areas of human action are rarely neutral and Likert scales work particularly well because they can capture this kind of emotional diversity and experience.

Response categories for Likert scales can vary depending on what kind of data and what kind of analysis the researcher feels they need. For example, the classic Likert scale consists of five response categories from strongly agree, agree, neither agree nor disagree, disagree, and strongly disagree (there are at times additional categories such as 'don't know' or 'not applicable' to take account of context), yet there are Likert-scale variations that include seven and even up to eleven categories that measure strength of accord with a statement with greater diversity of strength of sentiment. Often the response categories are increased to provide greater nuance, and to allow a variable greater flexibility in the analysis phase.

Likert scales have a number of advantages. These include an effective and efficient means of asking a number of related questions concerning a concept that can be adapted to a scale for analysis that lends itself to a variety of statistical possibilities. Another advantage is that they can capture the affectual and emotional nature, albeit somewhat opaquely, of a number of key social and behavioural issues that are often experienced as such in real life. A further advantage of the Likert scale is its use of statements that are often direct and precise summaries of events, decisions, possibilities, and states.

Let's take a look at a few examples.

This statement is central to the Likert scale question format:

Government should redistribute income from the better off to those who are less well off

The response categories allow:

Strongly agree ☐

Agree ☐

Neither agree nor disagree ☐

Disagree	☐
Strongly disagree	☐
Can't choose	☐

Often Likert scale questions are banked together in clusters to measure different dimensions of a concept which then allow researchers to combine measures into a scale. For example, the above question is part of a series of Likert scale questions measuring attitudes towards welfare, business and the law in the UK, as shown in Figure 6.3.

		Agree Strongly	Agree	Neither agree nor disagree	Disagree	Disagree Strongly
A	Gov't should redistribute income from the better-off to those who are less well off	☐	☐	☐	☐	☐
b	Big business benefits owners at the expense of workers	☐	☐	☐	☐	☐
c	Management will always try to get the better of employees if it gets the chance	☐	☐	☐	☐	☐
d	People who break the law should be given softer sentences	☐	☐	☐	☐	☐
e	For some crimes the death penalty is the most appropriate sentence	☐	☐	☐	☐	☐
f	Schools should teach children to obey authority	☐	☐	☐	☐	☐
g	The law should always be obeyed even if a particular law is wrong	☐	☐	☐	☐	☐

Figure 6.3   Likert questions from the British Social Attitudes Survey

Not all Likert scale questions have exactly the same response categories such as strongly agree, agree, and so on. There are many of these types of questions that use different forms of response category, but they all aim at measuring different levels of agreement or disagreement in response to statements. Indeed, authors such as Fowler (1995: 65) make a case that less emotional and more cognitive response categories in Likert scales should be preferred at times. Figures 6.4 and 6.5 are a couple of examples from the General Social Survey (United States) and the British Social Attitudes Survey that highlight Likert-style question formats with variations on the classic response categories

On the whole, do you think it should, or should not, be the government's responsibility to give financial assistance to college students from low-income families?

Definitely should be ☐
Probably should be ☐
Probably should not be ☐
Definitely should not be ☐
Can't choose ☐
Not applicable ☐

Figure 6.4 Likert-style question

Discounting the last two response categories, we can see that the distinction between *definitely* and *probably* works in much the same way as *strongly agree/disagree* and *agree or disagree*. Here is the other example with a different variation again from the British Social Attitudes Survey.

How sure are you about what would happen if Great Britain were to leave the European Union?

I am very sure ☐
I am quite sure ☐
I am quite unsure ☐
I am very unsure ☐
Don't know ☐

Figure 6.5 Likert-style question – survey

Levels of surety are measured here as an indicator of the level of confidence or conviction about the consequences of a phenomenon such as Brexit.

Likert scales, like so much of contemporary life, have also come under the influence of various forms of web-based communication and social media influence and it is not uncommon to see Likert scales use emojis as response categories (Figure 6.6). A respondent's 'emojiscore' is the metric and serves the same purpose as the orthodox forms of agreement. Emojis, however, can be ambiguous and even nonsensical for some respondents who may have no idea what they are.

Figure 6.6 Likert emojis

When would you use a Likert scale?

Typically, you would use a Likert scale when assessing attitudes or opinions that are associated with issues that are to some extent emotionally divisive or consequential, such as moral issues, government policy (such as attitudes towards welfare cited above), or real-life events or experiences that assess the strength or weakness of how people feel towards them. Likert scales are at heart measures associated with subjective states of opinion and feeling based on statements.

There are some views about middle categories such as neither agree/disagree. Some authors suggest that it is preferable to leave out these response categories and force respondents into an opinion. This has its merits as some respondents will simply indicate a 'neither', but most experts in survey design are happy to see them included (Groves et al., 2009). There are some good reasons for this, such as respondents who may not have experience or knowledge of the question's statement and are therefore genuinely unable to agree or disagree.

Semantic differential and horizontal rating scales

Semantic differential question formats use words such as oppositional descriptors or adjectives to indicate extreme states of difference concerning something to measure different opinions, attitudes, or experiences. Between the extreme states indicated by two words are a series of lesser states representing weaker or more neutral responses. The response category continuum is scored usually from 1 to 10, 1 for one extreme and 10 for the other. Semantic differential measures are usually employed to measure feelings and affect associated with evaluation. A semantic differential essentially is employed to evaluate a service, policy, person, experience or programme, depending on the context. The response categories are often indicated with numbers to complement the descriptors at each pole because it is very difficult, if not impossible, to load up a continuum with appropriate adjectives compared with numbers to indicate intermediate states (Fowler, 1995).

The advantages of semantic differential questions are that they can give an accurate scale of difference of opinion or feeling with precise states at the extremes. The response format also allows considerable ability to perform many statistical analyses with the data it collects given its range.

Some examples are shown in Figures 6.7–6.9. Classically they are employed in service or product evaluation.

Your stay with us at the Continental Hotel overall was

Excellent	.	.	.	.	.	.	.	.	.	Poor
10	9	8	7	6	5	4	3	2	1	0

Figure 6.7 Semantic differential example 1

My experience of the community health service assessment process today was

Exceptional	.	.	.	.	.	.	.	.	.	Poor
10	9	8	7	6	5	4	3	2	1	0

Figure 6.8 Semantic differential example 2

The candidate's performance in the recent debate, I thought was

Brilliant	.	.	.	.	.	.	.	.	.	Terrible
10	9	8	7	6	5	4	3	2	1	0

Figure 6.9 Semantic differential example 3

In addition to semantic differential questions, survey designers also use horizontal rating scales. Horizontal rating scales operate in the same way as semantic differentials, but instead of proposing opposite descriptors or adjectives at the extremes of a continuum, they propose to respondents opposite statements associated with a theme or concept. They are horizontal in that they seek not to rate as better or worse, higher or lower, but more to one side than the other. Horizontal rating questions often use a 1 to 7 scale or 1 to 10 scale. To some extent they share a similar format to a Likert scale, but differ subtly by not asking respondents about disagreeing with a statement as much as favouring its opposite. An advantage of this form of question is that it allows researchers to get a definitive positive answer rather than getting an opinion through levels of disagreement, which can be complex and convoluted. An example of a horizontal rating scale is shown in Figure 6.10.

Government should never restrict civil liberties in response to terrorism						Government should always restrict civil liberties in response to terrorism
1	2	3	4	5	6	7

Figure 6.10 Horizontal rating scale

When to use a semantic differential scale

Mostly semantic differential questions are used when you want to evaluate qualities and experiences associated with products, services, or performances. These question types aim at a personal response that indicates some form of experience or value, unlike the Likert scales that seek levels of affect and agreement. The response categories must warrant significant variation in order for the format to be valid. For example, you do not want to ask a question with a semantic differential when a yes or no will do. For example, I once went into a bank to make a deposit. This took only a couple of minutes and was not an especially complex interaction. After my transaction had been completed, the bank teller asked me a question about the service I had just received in a semantic differential format. 'So, on a scale of 1 to 10, where 1 to 8 is good, 9 is very good (think of 9 as some kind of mid-point), and 10 is exceptional, how would you rate your service with us today?' The service was effective, but not exceptional or even good, and there was no difference between 1 and 8! The nature of my need from the bank was not complex. A yes or no response to a basic question of satisfaction would have sufficed but the bank had its reasons for such a metric I am sure. I gave the service a 4.

When to use a horizontal rating question

Horizontal rating questions can be used to assess related but opposite statements associated with a general topic. They differ from semantic differentials in that they are not necessarily an evaluative tool about qualities associated with a person, thing, or experience, but share more with a Likert scale in trying to measure subjective thoughts or opinions. Opinions on topics such as policy, decision making, and suggestive-type social scenarios with potentially extreme outcomes are suitable for horizontal rating scales, as the example suggests.

Feeling thermometer

Feeling thermometers use a temperature metaphor to rate responses to various things. Researchers usually use feeling thermometers to gauge a feeling of warmth or coldness to individuals such as politicians, people, or groups with particular identities such as ethnicity, involvement in social movements such as environmentalism, or certain professions. Researchers can also use them to indicate general emotional responses to measure states such as anxiety. The response categories are usually between 0 and 100 'degrees', with 0 usually indicating extreme coldness and 100 extreme warmth, but ratings from 0 to 10 are not uncommon. Feeling thermometers are often presented in a survey as a diagram of a thermometer with the temperature to one side or, if administered face to face or over the phone, read out. An excellent example of how feeling thermometers are used from Pew Research is shown in Figure 6.11.

When to use a feeling thermometer

Feeling thermometers, as their name describes, are often used to gauge feelings up and down a lengthy continuum. In social surveys they are mostly used to measure general feelings towards individuals of note, such as public figures, but can also be used to measure feelings associated with identities that a population may have some response to for a variety of reasons, but usually because there are extremes of devotion and repulsion involved. Your survey should use feeling thermometers when you think your survey may measure attitudes towards such individuals or identities. To some extent the method can be used as a ranking question also, as the example suggests.

We'd like to get your feelings toward some different countries in the world on a "feeling thermometer." A rating of zero degrees means you feel as cold and negative as possible. A rating of 100 degrees means you feel as warm and positive as possible. You would rate the country at 50 degrees if you don't feel particularly positive or negative toward the country.

How do you feel toward?

Enter the number in the box between 0 and 100 that reflects your feelings

The countries put to respondents for this question were Britain, Germany, Iran, China, India, Canada, Japan, North Korea, Russia, and Mexico. The results reflect clusters of warmth and coldness meaning various levels of feeling towards the different countries, from "very cold (0–24)", "somewhat cold (25–49)", "neutral (50)", "somewhat warm (51–74)", and "very warm (75–100)". A graphic of the results is below.

Public is warmest on Canada, coldest on North Korea

Average ratings for ___ on a "feeling thermometer" from 0 to 100

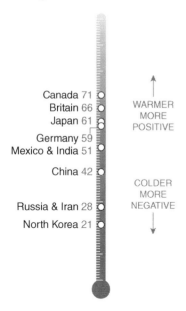

Figure 6.11 Feeling thermometer

Source: Pew Research Center (2018)

Ranking question types

Ranking question formats ask respondents to rank in order of preference their likes and dislikes, priorities and orientations, on an issue. Ranking has the distinct advantage of enabling the respondent to order in terms of preference a number of related categories associated with a dimension or concept. This allows the respondent to indicate the relative importance, strength, or meaning of a category in relation to the other categories within a response set. Ranking's other advantage is that it can allow respondents to give multiple responses to a question, where more than one answer is appropriate. This is advantageous when comparing dimensions or sub-dimensions of a concept. Compared with rating question formats, ranking question formats can give researchers more complex indications of a phenomenon or experience.

Types of ranking

Ranking in survey questions can take a few different forms. There are ranking questions that ask respondents to rank all response categories from 1 to 10, or whatever, while others ask respondents simply to indicate the most preferred from the options available, with the assumption that the one chosen is ranked higher than the others. Another variation on ranking is to rank a top three from a given list of response categories. Ranking a lot of categories can be tedious so a short list of favourites gives a good indication of preferences. The other common use of ranking-type formats is to have respondents indicate a score associated with a particular issue, person, or experience, in relation to other issues, people, or experiences, such as occupational status scores where respondents rank a range of occupations as more or less prestigious.

Let's consider some examples shown in Figures 6.12–6.14.

From the list below, select your three favourite music genres by putting a 1 beside your most favourite, a 2 beside your second favourite, and a 3 beside your third favourite.

Classical	☐	Avant-garde	☐	Folk	☐
Light Classical	☐	Easy Listening	☐	Rock	☐
Opera	☐	Musicals	☐	Techno	☐
Traditional Jazz	☐	Blues	☐	Alt Rock	☐
Modern Jazz	☐	Soul	☐	World	☐
Big Band	☐	Top 40 pop	☐	Religious	☐
Heavy Metal	☐	Country & Western	☐	Other.........................	

Figure 6.12 Ranking question example 1

Which mode of transport do you use most to travel to work? Please select the single mode you use most, only.

Bus ☐
Car ☐
Train ☐
Walk ☐
Bicycle ☐
Other, please specify.........................

Figure 6.13 Ranking question example 2

From the list below please indicate how important the following values are to good parenting. Please rank the values in order of importance from 1 most important to 10 least important.

Discipline	☐	Love	☐
Kindness	☐	Obedience	☐
Creativity	☐	Tidiness	☐
Independence	☐	Hard Work	☐
Imagination	☐	Determination	☐

Figure 6.14   Ranking question example 3

Descriptive/demographic question types

There is always a need for questions that seek to ascertain basic demographic data in social surveys. These data provide researchers with descriptive parcels concerning individuals and whole samples that are extremely useful in discerning how various attitudes, opinions, values, and experiences are distributed demographically, as well as learning about the sample. Many of these can be asked simply and are not usually difficult or complex. These questions relate to what Fowler (1995) calls 'facts' and are cognitive rather than affective. A typical set of demographic questions asks about the following concepts in the following ways (Table 6.1).

Table 6.1   Typical demographic questions

Concept	Questions
Age	How old are you in years? What year were you born?
Gender/sex	What gender/sex do you identify with?
Educational qualifications and experience	What is your highest level of education attained?
Employment type	Are you currently employed? If so, what is your employment type?
Occupation	Please state your occupation.........................
Income (personal or household)	Please state your (p/h) income (after or before tax)
Geographic region where one lives	Would you say you live in a large city, regional centre, small town?
Country of birth	In which country were you born?
Religion and religious practice	Do you identify with a religious group? If so, which one?
Marital status/family	What is your current marital status? Do you have any children currently living at home? Living away from home?
Ethnicity and languages spoken	What is your ethnic [some questions ask about 'ancestry'] background? Which language(s) do you speak mostly at home?
Dwelling/housing type	Can you indicate the type of dwelling you currently live in?
Political orientation	Many people identify as either left of right in politics, where would you place yourself?

Depending on the needs of the research and the specific concepts associated with it, various kinds of questions might be put to respondents about different aspects of demography and social background. Some research will want to question respondents in depth on these issues. For example, if a research question is interested in the impact of education on social status, the survey will contain questions about educational backgrounds in terms of school type attended, subjects studied, rating of teachers, university or college experience, and parents' educational background. Other studies will be satisfied with one or two measures. Some demographic or social background questions may need an initial then a follow-up question to establish properly a particular fact, such as employment type and religious identity, to allow for the fact that some respondents may not be employed or belong to a religious community.

Knowledge questions

Research using surveys may have occasion to ask respondents questions about their knowledge of various phenomena. Knowledge questions are used widely for a range of purposes and contexts. Knowledge can include external events to an individual, but also a range of behaviours and experiences that pertain to the individual at a certain time, be it in the present or the past. There are some general cautions around knowledge questions that aim to reduce measurement error. First of all, the knowledge that the survey question seeks to test should be relevant to the respondents and they should have some chance of being able to answer the question. Therefore, knowledge sought to be measured cannot be too specialized or obscure, unless the sample is a specialist one, such as an occupational group with particular skills or certain forms of knowledge relevant to a profession. The other problem with knowledge-type questions is memory. Often respondents are asked to recall events, behaviours, feelings, or experiences from times past. Most respondents are quite good at recalling general details, but can be hazy on specifics, especially if it concerns events from many years prior.

I discern two dimensions associated with knowledge questions: external/societal questions that aim to measure knowledge of institutions, events, and/or experiences that are external to the individual but may have influenced or affected them or made an impression on them at some time; and internal/personal knowledge questions about actual behaviours or experiences had by the individual respondent. Knowledge questions do not need to be direct questions about phenomena such as those encountered in a test or exam, or a trivia competition, although they can be. Many knowledge questions are indirect and ask respondents to rank or rate various events as a means of measuring their impact on identity or meaning.

Below are some common topics used in social surveys for both dimensions. Of course, it is possible in some instances that external and social knowledge questions are indeed internal and personal to some respondents who might have had direct experience of an event such as a war or other political event, but most respondents will not. Further, the way in which these kinds of questions are asked can discriminate between an external and personal experience.

External/societal

Political or historical events: moon landing, assassinations, wars, economic catastrophes, political leaders, and administrations.

Sporting and cultural events/achievements: Olympic Games, football world cups, world series wins, actors, musicians, and festivals.

Health or medical knowledge: nutrition, medication, illness, and disease awareness.

Internal/personal

Employment history: jobs worked, how long, which occupation, who for.

Educational history: schools attended, achievements/awards, courses completed.

Health: diet, smoking, alcohol intake, medication, fruit and vegetable intake.

Activities and habits associated with daily life: exercise, reading, media consumption, health check-ups/doctor visits, vacations, various routines.

Regarding formats, knowledge questions can be arranged in different ways and be constructed as both rating- and ranking-type questions. Let's take a look at some examples shown in Figures 6.15–6.18.

There have been a lot of important national and world events over the past 100 years that have helped shape Australia. Different individuals and groups, however, relate to some historical episodes more than others. On a scale of 1 to 7, where 1 is Not at all important, and 7 is Very important [another category was 8 'Can't choose' allowing for respondents who had no knowledge of the listed events], how much importance do the following have for you?

World War I;
Great Depression;
World War II;
Moon Landing;
Vietnam War;
Dismissal of Gough Whitlam;
Chernobyl Nuclear Disaster;
Port Arthur Massacre;
September 11 Terrorist Attacks;
2002 Bali Bombings;
The 1932–33 Ashes 'bodyline' cricket series;
Australia's soccer world cup qualification over Uruguay in 2005;
Australia II 1983 America's Cup victory;
Cathy Freeman's Gold Medal at the Sydney 2000 Olympics.

Figure 6.15   Knowledge question example 1

I am going to read out a list of different types of music. For each one please use this card to tell me how much you like it by giving it a ranking of 1 to 7, where 1 means you like it very much indeed, and 7 means you do not like it all. If you don't know or haven't heard of it, just say so.

Rock, including Indie.

1 – Like it very much indeed

2

3

4

5

6

7 – Do not like it at all

8 – Have not heard of it

Figure 6.16   Knowledge question example 2

Consider your recent physical activity. How often over the last six months have you?

	Often	sometimes	hardly ever	can't recall
Hiked	☐	☐	☐	☐
Gardened	☐	☐	☐	☐
Swam	☐	☐	☐	☐
Jogged or ran	☐	☐	☐	☐
Walked a long distance	☐	☐	☐	☐
Cycled	☐	☐	☐	☐
Played sport	☐	☐	☐	☐

Figure 6.17   Knowledge question example 3

People who are in the U.S. illegally do not have any rights under the U.S. Constitution.

Accurate	☐
Inaccurate	☐
Don't Know/refused	☐

Figure 6.18   Knowledge question example 4

When to use knowledge questions

One consideration to bear in mind with knowledge questions is what concepts are they measuring? Knowledge in and of itself certainly can be a concept, but knowledge often has a purpose and a context relevant to the research, so there is a concept that should be lurking somewhere near the surface if you are to use these kinds of questions. To some extent this is not a complex question. This is one reason why we might discern between internal and external aspects of knowledge. Some knowledge questions aim to measure various aspects of identity, and can be an important adjunct to the demographic social background questions we encountered above and pose no great challenges to the survey designer. External knowledge questions, however, may aim at more obscure or complex concepts, such as national identity, conservatism, or cultural and political engagement. That was the aim of the example question about important events in Australia. Other concepts that are well measured using knowledge questions are 'literacy' or engagement-type questions, such as health literacy, religious literacy, or political/civic literacy/engagement as the example question about the US Constitution highlighted. If you are seeking to use knowledge questions make sure that you have a clearly defined concept that they will measure, that all respondents have had access to knowledge so that it is possible that they know of an event, or have had some access to the knowledge of an event such as some basic schooling, and that the categories are not too specialist or obscure, unless the survey is for a specialist sample of respondents.

Vignettes/scenario-type questions

Some questions, and by association responses, benefit from a more detailed context to illustrate their meaning. Such questions use what is known as a **vignette** or scenario to set the scene for respondents and attempt to communicate better a concept to be measured or provide some context for the question. Vignettes and/or scenarios are typically short and hypothetical introductions to survey questions. They are typically used to relay specific circumstances around phenomena to give respondents information about options. Vignette- and scenario-type questions are often used in controlled experiments in psychology, some training instances in psychiatry, and other fields of study, but are also quite common in social surveys. They can be quite simple and more elaborate depending on the need. Vignettes have included audio and visual props such as photos, films, or artworks in addition to mere words. Figure 6.19 is an example of how a vignette question can be used in a social survey.

Adrian is a part-time employee at a government department. Adrian is also a member of an amateur theatre group that is currently performing a play in which he has a minor role. While at work at the government department Adrian prints out a copy of the short script for one of the scenes his character appears in on his employer's printer. Is Adrian's behaviour appropriate?

1   Yes. Adrian should be entitled to use the government department's printer to print out the script, especially if it is short.

2   Maybe. Adrian should only be allowed to print the script on the government department's printer with permission from a supervisor.

3   No. Adrian should not use the government department's printer for material that is not relevant to his employment.

Figure 6.19   Vignette question

A question such as this may be associated with a specific policy or rule for which the vignette or scenario may be relevant, but not necessarily so. The question may aim to measure knowledge of a company's policy or rules or be a measure of a more general concept such as compliance or obedience.

Scenario-type questions are also used to present background to respondents, present scruples, and get respondents to think about various issues. Scenario questions often portray a fictional set of circumstances that can relate to real attitudes regarding social, political, or cultural issues, such as the example in Figure 6.20 from the 2007 Australian Survey of Social Attitudes.

Suppose there was a medication available to enable parents to choose the sex of their children. Couples simply had to take a blue pill to ensure the birth of a boy, or a pink pill to ensure the birth of a girl. Do you think such a medication should be legally available?

Yes ☐
No ☐
I don't know ☐

Figure 6.20 Scenario question

Source: Australian Survey of Social Attitudes (2007)

When to use a vignette or scenario question

Vignette and scenario questions are often very useful for ascertaining knowledge and understanding of complex phenomena for respondents within specific contexts that rely on some detail, from the more technical and specific requirements to the more abstract. They can also act as a good measuring format for moral/affect-type questions surrounding behaviour and discernment of judgements based on certain criteria. They are also very good for controlled experiments using survey research.

Question responses

To some extent we have covered question responses in the examples above, with respect to rating and ranking formats, but there are some key distinctions between question response formats and general points about question response that need to be discussed briefly. Question responses provide respondents with formats for answering questions and researchers a means of coding responses to translate them into data enabling later analysis. There are two broad types of question response used in survey question construction: open-ended and closed-ended question responses. Both forms of response have advantages and limitations. In the same way that many surveys neglect the concerns of question construction, response formats can also be neglected resulting in measurement error and poor data quality.

A crucial aspect of question response formats is that they create variables of different levels of measurement thereby affording different data analysis capabilities. One of the primary aims in question response creation and selection is to allow for variation in answers from high to low, more or less, stronger or weaker, enabling the data to best reflect the true breadth of variation in the thoughts and experiences of respondents. This is one of the reasons why rating scales and ranking questions, as we have seen, can have quite generous numeric ranges in their response formats, and why also simple binary yes/no formats are not necessarily adequate. This is consistent with the logic of quantitative research techniques.

The selection of different response formats should meet the needs of the measurement problem for each indicator. At times a simple dichotomous yes or no will be adequate, but often the research question will need a more complex response format to best capture more complex or nuanced variation that exists with respect to affectual states and facts associated with respondents. How do you judge which response format for which question, however? Most surveys use closed-ended questions because the categories associated with the question are usually relatively well known due to knowledge of a concept, previous research, and/or pre-testing of questions using qualitative research such as interviews and focus groups, and other tests.

Open-ended response formats

Open-ended responses leave the respondent to fill in the blanks, so to speak. A given question, of any kind, is open ended in its response when the respondent is asked to record what they think, feel, or have done for a question when no pre-recorded categories exist for the question. This response format also allows the survey to collect qualitative data, as the respondent's answer can be, if space permits and the question warrants, an extended textual response. Other open-ended responses can simply be a word. One of the challenges of open-ended questions is how to code the responses after the data have been collected due to the sometimes large amount of text and narrative that these response formats generate. This can be difficult if the respondents have given a very wide range of responses, but also an advantage in that there is a rich source of data that can inform the research.

When to use an open-ended response?

Researchers often use open-ended response formats when there is no or only a weakly established set of valid response categories for a question, or if the question is a straightforward single-word or number response such as *how old are you in years?* Or, *what is your profession?* **Open-ended questions** are also used when the research requires qualitative data; this allows the respondent to elaborate on an experience, attitudes, opinions that the survey seeks to measure, or even about the survey itself. Many good survey designs ask respondents to comment on the survey itself, often through the use of an open-ended response format. Many surveys allow respondents to elaborate through open-ended response formats at the end of the survey by simply asking if they have anything to add that they feel important about the topics covered and their experience of them.

Closed-ended responses

Closed-ended responses differ from open-ended responses primarily by having a discrete number or restricted group of answer categories that respondents can choose from, as the examples in this and other chapters demonstrate. The greater majority of survey questions use **closed-ended response formats**. This format matches the question types that are mostly used to measure concepts through rating or ranking within certain types of continua such as a Likert scale. Using closed-ended questions is also far more effective and efficient overall and can mitigate **survey fatigue** issues that can burden respondents from time to time, resulting in non-response and missing data.

In addition to open- and closed-ended response categories, authors such as Dillman et al. (2009: 75) present a hybrid combination of the two in the form of a 'partially closed question' format. This format works on the basis of a closed-ended question that adds an additional option that is effectively open ended and allows the respondent to include an additional category that is not covered in the original response categories. Other authors suggest that this is more simply another version of a closed-ended question. Nevertheless, despite whatever it might be called, the advantages of this kind of inclusion are obvious, and this is a frequently used strategy for survey response formats. Typically, the partially closed question format (Figure 6.21) includes an 'other' option in addition to the set responses.

What is your most preferred movie genre?

Drama

Comedy

Romance

Action

Thriller

Horror

Other..

Figure 6.21 Partially closed-ended question

Coding

Your question response formats need to be given scores or a metric, that is translated into a number that indicates higher or lower, more or less, stronger or weaker, and so on, to make them amenable to analysis and able to generate meaningful statistics or estimates. There are a variety of ways in which researchers code response categories, but most often it is on a scale of somewhere between 0 and 1 or more. Coding in this way makes possible and clear the variation in the distribution for the variable once it is analysed. Most coding denotes an increasing progression of quantity from a zero, an absence, or 'low' through to 'high'. Typically, you do not reveal the codes in a question on a survey paper or schedule, although question formats such as semantic differentials often do so to be instructive. You do, however, for very good reasons, record them somewhere else, such as in a codebook. The production of a codebook is a common practice for survey researchers, and especially large-scale surveys that may have hundreds of questions with numerous question types and different response types. Coding also has a translating mission for questions associated with analysis of survey data. The enumeration of a question through the measurement metric (via response categories) signals the translation from question/measure/indicator to variable in readiness for analysis. Variables (recall 'independent' and 'dependent') are the survey questions and responses in coded numeric form.

Coding is primarily the process of assigning scores to response categories, enabling the translation of questions into variables. Coding also involves the broader classification of questions, possible instructions to interviewers, and a list of cases that make up the survey sample. For the main task of coding we need to consider both broad forms of response formats introduced above.

Coding closed-ended question–answer formats

Coding closed-ended questions is relatively straightforward (Figure 6.22). For each response category there is assigned a number, usually from 0 or 1 through to the highest rank or rated category or number of possible responses, such as '1' for 'Yes' and '0' for 'No'. Coding should also include non-response and missing data. Survey researchers often assign a number well beyond the chosen sequence to indicate missing data or categories such as *don't know* or *not applicable*. The break in the sequence is easily recognizable when using a data set in SPSS or other data analysis software packages. For example, on a typical Likert scale from 1 to 5, 9 or 99 is chosen as the code for missing data, *don't know*, or *not applicable*. 'Other' categories also need a general code and may require further enumeration consistent with however many other responses are produced by the question.

Government should redistribute income from the better off to those who are less well off

Strongly agree	☐	5
Agree	☐	4
Neither agree nor disagree	☐	3
Disagree	☐	2
Strongly disagree	☐	1
Can't choose	☐	9

Figure 6.22   Question with answer format coding

Not all closed-ended categories need to be pre-coded, however. Ranking questions which have numerous answer categories such as the question above regarding parenting styles (Figure 6.14, see p. 155) don't need to be pre-coded to indicate strong or weak, high or low, as respondents essentially do that with the responses which can be recoded at the analysis stage. Answer categories for ranking-type questions do need to be included in a codebook, however.

Coding open-ended question–answer formats

Open-ended questions are mostly coded into numeric data and/or thematic data after the data are collected. Very often open-ended questions provide data that are simple descriptive answers relating experiences or attributes that do not indicate more or less or levels or quantities. Sometimes, however, data from open-ended questions can be ranked or rated in terms of greater or lesser quantity, as in the case of self-reported health (where no pre-defined categories are offered to respondents) that respondents may describe in some manner as more or less, higher or lower, such as 'poor', 'OK', 'good', or 'very good'. Other open-ended responses such as age in years, precise income, are simply the numbers given by the respondent, which can then be coded differently later if necessary, to reflect general categories of low to high. Coding such data relates to the earlier point about classification and how researchers think about what they aim to measure, which in turn is related to our prior discussion concerning concepts. How we define concepts will determine how we classify differences, and consequently how we code and enumerate after data collection.

———————— Coding open-ended responses to incivility ————————

As an example of how survey design requires open-ended question data to be coded, Phillips and Smith (2000) had the task of defining the concept of 'incivility' in their study of rudeness that used a survey to record incidents of incivility that respondents had experienced in public from strangers. From their definition the authors classified forms of incivility and coded events that respondents described from open-ended questions. Respondents described in words various incidents that they considered to be representative of uncivil behaviour that they had experienced in public, such as a push, or a shove, or a punch, and the researchers then coded the responses to create a continuum of incivility from low through to high based on the nature of the incident recorded. This is a great example of how researchers can put an open-ended question to excellent use in a survey because there was no existing empirical benchmark for the concept of incivility in everyday life prior to the research.

Coding of certain open-ended questions can be relatively simple while other responses can be immensely complex and difficult. Take industries and occupations, for example. A government census or social survey with questions concerning respondents' work will garner many thousands of different answers because there are many thousands of professions and job titles across hundreds of industries that respondents report. Classification schemes and coding of such immense divisions are complex tasks but ones that have been benchmarked for some time within national statistical agencies and to some extent internationally, giving guidance to survey designers who are interested in such measures and their classifications. Other aspects of human behaviour and attributes that are often measured in surveys that share a similar classificatory complexity are crimes, countries of birth, ethnicities and language groups, and religious groups. There are efforts to attempt to standardize various codes so that researchers can do comparative work. The United Nations, the World Health Organization, and various labour and work agencies have produced coding schemes that allow researchers to compare levels of disease, work and occupation activity, and crime across the world.

Coding questions in a survey

Coding also includes the questions in a survey themselves, in addition to the answer categories. Many surveys are composed of different modules or sections that reflect the different concepts that the survey is attempting to measure. Each module of questions will have within it the questions designed to measure the particular concept of interest. This helps organize the survey, but also uses a form of enumeration to follow so as to be recognized during administration and analysis. In a large survey there may be 15 or more sections, with potentially hundreds of questions. Modules and the questions therein are often coded with numbers or letters and numbers. For example, Section B4 may have 10 items that measure political action. One coding solution that is common for such an example is to code the items from B4a through to B4j. Sections B1 through to B3 may also measure different dimensions of politics such as party affiliation, attitudes towards democracy, and so on. A logical system of tracing and recording question arrangement is valuable in survey design.

Codebooks

Once codes for response categories in the measures that compose the survey have been agreed upon, they are recorded in a codebook. Any given survey has numerous measures that need to be coded. The way in which researchers keep track of what question is coded and how is with the aid of a codebook. A **codebook** is a comprehensive record of the actual questions, response categories with scores, and other details such as instructions to interviewers. A codebook benefits survey research projects in numerous ways, from referencing data and responses to replicating a survey and/or performing secondary analysis (that is, using survey data for research that someone else has collected). The advantages and necessity of a codebook are best exemplified by looking at large-scale surveys such as the World Value Survey or the General Social Survey that have many hundreds of questions with a variety of response categories. Codebooks for these surveys are available from study websites. Putting a codebook together is essential even for a small-scale survey. Instructions on putting a codebook together for your survey are in the YOUR SURVEY section near the end of the chapter.

Levels of measurement

Your measures indicate something other than concepts in a survey. In statistical terms the type of question you ask can determine the type of analysis that you can perform with your data and in turn the types of research questions you can answer through various relationships between variables. Response categories for questions and how they are coded translate to what is known as the **level of measurement** (each question in a survey becomes a variable during the analysis phase through the nature of the question and its numeric expression). The response categories you elect to accompany your survey questions translate into scores through coding; these scores (also known as metrics) indicate the level of measurement for a variable. Typically, we think of and use four in survey research, after Stanley Smith Stevens' seminal paper 'On the Theory of Scales of Measurement' (1946):

1   Nominal
2   Ordinal
3   Interval
4   Ratio

Nominal

Nominal measurement is also called categorical. There is no meaningful numeric or quantitative difference between categories for nominal measures. While nominal categories are coded and scored much like categories in other levels of measurement, this does not have the same meaning. In other words, there is no meaningful quantitative difference between categories in a **nominal variable**. Many demographic or descriptive questions translate to nominal variables. A few common examples are shown in Figure 6.23.

What is your religion?
1. Catholic; 2. Islam; 3. Judaism; 4. Hindu; 5. Protestant; 6. Baptist; 7. Buddhist; 8. No religion

What is your country of birth?
1. Australia; 2. China; 3. USA; 4. South Africa; 5. United Kingdom; 6. Netherlands; 7. France; 8. Cambodia

Which gender do you identify with?
1. Male; 2. Female; 3. Non-Fixed/Fluid

Figure 6.23   Nominal question examples

From these examples we can see the nature of nominal or categorical variables as derived from descriptive or demographic questions. Despite the fact that they are coded numerically in an ordered sequence from 1 through to 2 or 8, these numeric differences do not have any quantitative meaning. For example, there is nothing about 8. No Religion that is six or seven times more religious than being Catholic or Muslim. The same is true for country of birth: the fact that France is coded 7 and China 2 does not mean France is more, greater, or higher than China in any way. And the same is also true for gender categories: 1, 2, or 3 do not denote any greater or lesser quantity of any sort to men or women, or those who do not identify with a fixed notion of gender. The fact is, as categories and response options, these all need to be coded so some kind of analysis can occur.

Ordinal

Ordinal variables are derived from measures that are coded with scoring schemes from 0 to 1 or more. Unlike the coding and scoring of nominal variables, there is a meaningful numeric or quantitative difference between the categories, but that difference is not precise in a literal sense, nor does it refer to a 'natural' metric such as time or currency. Rather, ordinal measures are arranged in some kind of general order, and that order can be from high to low, strong to weak, more to less, and so on (Figure 6.24).

The classic ordinal measure is the Likert scale:

Government should increase taxes for wealthier groups?

1. Strongly Agree; 2. Agree; 3. Neither Agree nor Disagree; 4. Disagree; 5. Strongly Disagree

Other classic ordinal measures include attendance at religious services:

Apart from weddings, funerals, and baptisms, how often do you attend religious services?

1. Most days; 2. Weekly; 3. Two or three times a month; 4. A few times a year; 5. Hardly ever; 6. Never

Figure 6.24 Ordinal question examples

From the categories on display in the above examples, the notion of 'ordinal' categories is evident. The categories are ordered in a numbered sequence that is meaningful but not in any real sense natural. Agreement and disagreement, strength, or affect associated with rating questions in particular need to be scored somehow, but they do not lend themselves to a natural metric. We do not really know what the precise numeric difference between *strongly agree* and *agree* is, compared with a measure that precisely deliberates between categories such as age, but an ordinal metric allows us to state that it is at least one point more. Similarly, attendance at religious services, while perhaps somewhat closer to a natural and meaningful metric such as time, is also ordered into general categories of high and low, or more or less. Ordinal-level measures make up a large majority of rating- and ranking-type questions.

Interval/ratio

Interval and ratio-level measures share an ordered ranking of categorical differences on response scales the same as ordinal-level measures, but differ from ordinal measures in that they have a precise and natural metric that distinguishes categories. Interval and ratio are often combined, but ratio-level measures differ slightly from interval in that they have a 'true zero' allowing ratio analyses to be performed. Experience tells us that ratio measures are rare in social surveys.

Examples include income stated as a precise figure in a currency, age in days, months, and/or years, education in years, height in centimetres or inches, the number of children in a household, and test scores. Note that these concepts can be measured ordinally with more general categories such as income groups, for example $0–$15,000, $15,001–$30,000, etc., age groups such as 18–25, 26–35, 36–45, etc., and educational qualifications such as 'some high school', 'completed high school', 'some college or university', or 'bachelor's degree'.

The various levels of measurement have consequences for the types of analysis that can be performed. For example, **descriptive statistics** such as different measures of central tendency are only permissible with specific levels of measurement. Interval and ratio levels allow the arithmetic mean, the mode, and the median, while ordinal measures do not, conventionally. Selecting specific measures with response formats is important because it translates into data with certain properties allowing certain analyses.

Ethics in question construction

One of the fine lines in survey design, indeed any research involving humans, is how to ask sensitive or personal questions of respondents (Tourangeau and Yan, 2007). Firstly, what is a sensitive question? A sensitive question can be different in different contexts, but common to the notion is a feeling that under normal circumstances someone who is unfamiliar to someone else would not ask about a topic, attribute, or form of behaviour. Even if they are familiar to them, they still may not ask, depending on the relationship. In survey research, relationships between researcher and researched are more or less contractual (but voluntary) and can be emotional even if distant. It is a fine line because the more data you have about a phenomenon and an individual, the better the research outcomes and the greater our knowledge, but at the same time the intrusive nature of survey research can cause harm, so deciding which questions to ask, and how many of them, is important in some contexts. Mostly this concerns only particular contexts and types of experience. For example, many legitimate research areas that seek to understand individual experiences of concepts such as crime, health, wealth, and relationships require researchers to ask respondents questions that can be embarrassing, unpleasant, and even painful. For many people these are not topics you would even discuss with friends, let alone a stranger from a university, government department, or research company. Yet experiences such as forms of illness, sexual activity, drug and alcohol consumption, and committing or being a victim of a crime are essential to understanding various aspects of behaviour. Less sensational forms of behaviour and attributes such as voting and income earnings can still be problematic for some respondents.

In pretty much all professional settings researchers who are planning to ask respondents a series of questions in a survey are required to submit an ethics proposal outlining the nature of the questions, their relevance to the research, and how the researchers plan to minimize harm to a potential respondent, where harm may be deemed possible. What ethics committees often have to decide in cases where there may be some distress caused through certain questions is whether on balance the data collected from the question are of greater potential value to the research, policy outcomes, and potential human improvement than any distress caused. Social settings for surveys are increasingly international. As a result, social and cultural customs, etiquette, hierarchy, and forms of communication need to be understood and respected before someone might be recruited to be a respondent. In some contexts, such as the modern west, being asked a range of questions about your thoughts and attributes by a stranger representing an organization might not be particularly problematic, but it may well be in non-western settings.

As for ethics and survey question construction, the main objective is to word questions that aim to measure sensitive content without value judgement or prejudice. Questions should be worded so as not to be or give the appearance of being judgemental. Whatever the views and opinions of the researchers, it is not their place to judge a respondent and reflect this judgement or prejudice through the way a question is constructed. For example, a famous, or perhaps infamous, item that surveys have used to tap attitudes towards homosexuality reads thus:

Homosexuality is wrong

1   All of the time?
2   Most of the time?
3   Some of the time?
4   None of the time?

Levels of 'wrongness' ending in no 'wrongness' portray a question somewhat loaded with a particular orientation. Besides the heavily judgemental tone of the question and responses, the notion of ordinal levels of wrongness do not make much sense without any context. There are many other ways in which survey questions can measure attitudes towards sexuality. Various questions that raise controversial or sensitive issues are asked in rating formats through statements; these are relevant to the purposes of the research that might want to measure attitudes to moral issues – they are not unethical.

In addition to wording of questions, response categories need care and thought. Survey question design would do well to include response categories that reflect specific cultural sensitivities around gender, sexuality, ethnicity, and other aspects of personal or collective identity across cultural settings. Consider gender, for example. The great majority of surveys simply ask respondents if they are male or female, yet there is a broader and more diverse set of gender identities that some individuals identify with. A similar problem exists for categorizing ethnicity, especially for First Nations peoples in relatively modern nation states. Consultation with under-represented groups and people otherwise ascribed to a range of set categories reflecting the knowledge and values of the researcher, who may well not be a member of the group responding to the survey, is a way forward to represent accurately the identities of particular individuals and groups.

Anonymity and confidentiality

The survey is predicated on a relationship of trust between researcher and researched. One aspect of trust in the relationship is that a respondent will not be able to be identified. Any answers you are given are anonymous, and also confidential. Usually there are few problems with anonymity and confidentiality with surveys as names are not required for the purposes of completion. While other personal details are often taken, such as demographic and geographic details, these are not likely to lead data users to identify the respondent. Despite the low probability of a respondent being identified, there is often no need to collect names and specific addresses through measures as part of the survey.

Some projects such as a government census where names and addresses are often taken do need a strict assurance that data will be used ethically. Understandably some objections have been raised by citizens where governments have requested names and addresses to be stored, as in the Australian Census of 2016.

Voluntary

Another dimension to asking and answering survey questions is the voluntary nature of any survey questions. Participation in surveys requesting respondents from a general public population are or should be entirely voluntary, with no part compulsory.

Even when respondents agree to complete a questionnaire, they do not have to complete each question, and do not have to offer responses if they so choose. This can be frustrating for survey researchers given the problems associated with missing data, but any compulsion is not ethical. A survey project should outline the voluntary nature of a respondent's participation in a separate letter accompanying the survey. For many respondents, surveys encountered through government departments, universities, agencies, or companies may look authoritative or 'official' and many people, especially older people, can be compliant and trusting. Many researchers can offer incentives for completing a survey such as a voucher for a product, a small monetary payment, or a ticket for a raffle.

Data protection

Surveys and the data they contain need appropriate storage and access. Professional surveys are securely stored electronically, or under lock and key in a secure place in an office if they are paper copies. While a lot of survey data is made available for public use, there are often strict protocols around use beyond that of the original purpose of the primary researchers. Data protection and privacy are fast becoming a potent issue with the advent of the online environment and increased technical capabilities of data companies in an age of massive social media use.

Measurement error (bad survey questions)

A crucial aspect of the total survey error framework is measurement error. Measurement error can take different forms, such as the original concept attempted to be measured – recall the discussion on concepts and dimensions. Another vitally important and obvious aspect of measurement error is question design or construction. The preceding discussion has taken into account the various formats and responses that survey researchers typically use to collect data with the various advantages that attend them. Knowing the variations of how survey questions are composed is only half of the necessary requirements to designing a successful survey, however. There are common problems with measurement error that relate to all of the question formats discussed in this chapter that survey researchers need to be aware of. Measurement error associated with question construction mostly pertains to how questions are worded, rather than how they are formatted (or arranged in a survey), although formatting can be the source of measurement error to some extent. The common pitfalls that lead to measurement error, listed below, relate to question wording.

---------------------------------- Bad survey questions ----------------------------------

If you are on Twitter you might be interested in an account called Bad Survey Question (@BadSurveyQ). This account posts an instructive collection of bad survey questions that highlights – often comically – some of the real-life measurement errors associated with question construction. The account is a gold mine for bad survey questions that highlight all of the key errors that you need to avoid. Peruse the account while considering the following problems in survey questions.

Common problems with indicator construction:

- Ambiguity and vagueness
- Double/triple-barrel questions
- Verbosity and obscurity
- Recall
- Leading questions
- Over- and under-reporting
- Questions in different contexts – how do they translate?

Ambiguity and vagueness

Overcoming ambiguous questions is perhaps the key challenge for survey research-ers. Much like the way in which we may assume we know what a concept is, we make assumptions about particular forms of behaviour which can mean different things to different people. Again, recall our key principle from the beginning of the chapter: question construction is communication between experts and non-experts. We need therefore to take the time to define properly, separate out, and limit key concepts in a question. The main problem with ambiguity in a question is that deep down we have no idea what the question is measuring as whatever we have posed as the key concept to be measured could be interpreted in different ways, might suggest radically different things, or suggest very different contexts or forms of whatever it is we are interested in learning from the questions. Let's take a look at a few examples.

Who in your household is mostly responsible for home maintenance?

What do you think 'home maintenance' means? Home maintenance could mean any number of things, although we might assume it is more to do with fixing something broken with the actual house such as a leaking tap, roof, or broken fence, but we can-not be sure. Our respondents may assume it to mean this or other aspects of house care such as laundry, food preparation, or childcare. We should instead seek a definition for what we mean by the concept of home maintenance and perhaps include a specific range of tasks that meet that definition. For example, if we went with home maintenance as a form of repair to the home, then we might suggest a question that states specifically what it is, or at least provide a list of valid tasks within a closed-ended question.

How might this question be made less ambiguous? Perhaps one way to improve this question is to state what is meant by 'home maintenance' (Figures 6.25).

There are many definitions of home maintenance. Home maintenance for our purposes entails a series of repair jobs associated with the house itself such as a leaking tap, broken fence, or lawn that needs mowing. If your household has more than one person in it, who in your household mostly does the following home maintenance?

Lawn mowing

Fence repair

Fixing fittings such as doors or windows

Taking out garbage

Figure 6.25 Improving an ambiguous question

Here is another example of an ambiguous question:

> *In our society there are people that tend towards the top and people that tend towards the bottom, where would you put yourself on this scale?*

While we might intuit what top and bottom (as well as middle) might mean, it is something of a guess, without specific parameters. The ranks of 'top' and 'bottom' might pertain to a number of socially valuable attributes that this question could be referring to, such as income, occupation, and credentials, but also cultural or political attributes such as ethnicity, gender, geographic region, or even more personal states such as mental health and/or disability. The answers respondents indicate will depend on how a respondent interprets the notions of 'top' and 'bottom', which may or may not be in accordance with what the researchers are interested in measuring.

In our society, there are groups that tend to be towards the top and groups that tend to be towards the bottom. Consider the following categories, where would you put yourself on each scale?

Income	Top	.	.	.	.	.	.	.	Bottom
Occupation	Top	.	.	.	.	.	.	.	Bottom
Qualifications	Top	.	.	.	.	.	.	.	Bottom
Ethnicity	Top	.	.	.	.	.	.	.	Bottom
Where you live	Top	.	.	.	.	.	.	.	Bottom
Gender	Top	.	.	.	.	.	.	.	Bottom
Physical health	Top	.	.	.	.	.	.	.	Bottom
Overall	Top	.	.	.	.	.	.	.	Bottom

Figure 6.26 Improving another ambiguous question

How might this question be made less ambiguous? I suggest two ways in which this question can be improved in Figure 6.26. Firstly, the question should be connected more precisely to the concept and dimensions it seeks to measure, which would mean separating out some possible dimensions mentioned above. Secondly, the question might be improved with some context such as an extended vignette or scenario to explain what 'top' and 'bottom' mean, and again by separating out and more plainly stating some of the possible signifiers that the question may be referring to (Figure 6.26). Further, answer categories might better record the notion of social value, as I think 'top' and 'bottom' denote, perhaps related to a hierarchy of status if not outright numeric such as income. A semantic differential format might include extremes such as 'greatly valued' to 'not at all valued'. At times the response formats can be ambiguous also. Some forms of ordinal response measures can be difficult to interpret. Take response categories such as *Hardly ever, Sometimes, Quite often, Regularly*. While we can certainly ascertain an ordered structure of higher or lower, or more or less, that is useful for a quantitative measure, just what do these categories actually mean to the researcher who poses the question and to the respondent? A common example is:

How often, besides baptisms, weddings, and funerals, do you attend religious services?

Never

Hardly ever

Sometimes

Quite often

Regularly

One problem here, other than the general ambiguity of the categories, is that depending on which religion you are, the categories will be interpreted differently without a benchmark against which to measure. If say you are an adherent of the Church of England, you need only attend religious services three times a year (Christmas, Easter, and Queen's (UK) Birthday). This can be thought of technically as 'regularly', or at least quite often, while Catholics are obliged to attend Mass every Sunday and a bunch of other days. Irrespective of how often members of these religions actually attend religious services, 'regularly' for a Catholic is potentially very different than 'regularly' for a member of the Church of England. Even within Anglican groups, some may think that the three days of obligation are regularly while other Anglicans may assume that every week is regularly. When this question is asked in surveys, it is mostly categorized in more precise terms of time, such as weekly, two or three times a month, a few times a year, etc. Response categories such as this can be improved with more precise categories, such as *daily, weekly, once every month, a few times a year, never*.

—————————— Absence makes the heart grow harder! ——————————

To some extent the following example (Figure 6.27) relates more to performing secondary analysis, but in survey design the utmost clarity is needed for answer formats so that data are correctly interpreted and used. Misinterpretation of an answer category caused chaos for British researcher Paul Dolan who misinterpreted the answer category 'Married – spouse absent' on a question measuring marital status in the American Time Use Survey. Dolan claimed that when husbands or male partners were 'out of the room' when the question about happiness in marriage was asked of female respondents, they reported being unhappy; however, the answer response refers to male spouses or partners who were 'absent' from the household, and not just absent from the room when the question was asked of their wives. Dolan was quoted in the *Guardian* newspaper (Cain 2019 (since amended)) as stating that: 'Married people are happier than other population sub-groups, but only when their spouse is in the room when they're asked how happy they are. When they are not present "f**king miserable", he said.' Below is a graphic showing the coding and categories of the variable in question, meaning that the spouse did not live in the same house for various reasons. Some surveys have extensive technical notes explaining such differences; some, however, are not very informative about the precise meaning of a response category, leaving a lot of room for potential measurement error as in this case.

Codes and Frequencies

● Category availability view
○ Case-count view

● Respondents
● Respondents and Households Members
○ Respondents and Non-respondents
○ Respondents and Non-respondents plus Household Members

An 'X' indicates the category is available for that sample

Code	Label	03	04	05	06	07	08	09	10	11	12	13	14	15	16	17
01	Married – spouse present	X	X	X	X	X	X	X	X	X	X	X	X	X	X	X
02	Married – spouse absent	X	X	X	X	X	X	X	X	X	X	X	X	X	X	X
03	Widowed		X	X	X	X	X	X	X	X	X	X	X	X	X	X
04	Divorced		X	X	X	X	X	X	X	X	X	X	X	X	X	X
05	Separated		X	X	X	X	X	X	X	X	X	X	X	X	X	X
06	Never married		X	X	X	X	X	X	X	X	X	X	X	X	X	X
99	NIU (Not in Universe)	.	.	.	.	.	.	.	.	.	.	.	.	.	.	.

Figure 6.27 Absence makes the heart grow harder!

Source: Bureau of Labor Statistics

Double/triple-barrel questions

Another often seen form of measurement error to do with question wording is the double- or triple-barrel question. These are questions that load multiple concepts or potential response categories into one question to the detriment of the data they aim to collect. They represent an obvious problem in trying to measure a concept in that the answer the respondent gives is not clear due to the response being aimed at two or more potential positions.

How do survey designers overcome double/triple-barrel problems? The way to overcome this specific problem of measurement error is to separate out the different concepts or response categories so that there is only a single concept or response category for respondents to consider. Let's take a look at some common examples.

> *How often have you have consulted a physician or other health professional in the last six months?*

This question is double barrelled by referring to physician or other health professional. The question is also ambiguous due to its use of the term 'health professional'. While we might be able to generate some data about the general level of consultation for health professionals that a respondent has reported when considering this question, we have no way of knowing whether that is for a doctor, practice or community nurse, specialist, surgeon, psychologist, or other health professional. We do not know either what the respondent considers to be a 'health professional', for example are Reiki healers or naturopaths 'health professionals'?

How might this question be improved? Separate out the different kinds of health professional and/or ask a general question about how often a respondent might have sought medical advice. One thing to keep in mind, in line with a concern mentioned above, is just how many health professionals do you list, without the question becoming burdensome to respondents?

How often have you consulted the following health professionals in the last six months?

	Often	Occasionally	Never
General Practitioner	☐	☐	☐
Specialist	☐	☐	☐
Physiotherapist	☐	☐	☐
Psychiatrist	☐	☐	☐
Psychologist	☐	☐	☐
Other, please specify..............	☐	☐	☐

Figure 6.28 Improving a double-barrelled question

This question might be further improved with more accurate or less ambiguous answer categories (Figure 6.28). What is 'often' or 'occasionally' in this context? Perhaps the answer categories could be once or twice (occasionally) and more than twice (often) or benchmarked against existing data for consultation with health professionals.

> *How often in a given week do you do physical exercise such as jog, swim, or cycle?*

This question is similar to the previous one. There is a key concept, physical exercise, but then three examples (unambiguous, however). As a general question, this, like the health professional question, may be able to gather some useful general data, but then again, depending on how respondents read the question, it may not due to its attempt at some specificity. Moreover, the question can be misleading in that if respondents do physical exercise (such as hiking or play tennis) but not any of the three forms listed in the question, they may not answer, even though they qualify to do so. Further, if respondents walk or do gardening, or other physical activity that is perhaps lighter or less exertive, but are not interpreted as 'exercise' or a sport, are they to be included? This relates again to clarifying the concept to be measured.

How can this question be improved? This question can be clearer by separating out specific kinds of physical exercise and clarifying for respondents what exercise means (Figure 6.29). The question could include various forms of exercise inclusive of more or less exertive types, depending on the operational definition, thereby tapping a range of physical activity.

How often in a given week do you do physical exercise such as those listed below?

	4+ a week	2/3 a week	once a week	never
Jogging or running	☐	☐	☐	☐
Cycling	☐	☐	☐	☐
Swimming	☐	☐	☐	☐
Walking	☐	☐	☐	☐
Hiking	☐	☐	☐	☐
Gardening	☐	☐	☐	☐
Play an athletic sport	☐	☐	☐	☐
Other, please specify.............	☐	☐	☐	☐

Figure 6.29 Improving another double-barrelled question

Would you say that the current level of government spending on security, border protection, and defence is too much, about right, too little?

Again, what is a respondent to make of this? There are three very different and distinct aspects of national security jammed into this one question. And while we might intuit a similar theme among the categories here that relate to a broader concept, they are most probably different dimensions of the one concept, or even completely different concepts. Defence is associated solely with military, while border protection in many countries is not. Security might mean any number of things, from the protection of national infrastructure such as railways and water sources to the online environment.

How to improve this question? Again, let's separate out the different categories so as to make the questions more logical and easier to answer (Figure 6.30).

What do you think about the current level of government spending on

	Too much	About right	Too little	Can't choose
Security?	☐	☐	☐	☐
Border protection?	☐	☐	☐	☐
Defence?	☐	☐	☐	☐

Figure 6.30   Improving a third double-barrelled question

Verbosity and obscurity

Verbosity relates to how wordy our questions are, that is how long and convoluted they are. It is not just a matter of the number of words, but the actual words we choose to include in a question that can mean the difference between valid data and an undesirable amount of measurement error. In addition to avoiding verbosity, we also should avoid using obscure language or jargon in survey questions. This can be a challenge given that sometimes we are seeking to measure complex concepts that may be components of an academic theory that is itself communicated using language specific to that field. The problems of verbosity and obscurity are twofold: firstly, too longwinded a question, or too complex its language, then the less likely are respondents to answer it; secondly, verbose and obscurely worded questions will render potentially invalid data because respondents are answering such questions uninformed. Recall that one of the arts of measurement is to relate complex concepts for non-specialists; wording of questions therefore needs to be clear and simple, and the question itself not too long. What is clear, and what is not too long, however? Survey questions need to strike a balance between detail that is specific so that questions are not too ambiguous and a length that is not too burdensome to read, or to be heard (if a survey is conducted over the phone, for example).

Let's take a look at a verbose question (Figure 6.31).

Given the current dynamic flux of population through global migration channels due to flexible and precarious labour patterns reflecting the rapid shift of international capital in production, what do you expect will happen to the employment prospects of young people in the near future?

Positive	☐
Negative	☐
Neutral	☐

Figure 6.31   Verbose question example

This question is long and longwinded. The question is also concept laden and those concepts are unclear. To a non-specialist respondent phrases such as 'global migration channels', 'flexible and precarious labour patterns', and 'international capital' will be bewildering. Even to a specialist such as an economist this question would still need an explanation. We can intuit that the question is interested in what respondents think of employment prospects for young people under certain conditions, however. As for the front end of the question the survey designers need to simplify things somewhat (Figure 6.32). *How might they improve the question?*

Given the rapid nature of economic change and the ability of people from many parts of the world to come here and work, are the job prospects of young people in this country

At risk, because there is too much competition with economic migration?

As good as they have always been because the economy has created a lot employment opportunities?

Figure 6.32 Improving a verbose question

Can you state the name of your current employer, the hours worked for that employer over the last month, the type of work you did for the stated employer over the last month, and also indicate the industry that the work you did for your current employer over the last month is a part of?

Figure 6.33 Verbose question example 2

There are numerous questions all thrown into one question here (Figure 6.33). The question is convoluted, verbose, and hard to read. The nature of the question means that respondents will have to reread it many times to get a handle on what it is asking.

How to improve this question? The only way in which this question can be improved is to separate out its various components. Separating out the various components will make the measures clearer and will take less time to answer. The question is aiming to measure different dimensions of employment so it could start with a statement such as:

We are interested in some aspects of your current employment.

What is the name of your current employer?

Is your employment Full time, Part time, Casual, Other?

About how many hours have you worked over the last month for this employer?

What is the current occupation you hold with your current employer?

Are you able to identify the industry that your current employment with this employer is a part of?

Recall

There are numerous instances or occasions where researchers have a need to ask questions of respondents that ask them to reach into their own personal histories and recall information about some aspect of their lives. Researchers may want to compare experiences, attributes, and opinions of different generations within a sample, or changes associated with the one respondent from one time to another. Often research-ers ask questions that rely on memory and recall associated with work, family, health, and especially important historical events. Questions that rely on recall can provide researchers with a wealth of data that inform how people experienced change, so long as they can recall the experiences, impressions, and opinions relevant to the question. Herein lies the promise and the problem of questions reliant on memory. Memory is very often vague, confused, or patchy; this is the case for many respondents irre-spective of age or length of time across which a respondent's memory is stretched, although respondents should be able to recall events and experiences that occurred more recently. Another problem with recall questions is relevance. Questions may attempt to collect data on aspects of people's lives that are unremarkable to them, yet important to the research, reducing the likelihood of valid data. However, some aspects of people's lives are so powerful and meaningful that they recall all kinds of details about them. Hopefully it is these events or experiences that accord with the aims of the research and the questions laid out in the survey.

Recall and memory-related questions can also be impacted by the mode of survey administration. For example, if a survey is attempted on paper in the respondent's own time and in their own home, they may well be able to come back to the ques-tion or questions after a day or two recalling the necessary details. If the question is asked over the phone, however, that time allowance may not be possible, due to the interviewer's time and schedule, the same may be true for face-to-face interviews and electronically administered surveys if they have time limits. Some of these modes may allow respondents to follow up or resume the question when the respondent is ready. Otherwise interviewers in face-to-face or phone interviews may be able to probe and to assist respondents to recall specific details. Some examples of questions requiring recall are:

What religion did you belong to when you were 16?

Think about your first full-time paid job. What was that job? Who were you employed by?

If you have been married previously, what was the main cause leading to the end of the marriage?

Leading questions

Leading questions create measurement error by coaching or leading a respondent to answer in a certain way, thereby creating answers that can be falsely positive or neg-ative. Questions of this nature are mostly scenario- or vignette-type questions, where there is enough 'lead in' to have a respondent agreeing with a premise or proposition the question is based on, but they can appear in any question format. Leading ques-tions compromise answers through creating a false or biased vision of a phenomenon in the minds of respondents. Leading questions can over- or under-state a problem or situation, use emotive or evasive language in the question wording, or simply use false statements. One way of detecting leading questions is to enquire about the agency or organization that is undertaking the research and who designed the survey. Do they have political, commercial, industrial, or ideological connections or interests? Some news outlets can be guilty of this in polls after saturating coverage of an event in a particular manner.

In addition to the example cited earlier about homosexuality, another common example is:

Over the last two years the city has experienced a very high increase in the rate of certain crimes. How fearful are you that you will be a victim of crime in this city?

How might this question be less leading? The obvious answer is to remove the premise and simply state the question (Figure 6.34). Further, the question might benefit from stating particular sorts of crime that may give interesting variation in a sample.

How fearful are you of being a victim of crime in this city with respect to the following crimes?

	extremely fearful	very fearful	somewhat fearful	not very fearful	not at all fearful
Home invasion	☐	☐	☐	☐	☐
Burglary	☐	☐	☐	☐	☐
Physical assault	☐	☐	☐	☐	☐
Stolen property, e.g. car	☐	☐	☐	☐	☐

Figure 6.34   Improving a leading question

Over-reporting/under-reporting

Survey questions, while having a veneer of objectivity and value neutrality, are not always interpreted as such by respondents. Many respondents may well feel they are being judged, or at least are offering data that they feel may compromise them or their reputations in some way. This may be the case even if ethical precautions around question wording are taken. There is a power relationship that needs to be considered as well as a social relationship that is circumscribed with cultural standards when asking questions in a survey. Questions about sensitive topics as discussed above are often prone to what is called over- and/or under-reporting, sometimes irrespective of how they are asked. This phenomenon in surveys often indicates levels of social desirability. Providing answers to questions is an act of trust and despite the many good assurances researchers give about confidentiality and anonymity, there are many instances of over- and under-reporting. Overcoming over- and under-reporting is a key concern for survey designers, and question construction and placement can mitigate this to some extent in line with some of the ethical concerns stated earlier. Very often, however, over- and under-reporting can simply be a limitation of survey research. A variety of topics are over- and under-reported. In countries where voting is optional many social surveys report levels that are well above the known rate of voters in a given election (Belli et al., 1999). Voting is seen as socially desirable and so many more people state that they vote than actually do. Consuming pornography is, as you could imagine, well under-reported in social surveys, even though other modes of data collection on this topic state much higher rates than surveys do. Being middle class is also often over-reported with as much as 80% of respondents in some survey samples stating they are middle class (Phillips, 2007) – there could be **sampling error** involved here to be sure.

Translating questions and meaning

As this text has highlighted and as you have perhaps seen for yourself, there are numerous large-scale comparative surveys that attempt to measure all kinds of concepts in various international and culturally different contexts. The job of asking the same

Table 6.2 Troubleshooting for question construction

Problem or potential problem	How to tell	What to do
Ambiguity/vagueness	The question will contain nouns, adjectives, or verbs that are not precise and could have a number of different meanings	Aim to be as precise and clear as possible. Use a brief definition, clarify through answer categories
Double barrelled	The question will have two or more response categories within it, when only one should be there	Separate out the different categories within a response format. Start question with a statement and list the different categories as separate responses
Leading questions	Usually an emotive or biased statement or premise at the beginning of the question	Eliminate the statement, or change the tone of the statement or premise to a more neutral one
Verbose/obscure	Language not applicable to non-specialists. Question is far too longwinded. The meaning is unclear	Keep the language simple, clear, and remember that respondents will not be specialists. Keep the length of the question short
Cross-cultural meaning	Seek out whether the concept or the wording of the question has the same meaning in the same context	Aim to have the concept the question indicates relate to the specific cultural context through previous research, pilot testing, or qualitative work

question in, say, over 100 different places is an immensely difficult one. Concepts have different meanings or no meaning in different cultural contexts, therefore there is a need to translate questions, not just into different languages, but into different terms to approximate consistency of measurement consistent with how different people see various forms of behaviour (Table 6.2).

Pre-testing and pilot testing

Given the extensive opportunities for measurement error through question design, how do survey researchers attempt to reduce measurement error associated with question construction? There is no way of eliminating measurement error entirely, yet there are ways in which survey design can reduce it. Firstly, we need to know how our questions might be contributing to measurement error: that is, how do we know if we have committed any of the above-mentioned 'crimes' in relation to question construction? There are a few telltale signs that measurement error may have occurred, such as some statistical anomalies revealed through some forms of analysis. Of course, this is bad news as there is little that can be done once the data have been collected. Prevention is better than cure (even though there is no 'cure' as such in survey research) so, mostly, researchers try and reduce measurement error by working through potential problems before the survey is put into the field, through pre-testing and pilot testing. Professional researchers will (or should) always attempt some form of pre-test or pilot test to gain knowledge of where potential sources of measurement error may arise or have occurred. But this costs money and time, and this form of check and balance therefore may not be possible for smaller organizations, research projects with small budgets, or businesses with little time and money for research. If this is the case, then the best advice is to use questions that exist, providing they are valid and reliable, work through possible question problems with the aid of a text such as this, or others, that have guides such as the above, or perhaps seek some limited, specific, and tailored advice from an expert.

Pilot testing

Pilot testing aims to run the survey on a small sample of respondents that will potentially have the characteristics of the larger sample, such as demographic attributes and research relevance. The small sample is given the survey to complete and then asked about the questions and gives feedback if time and money permit, or the researchers notice patterns of responses that may give cause for concern and be consistent with the potential errors discussed above. The problematic questions are amended and then the survey is re-piloted if, again, time and money permit. Once the errors have been fixed then the survey is sent out to the field proper.

Interviewer reports

Part of the pilot process or even the fieldwork process that assists in detecting measurement error is feedback from interviewers. It is rare for the researchers involved in large professional survey projects to do face-to-face or phone interviews to administer surveys. They often have trained students or workers from survey research companies to do it, so they are reliant on the impressions of interviewers for feedback about how respondents reacted to the various questions. Many projects work off interviewer reports that list potential issues or problems with questions that are sources of measurement error. These reports can be an excellent source of question problem identification as interviewers who administer a survey with many respondents can detect patterns of confusion, misunderstanding, or incomprehension in questions within a sample. Of course, it is imperative that interviewers themselves need to have a clear understanding of what the questions are trying to measure and what they mean before they can communicate sources of measurement error or attempt to clarify a question for a respondent.

This is of course not possible with surveys that are not administered face to face or over the phone, such as mail-out surveys or online surveys. With these modes, however, detailed instructions can be left to someone administering the survey on questions that may be deemed difficult to interpret or need further clarification or contact details.

Cognitive interviewing

Cognitive interviewing is a significant and at times complex means of ascertaining how survey questions are potentially or have been interpreted by respondents with the aim of reducing measurement error. Cognitive interviewing (CI) involves assessing potential respondents' impressions of specific ways in which questions are worded to clarify any ambiguity or confusion relating to question wording through a one-to-one process of questions and answers. CI is employed widely as part of professional survey research projects. One of its key premises and aims is to examine the meanings that respondents or potential respondents attribute to survey questions and to assess to what extent they correspond with the meanings intended in the questions by the survey question designers. That stated, it is not a process wherein there is a 'right' and 'wrong' party should there be discrepancies between meanings; the process of CI is one of refinement of meaning and eventual convergence of meaning in survey questions. A key dimension of CI is the relationship respondents have with the wording of questions and key concepts to be measured. Essentially, what do words in a question mean, and how are they understood? From the examples of potential measurement error above, we can appreciate how easily measurement error can occur. Coupled with the advantages that surveys offer to policy for large populations, testing of survey questions through processes and methods such as CI go a long way towards attempting to produce the highest level of data quality.

Much like pilot testing, CI in practical terms is subject to time, money, and expertise. CI in and of itself has become a complex science that is a key part of questionnaire construction and development (Willis, 2004). Larger complex survey projects use CI extensively.

Question banks and survey projects

At times there is no need to reinvent the wheel, so to speak. There are many questions that survey researchers use routinely because they have become valid and reliable indicators over time. A number of organizations, in both government and industry, have made attempts to standardize sets of survey questions so as to allow research to be comparable on the basis of those questions considered to be reliable and valid for specific concepts. There are numerous websites such as https://www.ukdataservice.ac.uk/get-data/other-providers/question-banks that list British and international question banks from professional survey research organizations, are accessible to the public and that list questionnaires from which survey questions can be used with proper acknowledgement.

──────────────── YOUR SURVEY ────────────────

Constructing survey questions

Constructing measures for your concepts is a crucial step in the survey design process. To ensure the best quality data possible you will need to take time to choose which kind of questions are required to measure your concepts. Survey questions exist in various forms; the challenge here is to attempt to devise your own and gain some feedback about them before you administer your survey.

Consider the various question and response formats that this chapter has presented. Which ones do you think are appropriate for your own survey, given your concepts and your research questions?

- Consider what your questions are trying to measure and in what ways – affective states, or facts?
- Which formats should you use for which purpose? Rating or ranking or both?
- What kinds of data do you need for your research question? Which level of measurement do you think your data need to be at? Do you need qualitative data at all?
- Open-ended or closed-ended questions? Are you familiar with some of the key categories associated with your concept? Can you confidently present a series of closed-ended questions?
- Do your closed-ended questions need to include an 'Other' option?

(Continued)

Work up a draft of the survey questions for each concept.

- Work through the questions as a team or between class members to take a step towards eliminating possible measurement error.
- Consider the main problems with question construction between team members, such as being ambiguous, double barrelled, verbose, leading, or judgemental.
- Discuss if any of the questions are potentially sensitive or problematic for potential respondents. Are they necessary for the aims of the research? As a rule, for such projects it is probably best if you seek to avoid research that is sensitive and demanding of potential respondents.
- Is there a cross-cultural framing to your project? Do the questions make sense to different groups who might be in your final sample? This will be important if you are working with a community organization perhaps.

Pre-testing and piloting:

- Once you have finalized your questions, attempt to pilot them with other members of your class, or the organization you are working with.
- Suggest a small pilot study, where some people relevant to the final sample can answer the questions (you may only need a few people) and give you feedback about their clarity and validity.
- Note any problems, and of what kind they were.
- If there are problems, redesign and attempt to re-test.

Codebook:

Develop a codebook with all of the question and answer categories labelled with appropriate labels and number codes. Use the same codes for the same answer formats, such as Likert scales. Section off each module of questions and code sections with a letter and number beginning with A1, then code questions within the module using the section code. For example, A1a, A1b, A1c. B1a, B2a, B2b, etc.

Key knowledge and skills

This chapter has introduced the various components of question construction. Key knowledge and skills in question construction are as follows:

- Questions can be designed to conform to different formats to measure states, facts, and other phenomena in a variety of ways appropriate to the nature of the question.
- Question construction is subject to a series of possible forms of measurement error which adversely affect the data. There are ways to avoid such forms of measurement error.
- Answer categories are open and closed ended. Open and closed categories are used in specific question types, the majority of answer categories being closed ended.
- Answer categories are coded numerically before the survey is administered to respondents. Answers to open-ended questions are numerically coded after the data have been collected, however.

- Answer categories in questions translate to various levels of measurement that enable different methods of data analysis.
- Codebooks are developed to keep a record of questions, the sequence of questions, and the various scoring of answer categories.
- Question construction is subject to various ethical concerns, power dynamics between researcher and researched, and respondent sensitivities.

Further reading

A classic text highlighting the problems associated with question construction including numerous examples of how survey question problems can be solved is Fowler's *Improving Survey Questions*. Robinson and Leonard's *Designing Quality Survey Questions* is a text dedicated to the development of survey questions with the survey design process in mind and well worth consulting also. The book has numerous chapters dealing with specific issues in survey question design.

Full text references:

Fowler, F. J. Jr (1995) *Improving Survey Questions: Design and Evaluation.* Thousand Oaks, CA: Sage

Robinson, S. and Leonard, K. (2018) *Designing Quality Survey Questions.* London: Sage

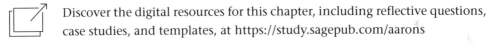 Discover the digital resources for this chapter, including reflective questions, case studies, and templates, at https://study.sagepub.com/aarons

Seven

Conceptual Models: Mapping Concepts and Preparing for Analysis

Concepts embedded in research questions and measured in a survey are relational, that is they will eventually be analysed in relation to one another. Survey research uses conceptual models to clarify the relationships between independent and dependent variables and to propose how the data analysis will proceed. This chapter will demonstrate how to:

- Create basic and complex conceptual models for survey design within the framework of the logic of quantitative analysis
- Illustrate the precise organization of the relationships between concepts in research questions with a conceptual model
- Propose relationships between independent and dependent variables for analysis consistent with the logic of quantitative research with conceptual models
- Incorporate conceptual models into the research process and survey design process clearly and effectively

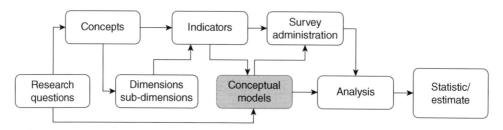

Figure 7.1   Survey design process: conceptual models/analysis

This chapter will discuss the importance of conceptual models to survey design and survey research overall (Figure 7.1). If you are designing a survey with research questions in mind that involve conceptual relationships, then you will need to map out the various relationships between the concepts and establish an analytic strategy before you collect your data and ensure that the relevant measures for each concept are included in the survey. Even if you are not designing a survey but are researching using survey data, you will need to map conceptually sets of relationships that drive your research questions. In Chapters 4 and 5 we considered the crucial role of concepts to survey design and their vital relationship to measurement in a survey. This chapter builds on the insights of the previous discussions of concepts, dimensions, and sub-dimensions by demonstrating how concepts relate to each other, and how the relationships between concepts, elaborated and graphically presented through models, also guide survey design. Further, **conceptual models** clarify the aims of the research more precisely through a consideration of how the research components such as theory, concepts, and data relate to each other in pursuit of research questions.

While concepts are often discussed as singular abstract entities, in a dynamic research environment informed by survey data they should nearly always be thought of in relation to other concepts. This is important for the fact that above and beyond the 'front end' notions of clarification and operationalization is the later work of the research process such as analysis, results, and theory testing/building. Conceptual models assist us in clarifying how our concepts relate to each other and consequently how we might structure the data analysis to best answer research questions.

Conceptual models, much like a range of other features of survey design, are given a variety of names just to confuse you and highlight the lack of consensus in scholarship! In addition to 'conceptual model' you will come across terms such as 'causal model' (technically more associated with how data analysis proceeds), 'flow diagram', 'thought map', 'variable model', 'process model', and perhaps others that, despite some nuances, are more or less the same thing. What is common to them all are ideas, boxes, and arrows deployed to give some sort of order to the morass of research ideas and concepts. Given our focus on the importance of concepts to survey design, we will stick faithfully to the term 'conceptual model' throughout this chapter.

The importance of conceptual models to survey design: Conceptual models and the relationship to research questions

Conceptual models help researchers design surveys in two important ways. Firstly, they allow researchers to map relationships between concepts and hypothesize the direction of influence that concepts have on each other. A conceptual model will graphically represent the empirical relationships between what we term dependent and independent variables or, more broadly, how concepts act on other concepts. This illustrates the logic of research questions appropriate for survey data in that we are expecting patterns of behaviour or human action to be the result of some factors influencing other factors. For example, we may state that, on average, the more education an individual has, the higher their income will be. Higher income is the result of (or is dependent on) more education. This allows the research to be planned more precisely and to help guide some forms of later data analysis when the data have been collected and cleaned up.

Secondly, researchers can map out clearly the relationship between concepts as they are portrayed in a discipline's theoretical perspective, thereby enabling the researchers to plan how they will theory-test (as is the case in deductive research) or theory-build (inductive). In doing so we produce conceptual models to elaborate on, explain, and illustrate some kind of plausible mechanism or process whereby what we think is happening is explained with reference to concepts embedded in theories. Conceptual models allow us to summarize and efficiently communicate a sense of 'how do things proceed?' or 'how does this (relationship or pattern) work?', relating this process to survey design through concepts and indicators in a manner that reminds us of the earlier discussion in Chapter 3 about plausibility and the relationships between concepts.

Recall also in Chapter 3 that we examined what kind of research questions are best pursued or suited to survey research. Survey researchers specify and pose types of questions that at heart seek answers to human problems for larger groups through the analysis of relationships between different concepts. It is the core of these research questions and relationships that you are graphically laying out when you produce a conceptual model. As any research question entails within it a number of concepts, it is the role of the conceptual model to specify their role in the research question and to align them in empirical relationships through analytic strategies that allow researchers to explain them theoretically.

The logic of survey research

Research informed by survey data follows a certain logic; that is, it proceeds in a certain way so as to be able to demonstrate that particular relationships between states, attributes, opinions, attitudes, and experiences 'exist'. Recall the advantages of survey research and the types of questions it is best placed to answer. These questions aim at discovering patterns through relationships best demonstrated with the use of quantitative data, for large relevant groups. 'Relationships' is the key word here. Relationships are found or revealed through analysis and the findings reflect some form of mechanism that is in operation in the area of human behaviour that the research is concerned with. The job of theory consequently is to interpret these findings and explain the patterns that are found within the data. Of course, if there is only one concept or a series of unrelated concepts that a research question using survey data is seeking statistics for, then models are not necessary. There are lots of occasions when survey research is only interested in measuring single variables, but the overwhelming majority of research using survey data aims to investigate relationships.

Positivism

It is important to note that survey design and its subsequent analytical logics framing data analysis are set within a philosophy of knowledge context called positivism. Positivism is not at all about being positive in the sense that we should enthusiastically embrace surveys (although I have pointed out the many benefits of survey research!). No, positivism is a philosophical term that attempts to describe a certainty about knowledge through empiricism. What we know is based on only what we can see. From such knowledge, and only from such knowledge, so positivists assert, can we deduce laws or more formal rules of human behaviour based on how we interpret what we see. Of course, how we conceive of concepts to explain what we see, in the first place, tends to shape how we record or observe them. You see the potential problem here: we need to theorize something first, then define it, then define it to measure it, and then interpret it. A lot can and does go wrong in that process, hence the focus on concepts as important relating to data and theory. Survey research has gone through a lot of changes to overcome forms of limitation, bias, and ethnocentricity associated with positivism. Many researchers these days are reflexive about how they measure concepts in specific contexts in an attempt to accept the limits of empirical research and inform survey design with alternative knowledge paradigms.

Conceptual relationships: Dependent and independent concepts and variables

With these concerns in mind then, we tend to proceed with caution when we discuss relationships between concepts. The most elementary relationship that a conceptual model aims to show is the relationship between independent and dependent concepts, or more precisely in the language of data, independent and dependent variables, as we saw in Chapter 3. The nature of survey research and the way of survey design mean that we are seeking to demonstrate and explain variation in patterns in human behaviour or human experience with reference to relationships between opinions, attitudes, experiences, and attributes. Further, these relationships can be demonstrated empirically, that is numerically or statistically, from which we can say something of accuracy about the theoretical contexts concerning our research interests and identify specific patterns for groups and sub-groups within a population. Independent and dependent or predictor and outcome variables, as these are also sometimes known, are mostly straightforward but at other times less so, yet the basis of the conceptual relationship that survey design should propose is that one produces, influences, or causes the other.

Relationships between independent and dependent variables are described in various ways and indicate some important limitations and constraints on this kind of research. You will often read about how relationships between variables are causal, associated, or correlated. Relationships between concepts or variables can also be **linear**, **curvilinear**, or non-linear. Causation is something that we have to take with a healthy dose of scepticism in survey research because stating something is 'caused' by something else, especially for people, is fraught with problems. People are not mere chemicals (well they are, but you know what I mean!) and simply adding some measure of a chemical that causes a reaction in another chemical is not how the social sciences generally proceed or are understood. To suggest something causes another thing we have to have the direction of the relationship correct and as the independent variable increases or decreases, so too should the dependent variable in lockstep. As it happens, variation is often much weaker in survey analysis for a variety of reasons such as sampling error, measurement error, and conceptual error. Further, there should be very convincing plausibility that this is indeed how a pattern occurs. There are many chicken and egg scenarios and large amounts of doubt and error involved in social-science-type research that use surveys, so we tend not to speak of causes and defer with some measure of humility and open-mindedness to association and correlation to explain relationships.

Take the above example of the relationship between education and income. Might we flip this relationship and suggest the opposite to explain why some people are wealthier than others? Well, if you are relatively well off to begin with, you are more than likely to go on to achieve a higher level of education than if you are relatively not so well off, leading to your earning a higher income. There exists plenty of evidence to suggest that this is just the case! It is difficult for us then to suggest with any great confidence or certainty, as the positivists might claim, that education 'causes' higher incomes. Instead we state that it is associated or correlated with it and set this association or correlation within context. Another important reason why we generally do not speak of causes when thinking about relationships between concepts, especially more simple models such as those that contain only a couple of variables, is that there are sure to be other factors at play that may also contribute to particular patterns and/or attributes that differ for people. In terms of our example, why some people earn more than others may also be attributable to factors such as context, family, opportunity, health, and a range of other things (read concepts) that complicate the notion of a direct cause.

Association and correlation

A more accurate and appropriate analytical approach to these kinds of problems is to suggest that variables or concepts are associated and/or correlated with each other rather than the product of a causal relationship. These terms suggest less of an impact that can be attributed to a relationship than a concrete notion of a cause, but more appropriately delimit its scale, leaving room for doubt, further analysis, survey error, and the proper place of theory. Association and/or correlation between two variables in data analysis is established through various forms of statistical patterns informed by valid and reliable data. Essentially, we can demonstrate a relationship using some statistical tests and rejecting the premise of the null hypothesis (a scientific assumption that two variables will not be associated).

Association refers to a general relationship between an independent and dependent variable, while a correlation indicates the strength and direction of the relationship. As we saw in Chapter 3, a key aspect of any relationship is plausibility. If we find in our analyses that we have established a relationship between two or more variables, does this relationship make sense? Theoretically, conceptually, logically? Recall the saying in empirical research: 'correlation does not imply causation', which acts as a stop sign to remind us that before making any bold claims about data, and whatever our findings between independent and dependent variables in survey research, we must ask if the relationship is plausible, just as we asked about cheese consumption levels and the number of deaths by sheet entanglement in Chapter 3.

Conceptual models

Basic conceptual models

As with previous chapters, let's produce some diagrams to show what I mean here. A basic conceptual model, such as the one in the first figure below, is a straightforward relationship between an independent variable and a dependent variable. The arrow between the two boxes in the figure shows the direction of the relationship: that is, the independent variable acting on or being associated or correlated with the dependent variable.

While this sounds quite straightforward there is another dimension to this arrangement that is important and represents what the two boxes and an arrow mean. What does it mean to be associated or correlated with when we are discussing relationships? Here we need to recall what kind of data we are dealing with and how those data are used to demonstrate a pattern. As quantitative data are representative of concepts, survey data relate to themselves through rates, levels, and amounts, so that a rate, level, or amount in the independent variable should produce a variation in the rate, level, or amount in the dependent variable – although it should be noted that it need not at all times, and of course some proposed relationships between variables will not exist. In other words, if a change (higher or lower) in the independent variable produces a change in the dependent variable (higher or lower) then we can begin to consider a relationship between the two, that is an association or correlation, just as our research question or hypothesis suggested. This basic relationship that entails variation and change in the values of the two variables is demonstrated in Figure 7.2.

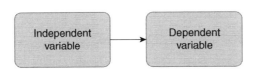

Figure 7.2 Basic conceptual model of a relationship between an independent variable and a dependent variable

Figure 7.2 represents a basic conceptual model showing that the independent variable (a clarified concept) will influence or effect the dependent variable (another clarified concept). Figure 7.3 is a basic conceptual model in action, in that it communicates that as independent variables increase or decrease, that is scores on them are higher or lower, so too will the scores on the dependent variable. This of course is not the case for all conceptual models and research questions. For example, there is no 'movement' as such for nominal-level variables such as nationality, gender, or occupation, despite there being differences. Variables in Figure 7.3 are therefore always ordinal or interval/ratio.

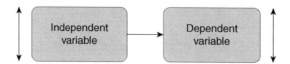

Figure 7.3 Basic conceptual model of a relationship between independent and dependent variables that are ordinal or interval/ratio

Figures 7.4–7.8 show a few examples to illustrate how researchers might use basic conceptual models to plan, summarize, and communicate survey research and elaborate or establish key relationships involved with the research questions or hypotheses.

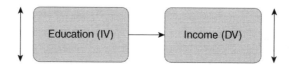

Figure 7.4 Basic conceptual model of a relationship between education and income

In Figure 7.4 we are interested in why there is a variation in wealth in a society. Figure 7.4 proposes or hypothesizes that an increase or decrease in the rate, level, or amount of education will produce variation in the rate, level, or amount of income. Put another way, as education increases (or decreases in terms of years spent or the higher the qualifications gained) so will the level of income, thus we can think of education and income being associated or correlated. Education is the independent variable (IV) influencing the dependent variable (DV) income. The relationship is also plausible in that we can readily intuit that this makes sense, but also there is ample theory to provide an explanation as to how this might occur and why, and previous empirical research that has demonstrated the relationship previously.

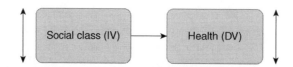

Figure 7.5 Basic conceptual model of a relationship between social class and health

Figure 7.5 displays a proposed conceptual relationship between social class and health. Here the research is interested in what might account for presumed differences in the quality of health in a population. Social class is the IV and health the DV. The more social class increases (that is, the 'higher' one's social class) or decreases (the 'lower' one's social class), the greater or lesser will be one's health.

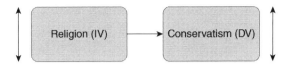

Figure 7.6 Basic conceptual model of a relationship between religion and conservatism

Figure 7.6 presents a conceptual relationship between religion and conservatism. The proposed research topic is interested in which factors (such as religion) might contribute to individuals and groups in a population having or not having conservative opinions, attitudes, or values. The diagram suggests that the more or less religious you are, the more or less likely you will have conservative opinions, attitudes, or values. Note that the measure of religion would have to be ordinal or interval/ratio. Religion can be measured in a survey in lots of ways. Identifying as 'religious' or not is one way to measure religion ordinally, as in having or not having religion. A nominal measure of religion such as which religion would not fit this model.

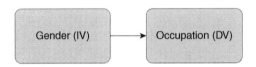

Figure 7.7 Basic conceptual model of a relationship between gender and occupation

Figure 7.7 illustrates a proposed relationship between gender and occupation. This model might relate to previous or existing empirical patterns that suggest many occupations are overrepresented by women or men, such as nursing (women) and carpentry (men). Similarly, occupational status such as manager or subordinate has often been cited as 'gendered'. Notice that there are no vertical and horizontal arrows in this diagram, and for good reason. At times there are relationships between concepts that are not what we call linear: that is, as one variable increases or decreases then another increases or decreases, as the examples in this section have usually expressed. Here we cannot measure gender as we would other concepts such as high and low or more or less, because gender is a nominal variable, but as states of being that do not change, the same is proposed for the DV occupation. We have not proposed here that occupation is a variable that in some way denotes more or less, higher or lower, although there may be ways in which researchers may seek to do so (occupations as an indicator of greater or lesser status, for example). Yet, we may still hypothesize a relationship between the two and seek to investigate if occupations are influenced, associated, or correlated with gender.

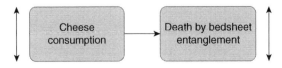

Figure 7.8 Basic conceptual model of an implausible relationship

Finally let's consider Figure 7.8, a conceptual map relating how plausibility is an important factor in survey design. Recall Tyler Vigen's spurious correlations between numerous IVs and DVs, one of which was presented in Chapter 3. Indeed, the chart he presents suggests that there is a correlation between the level of cheese consumption and deaths by being entangled in bedsheets. Vigen states that the correlation coefficient for this relationship is $r = 0.94$, which is an immensely impressive statistic indicating a very, very strong positive relationship – as cheese consumption increases, so too does death by bedsheet entanglement, almost identically. But the message here is all about plausibility and how possible the relationship is in a theoretical and real-world sense. The statistics are real, but the relationship is not, even if it has actually happened a couple of times, somehow. It is worth restating that just because two concepts or measures are related statistically, this does not mean that there is an association or correlation, and definitely not a cause. Here also is the value of previous research, theory, and perspective that contextualizes survey research and survey design.

In summary then, as we approach survey design (or secondary analysis with survey data) with our stock of concepts and indicators relating to our research questions that are operational or in development and refinement, we can use basic conceptual maps to plan out the hypothesized or theorized relationships between IVs and DVs from which we can refine and create more nuanced and specific research questions, and establish a guide or framework as to how data analysis will proceed once we have the data. Conceptual relationships, seen here as dynamic positions of influence and effect between IVs and DVs, allow us to operationalize how theories are empirically relevant and to map how concepts within theories relate.

Conceptual models are often more complex than a straightforward relationship between an IV and DV, however, and mostly entail numerous concepts and variables in a variety of relationships with each other, often reflecting a theoretical basis to the research but still proceeding based on the same logic of relationships between concepts. In the next section we will expand on the basic conceptual model and see how more complex models inform survey design, more specific research questions, and more complex data analysis.

Complex conceptual models

The first thing to notice about complex conceptual models is that they give us more concepts and more relationships to test. They are often more precise also, because they aim to provide us with dimensions and sub-dimensions of concepts to assess against dependent variables (themselves more refined). In so doing they provide the research with more sophistication and potentially more plausibility, aiming to test better elaborate theoretical frameworks and more detailed research questions as well as denoting what Davis (1985) calls a 'causal order', or the structure of the relationships between variables in complex models. Survey research aims to mirror various aspects of human life as best as possible, so adding more layers, background, or forms of explanation in the form of concepts will allow the research to approximate better some recognizable real-life patterns and inform our theoretical imaginations much more. So, what does a more complex conceptual model look like? Let's build on our basic model of education explaining the variation in income.

An important point to note is that with basic conceptual models we are tracing the operationalization of concepts again. The examples above show how relationships between concepts work in relation to a research question through concepts related to theory, but again they are vague. Here hopefully you can see clearly the importance of dimensions and sub-dimensions to concepts 'in action' as it were. For example, what is meant by 'conservatism'? Is it social conservatism, cultural conservatism, economic conservatism, political conservatism, or some other form of conservatism? This by now familiar process is also followed in the development of more complex conceptual models.

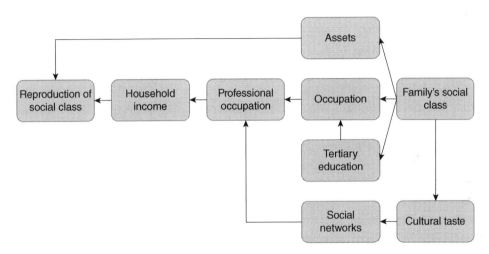

Figure 7.9 Complex conceptual model of relationships between social class and income

In Figure 7.9, we have moved from a basic conceptual model to a more nuanced and complex conceptual model with the addition of some more concepts that reflect theoretical or empirical elaboration on the question. Here there is still a concern for how education might be related to disparities in wealth, indicated by household income, but beyond variations in wealth this model is based on questions about how social class is reproduced, which is a much more complex but related concern. However, despite the upgrade in models, you can still make out the direction of the relationships that indicate the IVs and DVs.

Elaborating on our earlier enquiry, we can denote that the basic relationship between education and income (refined to a dimension such as household income), although still there, is embedded in a larger, more complex theoretical and conceptual framework akin to an archaeological dig that shows a small artefact that is actually related to a larger, more interesting find such as a mosaic. Further, although we have identified education as a key IV in our model, our analysis (assumed) of the previous literature would identify numerous other factors that explain income variation and the reproduction of social class, which we can test alongside education. Relevant dimensions of class such as occupation (high status), culture (tastes), and wealth (assets), related to a range of important social background experiences or attributes also pronounced by theory, previous research, or both, can be incorporated into a conceptual model that drives the design of the survey and the analysis of the data. With a more complex model such as this included in the survey design, we are in a position to assess or interrogate the best predictor of income and reproduction of a state such as social class. In such a model there can be a variety of relationships that denote **direct** and **indirect relationships** between concepts. For example, cultural tastes do not in and of themselves produce high incomes, but they are related to social networks, and having the right social networks may be directly related to the attainment of professional high-paying and high-status employment (think of the saying 'it's not what you know but who you know'!).

This form of conceptual model also allows us to make and communicate important statements and refinements associated with the research topic and research questions. The complex conceptual model provides the survey researcher with a mechanism to explain what is happening in the research and how. This is related to theory testing or theory building (deductive or inductive) as stated. It may follow and outline a theorist's conceptual scheme for how a phenomenon such as social class is maintained as a broad group phenomenon or explain one's own theoretical thinking on such a matter. Further, we can see the distinctions in this model between dimensions and even sub-dimensions, which allows us to select appropriately relevant aspects of a concept to be measured with valid and reliable indicators.

Let's take a look at another complex conceptual model.

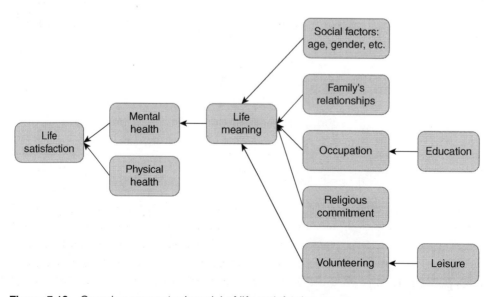

Figure 7.10 Complex conceptual model of life satisfaction

Figure 7.10 builds on our basic conceptual model that suggests that health is determined by social class. Here we can unveil a more complex picture and relate a number of hypothesized relationships that might speak to the broader concept of 'life satisfaction' or 'quality of life' of which health may be an important dimension. As we discussed earlier, health itself as a concept has its own dimensions, and, again, which ones we deem relevant are to do with our own research interests, the previous literature, and theory appropriate to our research. Let's go with the distinction between mental health and physical health. A dimension of mental health may be 'happiness', which we can include in the survey as well as other dimensions of physical health. Mental health may be mediated or impacted by the meaning or outlook an individual attributes to their life, which is a result of various IVs in addition to social class. Social class in this model we may restrict to education level and personal income which may have direct or indirect relationships with the DV. How does social class compare with more cultural aspects of identity such as what one does in one's leisure time, religious behaviour, and family relationships? Does gender matter to mental health?

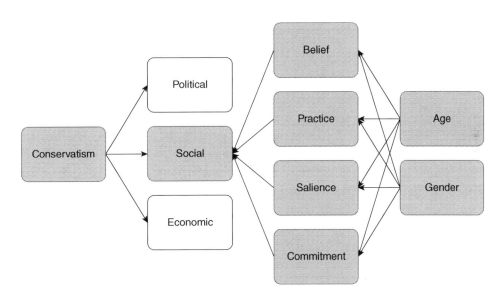

Figure 7.11 Complex conceptual model of religion and conservatism

Once again building on our basic conceptual model (Figure 7.6, see p. 197) of religion and conservatism we can see that Figure 7.11 offers a more complex picture of the circumstances, be they theoretical or empirical, surrounding the initial relationship that the basic model sought to test. Here in Figure 7.11 we have numerous options to explore that envelope, the basic model presented earlier. Importantly this example shows the importance of dimensions for the DV as I stated earlier (and if room permitted, the inclusion of sub-dimensions). In this example we have two sets of dimensions potentially impacting the others. For our IV, religion, we have four dimensions all reflecting different ways of being religious: belief, denomination/religious type, commitment, and salience. We also have three dimensions of the concept of conservatism, which may be thought of as a form of political identity, sets of social practices accompanied by certain values, and/or attitudes and opinions on economic behaviour. From the social, economic, and political dimensions of the DV, the research may be interested in the social dimension of conservatism only or all three.

The addition of IVs such as age and gender are also instructive for two reasons. Firstly, the literature on the social aspects of religion tells us that gender is a key social determinant of religious behaviour to the extent that women are often far more religious than men, and age is also an important factor in conservatism or being progressive. The older one is, the more conservative one is generally. Secondly, with the introduction of social identity or background concepts we can compare what we may call a 'social model' with a 'religious model', comparing models within models so to speak, as well as assessing if religious variables are mediated by gender and age.

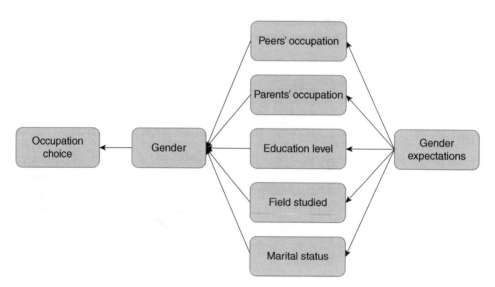

Figure 7.12   Complex conceptual model of gender and occupation

Figure 7.12 presents another complex conceptual model for developing research on the relationship between gender and occupation (Figure 7.7, see p. 197). Gender and occupation are modelled here with the aid of a range of concepts that give this example a slightly different form of orientation, although the relationships we may seek to explore with survey data here are much the same as for other questions. It is important to note that gender does not 'produce' or 'cause' an occupation (much like we might plausibly imagine education levels to produce higher incomes) in the sense that being masculine or feminine, male or female, automatically assorts one into a form of formal work; rather gender is related to occupations through various other experiences and attributes (or we are hypothesizing that they are) that lead to an occupational outcome. So we might explain that the occupational differences between women and men are a result of various influences such as family educational background, societal-level expectations reinforced through schooling and family, peer network experiences, as well as assessing different generations and cultures.

We might even suggest, going by this model, that gender is not so much an IV as it is an **intervening variable** – an in-between variable – between social and cultural factors and occupation. Or we could suggest that it is an IV but that it is one built by these other experiences that impact how society exerts pressure for men and women to act in certain ways (such as what work they do); either way we can still propose and test a relationship. Another important consideration in this example is that of a sense of the limits of survey research here, in that we are attempting to answer such a question with recourse to social and cultural tools and not genetic ones. Biological or genetic perspectives pertaining to sex differences and how they may impact occupational choice cannot be included (easily), so we are limited to an extent and our knowledge of these patterns constrained to a particular orientation of enquiry.

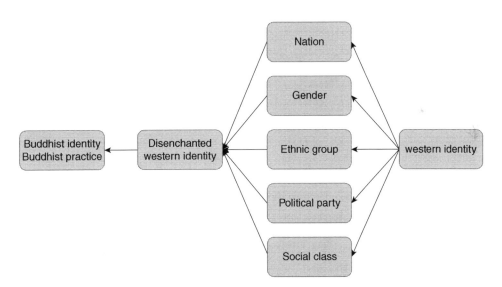

Figure 7.13 Complex conceptual model of western involvement in an 'eastern' religion

I have already described my work on my honours-year project on westerners turning to religions such as Buddhism. From the survey my supervisor and I were able to plan two research papers (Phillips and Aarons, 2005; 2007) that were published in good sociology journals. Figure 7.13 is a summary of one of the research papers we planned and wrote from my survey of western Buddhists. Besides trying to outline how Buddhism was practised and engaged in in a western context such as Australia, compared with a more traditional cultural setting, I was interested in what might explain western interest in Buddhism; that is, why did this group of people turn to Buddhism? This is perhaps the more interesting and pressing question for this topic. Now there are potentially any number of explanations ranging from the personal to the religious but, being a sociologist, I was interested in what social or cultural reasons might have been at work in this particular pattern, explanations that went to some extent beyond individual reasoning and could be found in the patterned experience of groups. In doing so we sought to include measures of group-based identity that many social surveys include to explain a variety of patterns in sociological explanations of the world. As modelled in Figure 7.13, the article employed the concept of 'western disenchantment' to help explain the variation in levels of Buddhist identity and practice – two dimensions of religious identity. Western disenchantment is based on a theory of general disenchantment proposed by the classical German sociologist Max Weber. We modified Weber's original idea to use it for our purposes.

Western disenchantment contained a number of dimensions for which we included indicators. Further, we sought to measure this experience by controlling for a number of social background experiences. The model represents a process or mechanism that related that those with higher levels of disenchantment – measured by lower affiliation with nation, gender, social class, political party, ethnic group – would have greater levels of affiliation with being Buddhist and would practise Buddhism more. So essentially, the more disenchanted one was with being western, the more one turned to Buddhism. The survey data supported the hypotheses and we could point to this explanation as a possible way to understand this particular pattern.

Complex models for complex analyses

Complex models can become even more complex, in the sense that they aim to represent quite sophisticated and detailed mechanisms of association and correlation between concepts. Many of the models I have discussed to date conform to specific types of analyses once the data have been collected. Conceptual models can also become even more complex for analysis depending on what forms of analysis are required for the research. For example, many researchers aim to analyse data in blocks or sets that can give the researcher a statistical indication about the strength and effects of different kinds of IVs on DVs akin to my example above of a 'social model' versus a 'religious model' in predicting who is conservative. The more complex and sophisticated forms of analysis include path analysis, multilevel modelling, and structural equation modelling. These forms of analysis that are amenable to survey data use conform to the basic operation of the establishment and assessment of relationships between IVs and DVs, and still seek to operate within a theoretical or conceptual frame of explanation that is circumscribed by plausibility.

Path analysis

Path analysis elaborates on the basic conceptual model and the complex conceptual model by proposing a number of paths to the same outcome. That is, there are a number of possible explanations for an event or phenomenon (DV) and this form of analysis will allow the researcher to assess the relative strengths and weaknesses among them. To some extent I have presented some examples of a basic path model that considers direct and indirect relationships as well as intervening variables, such as in Figure 7.10 (see p. 200).

Multilevel modelling

Multilevel modelling is a technique that seeks to assess a number of models that aim to predict one or more DVs at once. MLM achieves this by comparing variables or survey measures that measure different units of analysis. Recall that a unit of analysis can be an individual, a community, a postcode, a family or household, or organizational unit. The examples of complex conceptual models above all use individuals as the unit of analysis, but they could incorporate group- or community-level data such as crime levels, economic indexes for areas, or infection rates for areas also.

Structural equation modelling

Structural equation modelling (SEM) is a slightly different version of MLM. The main difference is that SEM seeks to identify what are latent variables instead of observed variables. Often latent variables are measured through scales or indexes that combine a number of similar variables that measure a larger concept.

Conceptual models and survey design

This chapter has so far indicated a number of important reasons for developing conceptual models as part of survey design, yet it has not mentioned perhaps the most important aspect of this relationship, one we touched on in an earlier chapter. When researchers are designing and constructing a survey, they need to include indicators for all that they need to explain and measure. However, for many concepts you have that relate to each other in your model, you need measures or indicators, including dimensions and sub-dimensions, so when you are planning a piece of survey research be mindful that whatever you consider to be relevant, in terms of concepts as they relate to a conceptual model, needs to be measured, and therefore needs to be in your survey. This can be easily overlooked with obvious consequences. But there are some considerations to be mindful of (which we will take up in much greater detail in Chapter 8). Too many concepts in your model means the number of questions in your survey will balloon. The problem here is that too many questions in your survey will seriously annoy your respondents and lower the response rate overall. Too few concepts in your model will compromise your research of course. The same rules or logic associated with the selection of dimensions and sub-dimensions as relevant or not to the research questions applies to conceptual models and indicators that go into your survey to be put to respondents. This practical restraint will serve to limit researchers' plans in survey design to explore more discrete research questions, and consequently selection of theories associated with the concepts in question.

Conceptual models and data analysis

Conceptual models indicate how your survey data – mapped and modelled as a series of related concepts – are organized to structure data analysis. The intention of this book is not to discuss or instruct how actually to analyse data – there are any number of excellent texts that can assist you with that – but outlining how survey design through conceptual modelling can provide the outline or the framework for later analysis is important. The research process suggests that after you have collected your data you then set about analysing them to answer your research questions. This is the logical way in which research proceeds, but in order to do so effectively you should plan to some extent how you will analyse your data. Where conceptual models help this process is through organizing the direction of the influences you are hypothesizing between variables or concepts, be they complex or basic. From the examples that we have considered so far in this chapter, we can discern that analysis proceeds with the intention of establishing or testing proposed relationships between IVs and DVs. There are many ways to do this as I will suggest in Chapter 9. Data analysis is also aided by the type of data you have collected, sourced from the kinds of questions you ask in your survey that produce variables associated with the different levels of measurement.

Pulling together the 'front end' of survey design

We have reached an important point in survey design with conceptual models. In the previous chapters I have been discussing and illustrating the various individual components of the research process and survey design process that we have considered separately but are in reality intimately connected to every other part. In this section, then, I want to show you how researchers pull all this (front end material) together properly to plan a survey research project through survey design. What do the various components of a survey design that we have been discussing in depth look like just before launch, so to speak? How do the various elements of the research process and survey design process meet at this stage and complement one another? How do they relate to each other in practice?

We can think of a survey or questionnaire as the centre of a research universe around which the other planets (concepts, dimensions, indicators, relationships, theories, research questions, and data) orbit. They all have functions and a relationship to the whole just like the planets in relation to a solar system within a galaxy. Once again taking the research process as our guide through this galaxy, I collate and illustrate this journey using an example to show how these various strands in survey design combine to structure a survey research project to this point.

Topic

Consider that a topic is a broad and somewhat vague area of research. Topics of course relate to perspectives and theories within disciplines. For our example we will consider the following topic:

Exploring economic disparity in society

Literatures and previous research

Having a topic is the beginning of the research process. Now there is a need to refine the topic into precise and answerable research questions. Recall the different literatures associated with a discipline and various perspectives within that discipline. These give us an overview of how the topic has been researched and what specific aspects of the topic have been considered and studied, as well as what has not been researched to any great degree yet. Recall my disappointment but slight joy over nothing written in sociology that I could find at least, about westerners involved in Buddhism, despite quite a lot having been written about new religious movements.

More specialized literature is needed later when clarifying and operationalizing concepts, such as specific theory and empirical studies, relevant policy literature, and industry based literatures that are directly related to the topic.

Method

Well obviously here our methodology will be a survey as the main means of data collection because our research will be empirical, but in any research project the choice of method needs justification. That justification is to some extent born of the literature, especially the empirical literature that specifies particular approaches to a topic or questions, but methodological justifications are also importantly bound to the types of research questions that are asked, as we have seen. Those for our example are below and justify the use of a survey. Further, our method of survey research will relate to the scope of the study – we typically will be interested in large groups and not a small number of individuals.

Research questions

I will posit two key research questions for this example that reflect our simple and more complex conceptual models that were introduced earlier in the chapter. Each question may have different perspectives and theories, contexts, and purposes, leading to different statistics. For example, question 1 is a question that a government department may want to ask so as to formulate policy around spending on education. Question 2, however, is more complex and less practical and may be directly related to basic research in a field such as sociology, economics, or social work.

1 *General economic disparity is associated with those with higher levels of education that lead to higher incomes.*
2 *Is general economic disparity related not just to higher levels of education influencing higher incomes, but also to a system that reproduces middle-class privilege such as a middle-class family background, providing a range of social advantages that lead to economic advantages?*

Concepts

Concepts, dimensions, indicators

In each question there are key concepts to identify and to operationalize. Recall the diagram of concepts and dimensions in Figure 5.11 for the extended definition of middle class, reproduced here in Figure 7.14.

I identified a number of key dimensions and sub-dimensions that are related to the broader concept of middle class embedded in my research questions, namely income, wealth, occupation, and culture in addition to education. Various sub-dimensions were also relevant to how middle class was defined, such as cultural tastes, tertiary education, and property such as buildings or other assets. These dimensions and sub-dimensions are grounded in the literature that discerns various ways in which the concept middle class is theorized by social scientists such as sociologists, economists, and social work scholars.

The model I introduced earlier in the chapter (Figure 7.4) is also reproduced here in Figure 7.15.

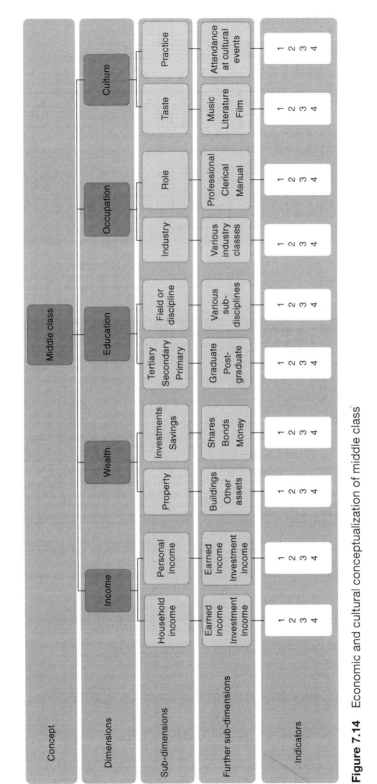

Figure 7.14 Economic and cultural conceptualization of middle class

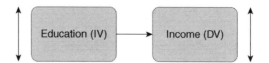

Figure 7.15 Basic conceptual model of education and income

The basic conceptual model represents question 1 in our research project. The more complex conceptual model shown in Figure 7.16, reproduced from earlier in the chapter (Figure 7.9), represents question 2. Consistent with the notions of narrow and extended conceptual definitions that we have explored, the basic and complex conceptual models here incorporate narrow and extended conceptualizations.

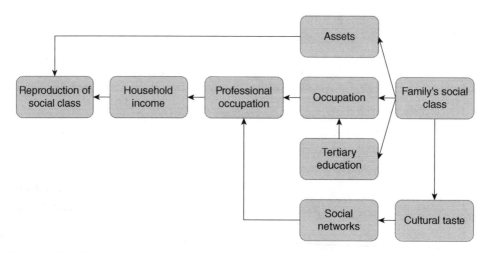

Figure 7.16 Complex conceptual model of relationships between social class and income

Indicators: Question and answer formats

Having produced conceptual models relating to our research questions contextualized within theories and perspectives, we now have to develop indicators to include in the survey. Which indicators are the most appropriate, valid, and reliable? I will not suggest actual questions here but importantly we need to consider the level of measurement required to produce data that will best answer our questions through appropriate forms of data analysis. Given our research questions, we will need ordinal- and interval-level indicators that will allow us to measure and pursue estimates for higher and lower levels of education and income. Recall that ordinal- and interval-level indicators produce data that are quantitative in slightly different ways.

For question 1 represented by the basic conceptual model, we need measures of education and income. We also need these measures to produce a metric of higher and lower education and higher and lower income. Typically, concepts such as these can be answered with either ordinal- or interval-level questions, and usually with closed-ended formats that list educational levels such as 'completed High School' or 'completed Bachelor degree', or open-ended formats that ask a respondent to record how many years (as a raw number) of education they have completed. Income is typically measured either as an interval-level variable with a precise monetary figure for a period such as a year or month using an open-ended answer format, or as ordinal with a closed-ended answer format composed of income brackets.

Question 2 demands a series of other indicators to measure the concepts within the question and the conceptual model. Questions need to be constructed not just for education and income, but also for family's social class, wealth, occupation, social networks, and culture that reflect the various dimensions of these concepts that are relevant to the research. Of these, occupation may be the one concept that is ostensibly a nominal variable, the others mostly ordinal and interval.

The types of indicators we select and develop to measure these concepts also enable us to establish a data analysis strategy allowing us to test the various relationships between concepts implicit in the research questions in the most efficient way to produce the statistics to answer the questions we have set. I will go into detail about this aspect of the research and survey design process in Chapter 9, but for now it is enough to appreciate the roles of conceptual models in further clarifying the research.

More broadly this section illustrates to an extent the culmination of the 'front end' of survey design. We can see how the various steps in the survey design and research processes are integrated and that each step in the process is aimed at producing valid and reliable data to answer our research questions.

─────────────── YOUR SURVEY ───────────────

Conceptual models

As a further step in the planning and clarification process for your survey design, leading to data analysis, develop a complex conceptual model that maps out the research question and the relationships between concepts.

Here you can combine the various 'front end' components of the survey design process thus far.

Be aware that your conceptual model takes into account the dimensions and sub-dimensions of the key concepts and that it follows/reflects your research question.

You may attempt to design a conceptual model using word processing software such as MS Word, using 'Insert' and connecting shapes with arrows.

You may also seek out conceptual model programs also. Draw.io is free, easy to use, and an excellent resource for constructing conceptual models.

(Continued)

Design a visual presentation of your survey design project thus far combining key elements of the research and survey design process, including a conceptual model, and present to your class or the organization you are working with and discuss. Include the following components.

Research process components:

- Topic
- Literature
- Research questions
- Why a survey is the most appropriate methodology

Survey design process components:

- Relevant concepts identified
- Conceptual model: relationships between concepts
- Survey questions for key concepts
- Briefly, a basic plan for potential analysis of the data as suggested by the conceptual model

Key knowledge and skills

This chapter has considered the roles of conceptual models in the survey design process by showing how concepts are related theoretically and empirically. Key knowledge and skills concerning conceptual models are as follows:

- Concepts in survey research are sometimes singular, but most often posed as relational, reflecting the nature of the research question.
- Concepts, through indicators, translate into variables. The logic of quantitative research determines that the basic relationship between variables is a relationship between an independent and dependent variable.
- Research using quantitative survey data assesses whether variation or change in the independent variable relates to variation and change in the dependent variable to determine a relationship.
- This relationship is proposed through a diagram representing basic and complex conceptual models.
- The conceptual model also proposes the direction and structure of the data analysis, to establish the relationship.

Further reading

Conceptual models are treated quite sparsely in the literature on survey design. However, the related notion of causal models is often associated with discussions and instructions on data analysis. A particularly good and accessible account of conceptual models in this vein is James Davis' *The Logic of the Causal Order*. Chapter 3 of de Vaus' *Surveys in Social Research* also has a brief and clear presentation of conceptual models in basic and complex form.

Full text references:
Davis, J. (1985) *The Logic of the Causal Order*, Sage University Paper Series on
    Quantitative Applications in the Social Sciences pp 7–55. Beverly Hills, CA: Sage
De Vaus, D. A. (2014) *Surveys in Social Research* (6th edn). St Leonards: Allen & Unwin

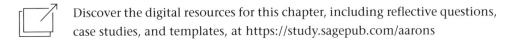 Discover the digital resources for this chapter, including reflective questions, case studies, and templates, at https://study.sagepub.com/aarons

Eight

Survey Administration

Survey design entails a range of applied considerations and tasks that are practical in nature. It is important to think carefully about how the survey is produced, implemented, and completed. This chapter will cover:

- Division of labour in administering a survey
- Components of the survey for potential respondents
- Sampling
- Modes of survey implementation
- Putting a survey together – arrangement and design of the survey

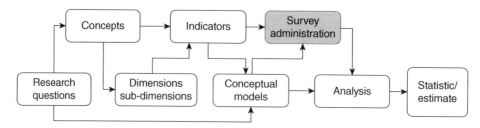

Figure 8.1 Survey design process: survey administration (mode, sampling, and survey construction)

Now that we have worked through the more intellectual and scientific components of survey design, such as research questions, concepts, and question construction, we need to consider the more practical aspects associated with the implementation of a survey (even though they are not really unscientific). Survey administration (Figure 8.1) involves how a survey is actually put together, delivered, and managed, and involves asking ourselves: how many questions; which questions where; what should it look like; who do we ask; how will it reach potential respondents; how do we manage the implementation of it; and how do we manage the data that the survey collects?

As a shift to the more practical applications of survey design, this chapter covers a great deal of what we in the social sciences call fieldwork. Fieldwork, while relating literally to work done in an actual field (à la archaeology), is the umbrella term given to various modes of data collection in any of the social sciences or humanities where observations are gathered from subjects or respondents.

Division of labour in administering a survey

We can divide the work of survey administration into survey composition and formatting, and implementation management. These two broad forms of survey administration are necessary for all modes of a survey, yet survey administration differs on specifics and needs depending on the mode. Aside from implementation of a survey via a certain mode, the administration of a survey entails a number of important tasks that a research team need to organize and allocate between them. Survey projects need people to collate the survey and survey matter, check addresses and contact details of the final sample, construct a website if need be, register, mail, and receive completed surveys, enter and store data. Large-scale survey projects with big enough budgets can outsource much of this work, but for projects without the budget to leave such tasks to a survey data company, these tasks will need to be done 'in house'. Not all of these components are absolutely necessary, however. Your project may not need a website but if you desire an online presence, and if you, like me, have no idea about website building, then social media platforms may be one way to give your survey project a public face.

Components of a survey for potential respondents

In addition to the actual survey that is given to potential respondents – irrespective of the mode of the survey – survey researchers need to give potential respondents some information about why they have been chosen and what the survey is about. This is for two reasons: (1) so that potential respondents are informed; and (2) as a courtesy. Remember that survey research relies on the goodwill, trust, and to some extent the kindness of strangers. Ethically, there is a relationship between researcher and researched so that if you are asking for individuals to answer questions about themselves, they are properly informed about why, and how the data they contribute will be used.

Cover letter/statement

Each potential respondent when contacted by the research team or researcher with the view to recruiting them to complete the survey deserves to know what the survey is about, of course. The broader aims and purpose of the research need to be communicated to potential respondents as an ethical act and as a courtesy, but also to provide context about the study. The description of the study need not be too detailed, however. The principal means of relating such information is in the form of a cover letter or statement. Some projects, however, particularly large and longitudinal ones, have detailed websites that contain a lot of information about the purposes and uses of the surveys that they administer. This is not always necessary, but it is good to be transparent and open about the research that the survey informs, and if the project is publicly funded there is a strong ethical argument for such transparency.

Other details should include who is conducting the study, the individuals involved and their positions within an organization; the institutional setting such as a firm, university, or government department is also important, as is relevant information for potential respondents. This information can also be important in establishing rapport with respondents and assist in establishing the study as legitimate research and therefore worthy of a respondent's time. A cover letter can also provide brief instructions about how the survey will be administered: if face to face or via telephone, indicate that someone will make contact and arrange a time and place to conduct the interview; if online, provide a statement about how to access the survey, such as a web address or URL; and if a mail-out and return, then where to send the completed survey. Cover letters can be sent via email, text, social media, or SMS, or an old-fashioned postal letter. A letter sent via the post is preferred and is often the official means of communication between parties for research purposes. Letters should state the name and position of a researcher who is available to discuss any matters associated with the research that the potential respondent may wish to discuss. Finally, the letter should have the organization's, university's, or government department's insignia assigned to an official letterhead. Notification of ethical clearance (if applicable) and a statement about the voluntary nature of the survey should also be included and prominent.

An example cover letter from my study of Australian Buddhists is given below.

Example cover letter

Australian Experiences of Buddhism Survey   La Trobe University

Dear.......................

As a member of the.................Buddhist Centre, I am writing to kindly invite you to participate in a study I am conducting as a part of my honours year in sociology at La Trobe University. For my thesis I am interested in why you and other members of the...............Buddhist Centre might be attracted to Buddhism.

You may be aware that Buddhism is one of the fastest growing religions in Australia and in other western countries as a result of immigration and its attraction to established populations. Yet, there is little knowledge of why it is attractive to people who are not from traditionally Buddhist countries.

My study seeks to understand how Buddhism is practiced in Australia and the different meanings Australians give it to their lives. Accompanying this letter is a questionnaire that should take no more than 20 minutes maximum to complete with questions about your experience of Buddhism. Your participation in the survey is entirely voluntary and all data from the survey are confidential and anonymous. The survey has the commendation of the President of the.................Buddhist Centre. Please answer all questions and then place the completed survey in the addressed paid post envelope that is included and post.

The survey has ethics clearance from La Trobe University, and I or my supervisor, Dr Timothy Phillips, can be contacted to answer any questions you might have concerning the study or the survey, on the following number: 000000000, or via email at Haydn. Aarons@latrobe.edu.au

I thank you for your time and consideration.

Yours sincerely
Haydn Aarons

This information can be included in a cover letter briefly, or more substantially via a separate statement. Either way, the respondent knowing that the research project has received ethical clearance from their or an independent institution is important, as is a statement that makes clear that the research (in most cases) is purely voluntary and that respondents do not need to answer questions they may find too personal, confronting, or difficult. Information such as this can be restated when the respondent attempts to fill out or respond to the survey questions via interview.

Incentives

There are many large-scale surveys that include incentives to encourage potential respondents to take part in a survey research project. Incentives usually include entry into a draw for a substantial prize such as cash, goods, or rewards such as paid holidays. These are generally fine and do not present any great ethical problems. Incentives aim at overcoming what is known as survey fatigue. Details of the incentives associated with the project can be listed in the cover letter, or separately. Of course, incentives associated with survey completion are subject to the resources of the research project; however, they need not be too expensive or grandiose (for example, I have won cinema tickets for survey completions before!). As an incentive, Dillman et al. (2009), for example, suggested US$5 a survey over a decade ago; the amount these days would be a nominal amount (perhaps US$10–15) that would cover the short period of time taken to complete the survey, but many organizations do not pay respondents. There are also companies that pay respondents to complete surveys (you don't earn a lot by any means for completing them), but you can sign up to them for a little extra cash.

Follow-up and reminder letters

Many survey projects do not achieve great response rates straight away so it is standard practice to leave the fieldwork open for a few weeks or a month – longer for bigger projects – to ensure that everyone in the sample has had an opportunity to complete the survey. Many responses will come within two weeks in most modes, but not all of the responses that are possible or that you may need might reach you in that time. What researchers often do, therefore, is send follow-up requests for potential respondents to complete a survey with a reminder letter. To some extent this depends on the sample you want or need for the study to be representative, but many researchers as a rule simply aim to get as many responses as possible, and therefore follow up on potential respondents irrespective of sample size. I would recommend one follow-up reminder letter, possibly two if responses are low and the sample is looking somewhat skewed or biased towards some groups. Beyond two follow-up letters you can be pretty sure that the contact details are incorrect or that the potential respondent is not interested in participating. Following up with potential respondents is common to all modes of survey administration. A follow-up or reminder letter should be brief and include a thank you note just in case the respondent has completed the survey during the time when the follow-up letter was sent. The follow-up letter should include all of the details of the invitation to complete the survey that were part of the original letter.

———————————— Follow-up reminder letter ————————————

Australian Experiences of Buddhism Survey   La Trobe University

Dear.......................

I recently sent an invitation for you to complete a survey on your experiences of Buddhism at the.................Buddhist Centre. I am resending the survey with a cover letter explaining the study with some instructions on completing the survey. I would be grateful if you would complete the survey and return via the addressed paid post envelope. If you have already completed the survey and returned it, thank you, and you can disregard this note.

Yours sincerely
Haydn Aarons

Once your team has organized the work associated with the above tasks then it is time to consider and plan the mode of survey administration. Perhaps the most important aspect of survey administration is the mode: that is, what platform will the survey take and how you will get it to the people you need to get it to? The mode of survey administration is also important because it affects how surveys are designed, response rates, and the quality of the data that you collect. The mode of survey administration has also undergone profound changes with the advent of technology. We consider in some depth the various modes of survey administration below.

Modes of survey administration

Three crucial concerns that govern the mode of survey administration are:

1   *The avoidance or reduction of non-response (non-response error) and consequently missing data.*
2   *Ensuring the best quality data from respondents possible, given the resources available.*
3   *Gaining the most comprehensive coverage of intended respondents as possible.*

In addition to issues such as question construction, a survey's mode of administration can strongly determine the quality of data that a respondent provides. We can think of the different modes of survey administration as ways of avoiding and minimizing this form of error in data collection.

Modes of survey administration are important for a number of reasons, but principally because they carry with them various ways of allowing and restricting respondents to answer questions that relate to a sample's coverage and to data quality, but also important for which questions you can ask, how respondents can interact with the survey, and how the researcher manages data. There are tried and true modes of survey administration which have stood the test of time, and some exciting new ones with enormous potential which are still being worked out. As no doubt you can appreciate, survey administration has undergone some tremendous changes associated with the changes in technology such as the internet. These all aid the cause of survey administration considerably, but they are also fraught with problems and challenges to be worked through. There are advantages and limitations with all the different modes. What is important, however, is that the researcher is able to identify the mode that best suits the needs of the research, the aims of sampling, and the resources at the researcher's disposal. With respect to resources, there are some important practical issues to keep in mind:

- *Time*: does your survey need to be done quickly, or can you tolerate some experimenting with modes?
- *Money/capacity*: what is your budget? Can you afford a graphic artist, website design and administration personnel? Can these things be created/performed by staff or team members?
- *Technology*: do you have the capacity to design and administer a website for the survey?
- *Personnel*: can you train interviewers, have them go door to door, and interview people?

There are four principal modes of survey administration that we will cover in this chapter:

- Face to face
- Telephone
- Mail-out and return
- Web-based and mobile devices

While most projects, especially projects that are subject to a low budget, use one mode, a number of survey research projects also often use multi-mode survey administration.

Face to face

The face-to-face mode of survey administration is the gold standard in survey administration modes. Face-to-face interviewing entails conducting the survey via an interview with a respondent at an arranged time and place, where a trained interviewer sits down with the respondent and talks them through the survey by reading out the questions and answers to completion. Face-to-face administration of a survey often occurs in an office of the organization administering the survey, or the respondent's home where they might feel most comfortable, but public spaces such as cafés are also good places to conduct interviews face to face, providing there are no interruptions and the respondent is comfortable. Where an interview is conducted is to some extent dependent on the nature of the questions also, that is how sensitive or personal.

There are many advantages of face-to-face interviewing that revolve around person-to-person interaction and having an informed representative of the study on hand. Interviewers in face-to-face situations are able to clarify questions and response formats if need be, instruct the respondent about which questions to answer exactly, assuming that some questions are not relevant, guide respondents through a complex survey, and assist them in answering all questions to the best of their ability, reducing non-response. Interviewers are also able to assist elderly and younger respondents such as children, and translate questions into another language for respondents, if need be. Interviewers are also able to discuss survey issues that have arisen in the course of the interviews with the researchers, providing feedback that might enable changes while the fieldwork is in its early stages, such as confusion about a question's wording, for example.

The face-to-face mode of survey administration is excellent for longer questionnaires that can require guidance through appropriate or relevant questions such as filter questions, and whose sheer length (some big surveys can take up to an hour to complete) requires assistance throughout. Larger surveys can be complex in their organization, so 'live' assistance allows the respondent and interviewer to clarify instantly. De Vaus (2014: 128) states that the face-to-face mode is the best mode for asking open-ended questions of respondents, because respondents can better answer such questions through verbalizing rather than writing. This mode is perhaps unsuitable and unnecessary for shorter or very short questionnaires, but is often conducted effectively in 'on-site' situations such as events, the street, and public places where researchers just want 'a minute of your time, to answer just a few questions about...'.

Process and requirements of implementation

Face-to-face interviewing follows an implementation process. Perhaps the most important aspect of this mode of survey implementation is the requirement of trained personnel to conduct the interviews. The interviewer must have a range of skills to conduct interviews effectively. This mode often requires the recruitment and training of interviewers. There can be a number of interviewers required if the project is large and covers a wide geographic area such as a national study. The interviewer needs to make the respondent feel valued and comfortable through some effort in building a rapport and establish a sense of trust about the research and the researcher. Once a time and place have been agreed upon, then the interviewer meets the respondent, and both make themselves comfortable. There can be some time for some informal discussion if the respondent is willing, and then the interviewer should ask if there are any questions about the survey and the use of the data before the interview begins.

Face-to-face interviews are surveys that are read from a schedule, question by question, entailing the preferred arrangement of survey questions in a given order to be given to respondents. Instructions for the interviewer about how to ask, and what to ask which respondent, are included in the schedule. This is important for household surveys that are interested in more than one respondent in a household, or where there is a survey for an individual and then one for the whole household.

Face-to-face interviews can allow the interviewer and respondent to consider a question, leave it if more time is needed to best answer it, and then return to it at another time during the interview (especially for questions that may require knowledge or recall). The interviewer can also clarify questions that respondents find unclear or difficult, prompt respondents, or at times reword or state the question in another way (this is rarer and must be treated with caution because the question can be inadvertently changed). The interviewer can mark down responses on paper or record them electronically – which is the more likely scenario these days given the portability of computers, phones, and tablets, saving time on data entry. The interviewer needs to record the details of the respondent and label the completed survey for administration records.

Face-to-face interviews mostly use technology to administer the survey and record the responses. Systems such as CAPI (Computer-Assisted Personal Interview) use computer-based applications to make the process of data capture more efficient.

Response rates

The face-to-face mode of survey administration generally garners a response rate of 70% or more (de Leeuw, 2008). This is the key advantage of the mode. Having a 'captive audience', so to speak, in a respondent who is seated and answering questions, and a skilled and informed interviewer, essentially allows the survey to be completed many more times than not when a respondent agrees to participate compared with other modes that rely on self-completion.

Most surveys are conducted in communities that are familiar to the researchers, and where mostly potential respondents are to some extent familiar with the very basics of survey research, and for whom the concepts aimed to be measured will be familiar. Face-to-face modes are often employed in alternative settings such as low-income countries where governmental or non-governmental organizations or agencies (such as the Red Cross, World Bank, United Nations, or the World Health Organization) aim to collect data associated with interventions, programmes, and policy initiatives in such countries. These contexts present a variety of challenges to a survey project, especially if the survey designers are not local (see Deaton, 1997). Face to face may be the best and indeed only mode of survey administration open to agencies whose work is in such contexts. At times the field may lack the technologies and transport necessary to conduct interviews. Researchers who are foreign to the countries and communities who are being studied require interpreters, a means of interpreting concepts in local cultures as respondents themselves experience them, and various ways of gaining access to potential respondents.

Limitations

There are not too many distinct limitations associated with the face-to-face mode of survey administration, but some do exist. The main problem with this mode can be contact with potential respondents whose details may be difficult to obtain or who may not respond to requests for interview (this limitation is not the sole preserve of the face-to-face mode, however). Of more direct concern is the fact that some respondents may simply not be very comfortable with a face-to-face interview and prefer another mode such as telephone interview, or to complete a survey via email. If interviewers are poorly prepared, not particularly personable, or have no training or insight into the research the survey is aiming to serve, a compromised interview can result. The quality of the data is to some extent determined by the interviewer, who can influence the setting, the interaction with the respondent, and how data are recorded. Limitations of this mode are also practical in that they can be very costly, require large numbers of interviewers to be trained and co-ordinated, who have to travel long distances at times, and the mode can be time consuming. Finally face-to-face interviews can be problematic for knowledge or recall-type questions, where a respondent needs more time, because the interview is usually a one-off occurrence completed within an hour, before the interviewer might have to go to the next interview.

Telephone

Telephone interviews are a very popular and effective mode of survey administration. They often contain many of the same advantages and convey similar benefits to the survey researcher as face-to-face interviews. This mode often costs less and takes less time than the face-to-face mode. Converse to the notion of a personable experience associated with the face-to-face mode, telephone interviewing can be personable and yet allow 'distance' between respondent and interviewer, making respondents comfortable and the experience of completing a survey less intrusive. For some respondents this is indeed preferable. They may be happy to complete a survey but not want the intrusion of a stranger into their home or have to meet in a public place. This mode of survey administration is often the principal mode used by data collection companies.

Process and requirements for implementation

Telephone interviews follow much the same process as a face-to-face interview would. There is a schedule in which the survey questions are arranged, allowing the interviewer to assist the respondent in clarifying question wording and answer formats. Telephone interviewing does require training similar to that of face-to-face interviewing. The main difference of course is that there is no travel or requirement to meet with a respondent. Telephone interviews are conducted from a single location and multiple interviewers can use phones simultaneously, cutting down the time of data collection. If the interviews can be conducted on the premises of the research organization near to the researchers, they can be on hand to clarify problems, receive feedback, and implement change.

As with face-to-face administration, one should not 'cold call' (call without previously informing the respondent about the nature of the call) respondents. Potential respondents should be contacted preferably with a letter or email, but an invitation call is certainly fine, informing them they have been selected to be a part of a study, and then asked if they can be contacted at a time convenient to both interviewer and respondent. Surveys administered over the phone mostly use computer-assisted telephone interviews (CATI). This technology allows answers from respondents to be directly entered into a computer program allowing analysis instantly.

Response rates

Response rates for telephone mode surveys have dramatically declined in recent years. This mode was once a standard mode for many data collection organizations but has been severely compromised as a result of the abuse of the method, decline of access to publicly listed numbers, and some public apathy towards surveys administered over the phone. For Pew Research in the United States such problems associated with telephone modes leading to dramatic declines in response rates as shown in Figure 8.2 has seen the company no longer use the telephone mode for its polling projects. To some extent the problems associated with response rates for telephone mode can be overcome with a panel of respondents that data collection agencies can reliably engage when needed, yet this mode in general is in steep decline.

Limitations

Perhaps the biggest limitation for the telephone mode is not so much the method itself as its use, or, should I state, abuse. There is something of a crisis in survey research that uses the telephone as its main mode and that is down to unscrupulous sales and marketing companies that have given the mode a bad name. The reputation of the mode has most definitely taken a hit with the saturation of trivial sales pitches at inconvenient

After brief plateau, telephone survey response rates have fallen again

Response rate by year (%)

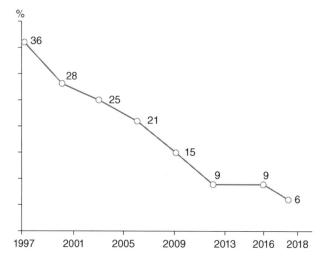

Note: Response rate is AAPOR RR3. Only landlines sampled 1997–2006. Rates are typical for surveys conducted in each year.

Figure 8.2   Response rates from telephone mode of survey administration 1997–2018

Source: 'Response rates in telephone surveys have resumed their decline.' Pew Research Center, Washington, DC (2019). https://www.pewresearch.org/fact-tank/2019/02/27/response-rates-in-telephone-surveys-have-resumed-their-decline/

times to millions of households. Few people are prepared to pick up their phones these days and complete a survey over the phone, without prior contact first. I would argue also, that, despite having many of the advantages of the face-to-face mode of survey administration, it is far easier for a respondent to cancel or withdraw suddenly from an interview that is conducted over the phone than it is when surveying face to face, potentially creating greater levels of non-response. Contemporaneously, another big limitation for the telephone mode of survey administration is the decline in publicly listed landline subscriptions connected to households or businesses. The rise of mobile or cellular phones, which are not listed in phone books, unless nominated, especially among younger segments of a population, creates an additional problem for this mode by making representative sampling increasingly difficult.

Mail-out and return

This mode of survey administration is still one of the most common forms of survey administration. As the name conveys, a paper copy of the survey is mailed out to the sample of respondents, who fill it out and then mail it back to the researchers, who then manually enter the data from the surveys into data analysis software such as SPSS. This is an old but tried and true mode of survey administration. Despite the rise of technology that has changed the way in which survey administration is conducted, the mail-out and return mode is still popular among researchers and still manages to gain respectable response rates.

Process and requirements for implementation

The mail-out and return mode entails printing and mailing out paper copies of the survey to all potential respondents on the sampling frame. The mail-out package should include a cover letter (as discussed above), a statement about ethics clearance, and crucially a return paid post envelope, enabling respondents to mail back the completed survey. The process will need to be repeated with follow-up notes and another survey to remind those respondents who have not completed the survey to do so. The researchers need to be careful to specify a unique address for the return of the surveys in the cover letter or include the address on the paid post envelope for return of the survey. A temporary mail-box or post office box is a good idea so that survey mail is not in together with regular mail for an organization, particularly if the survey is attempting to reach a large sample of respondents. Once the surveys have been returned, they should be marked or registered by number, or some kind of code for identification. After the data have been transcribed into data analysis software the surveys should be stored securely.

Despite being old methods, mail-out, paper-based, or postal surveys also are aided by the developments in computer technology. Mail-out surveys can be administered using what is known as CASI (Computer-Assisted Self-Interview) or DBM (**Disc By Mail**) where the survey is recorded on a disc and sent to the respondent who answers the questions on the disc and mails the results back to the researchers. Mail-out surveys can also include access to a web-based format of the survey by recording a web address. In all, the mail-out mode has the advantage of reaching potential respondents in greater proportions than some other modes since it can reach respondents at households for which physical addresses are still relatively easy to access and create a sample for.

Response rates for mail-out surveys, if done properly through adherence to good and careful survey design, are consistently between 50% and 70% according to Dillman et al. (2009: 236). This is one reason why, despite the rise of technology, mail-out surveys are still a preferred method of social surveys for many projects.

Limitations

There are some distinct limitations associated with the mail-out and return mode of survey administration. Compared with the face-to-face and telephone modes, the mode is characterized by self-completion, which has the potential for higher rates of non-response if respondents are confused by or have difficulty answering some questions. To overcome this a contact can be established to answer questions about the survey from respondents. The other major limitation to this mode is the simple rejection of the survey by ignoring it, hence the importance of follow-up notes and letters to encourage potential respondents to complete the survey.

─────────────── Meeting your respondents! ───────────────

I had an experience when I was at a garage sale one time during which I had sent out my survey of Buddhist practice and belief to Australian Buddhists. I got talking to the owner of the house. She told me that she had had this letter from the university about some Buddhist survey, which she had skimmed through, and she was simply going to ignore it because 'those things were annoying'. I confessed to being to the designer of the study and the survey author and told her of the 'importance' of the work, after which her tone changed to one of 'been meaning to get around to it actually, but we are moving etc. etc.' and an assurance that she would fill it in and send it off as soon as possible. There is really no need, nor would it be sound ethically, to follow up mailed-out surveys to unmotivated respondents by paying them a visit at their address, but, unwittingly, it worked that time for me!

Samples for mail-out administrated surveys have become more and more difficult to construct, given that they were once done via phone books (recording landline phone numbers) that listed addresses. In some countries such as Australia, sampling frames for mail-out questionnaires are constructed through electoral rolls that record the addresses for all who are listed. In the Australian example, everyone over 18 has to vote, and so has to be enrolled to vote, giving researchers an excellent sampling frame resource. Mail-outs can be expensive, if for large samples in need of repeated mail-outs of surveys, reminder letters, and thank you notes. In addition to these expenses, manual data entry can also be an expense for many projects that use mail-out surveys. Time can also be a limiting factor in mail-out surveys compared with other modes of survey administration, whereby there may be a lot of waiting around for surveys to be returned and data entered and cleaned.

Despite the limitations of this mode, and the advent of computer and internet technologies, authorities on survey research modes such as Dillman et al. (2014) suggest that the humble mail-out and return mode of survey administration is surpassing other modes in terms of response rates and data quality. There are a number of reasons Dillman et al. cite that might be evidence for why respondents prefer, and researchers might still consider, the mail-out mode. Many people prefer mail-out surveys compared with email or web-based surveys, for reasons of privacy and anonymity. Many people are also overwhelmed with email and may simply ignore messages to complete surveys. Mail-out surveys according to Dillman et al. also benefit the researchers in that they are easier to design and administer and can be enhanced with computer design packages. Technological innovations with address files such as the DSF (a comprehensive computer-generated list of all addresses associated with the US postal service) have overcome to some extent the problems with sampling frames drawn from phone lists.

Web-based and mobile devices

From the old to the new. With the advent of communication technology has come a new mode of survey administration that is internet based. Surveys administrated in this mode can be linked via email and social media and have a potential reach of millions. It is not too difficult to imagine the advantages of web-based modes, but equally not too difficult to see their limitations also. A survey based on the web through any of the existing software platforms that enable survey design can be sent instantly to any number of potential respondents, who can then open a link in an email and complete the survey with instantaneous data entry, providing the researchers with analytic capability a very short time after the survey has been sent.

Process and requirements for implementation

The process of administering a survey online can be mostly easy and user friendly, but, for larger projects, more complex and problematic. At the more basic end of the scale, the researcher needs to select a software platform (a wide selection exists) such as Survey Monkey or Qualtrics (for which basic subscriptions are not too costly) and enter the questions and select answering formats. Questions and answer formats including coding are written into these programs. A codebook should be developed for reference, however. The survey program will have a range of question and answer formats available to choose from but can also be entered manually. Once the survey is uploaded the survey can be accessed via a created web link to a URL. From here it can be embedded in an email or posted on social media or a website and sent to and accessed by relevant potential respondents. The responses are collected by the software and basic analytics can be performed instantly as the results arrive. The data collected via such programs can be converted into different readable files and made compatible with various data analysis programs such as SPSS, enabling more complex analysis. More complex projects will require greater technical capabilities usually provided by specialist companies. Researchers may want to assess the response rates after the first email with the survey has been sent, after a few days or a week, resend it, then reassess until a satisfactory response rate has been achieved.

Web-based surveys are an excellent mode of survey administration for organizations that have a defined client or staff list where all have internet access and a traceable email address. Organizations may seek opinions from staff or clients for a range of reasons, but in particular web-based surveys are used frequently for staff climate surveys, organizational change surveys, and client satisfaction surveys.

Social media platforms such as Facebook and Twitter now have inbuilt polling applications as part of their services allowing basic, short question polls. There is great concern, however, over the privacy of data ascertained from social media.

Increasingly there is a pattern of using mobile and hand-held devices to administer surveys. These are web based and often rely on web-based applications that respondents can download onto a smartphone or tablet and complete the survey. There are numerous apps that can facilitate this, and popular web-based survey programs such as Survey Monkey have smart phone and tablet apps facilitating this mode of survey administration.

Limitations

The great limitation with respect to web-based and electronic modes of survey administration is that those without access to the internet or who do not have email are excluded from the sample. This factor may exclude important sections of a population such as the elderly, those on low or very low incomes, those who live in remote areas, and those in various countries that do not have adequate access to the internet. Constructing a sample from email addresses represents similar problems to sampling using telephone modes, in that email addresses are not publicly listed like landline phone numbers. Other limitations include perceptions around data security on the web, potentially compromising important concerns such as anonymity and confidentiality. Expense can be a limitation if the study is a large-scale complex one, where specific skills in web design and maintenance are required.

Mixed modes of survey administration

Very often surveys are administered through a combination of the various modes discussed above. The principal benefit of applying mixed or multiple modes of survey administration is to ensure greater response rates and better data quality through greater coverage of an intended sample. Mixed modes of survey administration aim to cover the problems and pitfalls associated with each mode, which reflect the means and habits of the full range of potential respondents, be they old or young, language proficient or not, geographically isolated or not, subject to specific preferences or not. Administering a survey face to face or via telephone as the main mode of administration is great, but then having mail-out or web-based versions available enables potential respondents to choose how to engage with the survey and potentially overcomes various coverage problems.

Mixed mode survey administration enables the researchers to assess which modes work best, where certain modes work best – with specific questions, demographics of respondents, etc., enabling better planning for future research.

A summary of the advantages and limitations of various modes of survey administration is compiled in Table 8.1.

Table 8.1 Summary of the advantages of various modes of survey administration

Mode	Sampling	Time	Cost	Data quality
Face to face	Traditional	Longer	High	Usually excellent
Telephone	Increasingly difficult	Short	Moderate to high	Excellent
Mail-out	Traditional	Longer	Low to moderate	Good to excellent but can be poor
Web-based and mobile devices	Difficult if general, easy if a defined sample (employees in an organization)	Instant	Low	Excellent for specific samples

Sampling

An important part of survey administration is who you want or need to ask the questions you want answered. Sampling is subject to various practical concerns but can also require complex mathematical equations. In this section I will cover the basics of sampling. With the exception of a national census[1] and a census of a small group, nearly all survey research is based on samples of populations (Figure 8.3). Samples are used for two reasons: to lower costs; and for most projects the whole population is not needed. There may be specific segments of a population (which means any group of people that are of interest to a research project and not the total number of people in a country, for example), community, or organization that your research is relevant to, or indeed a whole population. Whatever the population relevant to your research, you will need to construct a sample to be targeted to take part in the survey. Samples are smaller representations of a broader population and cover all units of analysis. This holds for whoever the research may be aimed at, such as a group, community, organization, a specific demographic such as the young, an industry, a country, or also global populations.

Recall that survey research is an excellent research method for identifying patterns for groups, with these patterns representing real patterns in a broader population. Well it is, but only if the sample is what we call representative. To be representative a sample needs to be an accurate representation of the broader population.

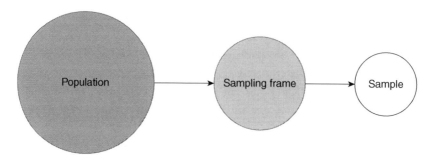

Figure 8.3 Population, sample frame, sample

Representativeness enables statistical findings from survey data to be generalized to a broader population via inference. If the sample of the population has a similar 'shape', that is it resembles the key segments of the population or represents desired attributes of the population in terms of proportion, then the findings can be confidently generalized back to the population.

Creating a sample

Creating a sample is subject to some important considerations. No sample will be perfectly representative of a population (with the exception of some smaller groups), so almost every sample will have some amount of bias; this is just the nature of how complex populations can be wedded to the limitations of various modes of survey implementation. We call this sampling error or standard error and can factor sampling error into our analyses later in the research when analysing data. There are some important steps in the creation of a sample: defining a population of interest, gaining an accurate sampling frame, developing a method of random selection from the sampling frame, and deciding on the size of the sample.

Defining a population of interest

It is crucial that the population of interest is properly defined, allowing us to direct sampling to the desired population. Who, exactly, is of interest in your study? Populations define the units of analysis that we use to answer our research questions. When we arrive at analysing the data we have collected through the survey, a clearly defined population is necessary, so the research is consistent with its intent. As stated, populations can be individuals, postcodes, businesses, political parties, and other groups. Populations may also have specific elements that the research is interested in. If our survey is interested in measuring work satisfaction for employees across an industry, for example, which employees are relevant to the research?

Full time, part-time, casual, or volunteers? Should the sample include employees across different departments of a business, and different businesses across an industry? Should the sample include employees engaged in different occupational roles? Defining desired respondents who meet a stated criteria clarifies the sampling process and gives a greater chance of the sample being representative. The shape of the sample, when considering these factors, will give us an indication of how biased it is, and how much our analyses are subject to sampling error, and, in turn, how reliable and generalizable our findings from the data.

Small or smaller groups such as businesses, schools, or sporting groups are less difficult to represent relatively accurately in a sample than larger groups. A lot of social research using surveys, however, is focused on national populations and is used for important policy directives in health, education, resource allocation, and employment. In this, researchers attempt representativeness by aiming to reflect as accurately as possible the various ways in which a population is differentiated (Figure 8.4). For example, take some important markers in a population such as gender, occupation, income, ethnicity, age, education level, geography, and political orientation. These are the main ways in which a population of individuals is distinct from another.

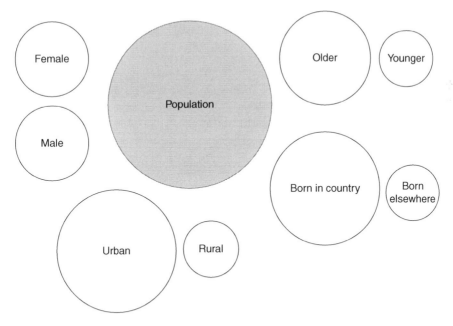

Figure 8.4 Population and sample attributes

Beyond these there are many other ways in which a population can be differentiated including: religion, leisure habits, genetic markers, citizenship, home ownership, marital status, sexual orientation, pet ownership, mobility, family size, internet connection, mobile phone use, etc. At some point the researchers have to prioritize some forms of differentiation over others and delimit the sample according to the attributes that are most important to the research. The logical way in which this is done is to be guided by the project's research questions and theoretical underpinnings that will emphasize particular attributes that will be theorized to explain various patterns to which some specific attributes within a population are not relevant. In addition to deciding on specific population parameters, many national samples have a defined age limit such as 16 or 18 to 90+ and exclude institutionalized individuals for practical reasons.

Samples and population attributes

To illustrate the point above concerning social attributes that are not overly prioritized in a sample, one aspect of large national surveys that I find a little frustrating is their lack of representativeness of religious groups in a society. Some of my research is interested in how religious identity is related to certain types of behaviour, such as musical tastes. While some groups (such as Catholics and Anglicans) are accurately represented, many are not (such as Muslims, Jews, and Buddhists). This limits what researchers can and cannot say about the role of religion on a range of attitudes and opinions that are important. In many societies that are multicultural, religious identities are important in shaping how people live and what they think. Constant under-representation precludes a lot of what we can learn about the experiences, attributes, and attitudes of minority religious groups. Religious groups are but one neglected factor in large-scale national surveys. A variety of ethnic groups and First Nations populations are also often under-represented in national surveys. These omissions often reflect the emphasis and priorities of the designers of large-scale surveys and are not simply a matter of probabilistic inaccuracy.

Sampling frame

For most samples, researchers start with or try to ascertain an accurate list of cases of the relevant defined population. The list is called the **sampling frame**. For large populations such as cities or countries sampling frames are constructed from contact information for individuals such as household addresses recorded in phone books, electoral rolls, and increasingly specific electronic lists of contact information. Accurate sampling frames for smaller populations such as clients of a service or business, university students, or patients of a clinic are easier to obtain but still should reflect the defined population.

From the sampling frame a proportion of respondents are selected to create the final sample. The researchers select a sample via a mathematical method such as nominating 1 in 10, or 1 in 20, or by use of a computer-generated selection method, until an adequate sample is constructed. For large populations such as cities or countries the researcher may require specific attributes of interest in a population that need to be included. The census or other accurate population data for countries, cities, or communities are excellent benchmarks to compare the sampling frame of the research, so as to best approximate a representative sample based on select demographic criteria. It is easy to see therefore how problematic some modes of survey administration can be, depending on the quality of the sampling frame through access to potential respondents via publicly available lists.

How is a sample representative?

Sampling is broadly divided into two camps, probabilistic and non-probabilistic sampling. The distinction is mathematical. Probabilistic sampling is based on the probability of all members of a sampling frame having an equal chance of being selected in the sample. Non-probabilistic sampling is not based on any equal probability of being selected for a sample. For example, researchers who conduct surveys on a street corner have no way of accessing an accurate range of individuals that make up a population of a city, because they are dependent on who passes them by at any given time. News polls are also non-probabilistic because they really only attract readers or viewers of a certain publication or broadcast: those who read the *New York Times* or watch Fox News, for example, compared with those who never read the *New York Times* or watch Fox News. Samples in this respect are biased. This is not necessarily bad, depending on the intentions of the research, but the research can only be generalized to a specific population or proportion of it.

———————————— Non-probabilistic sampling ————————————

Another example of a non-probabilistic sample is my work on Australian Buddhists, aspects of which I have shared throughout this book. The survey was administered to all the people on a database of a Buddhist Centre (my sampling frame) but that was only one Buddhist centre among the many that exist in Australia. If the sample were to be probabilistic and therefore representative of the population of Australian Buddhists, the research would need to have a representative sample of the number of total Buddhist Centres and Temples across the country, not to mention those who might be Buddhists but not aligned with a formal organization such as a Buddhist Centre or Temple. The result is that the research comes with the caution that it does not represent Australian Buddhists in total but that it can only be read as representative for the Buddhist Centre that the study was centred on. This does not problematize the work essentially, only that it is limited, which is fine, so long as the research is not claiming that the results are generalizable to a broader population of Australian Buddhists.

Sample size

Sample size is a matter of to what extent the researcher can reach the intended sample and is comfortable with rates of sample error. Sample size and accuracy determine the rate of sample error: for example, as sample size increases, the more accurate it becomes, lowering the rate of error. The size of sampling error will impact any relationships we find with the data to the extent that some relationships will be more or less a possible result of sampling error. But size, accuracy, and error reach a point where there is a diminishing pay-off for increasing the sample size, so most studies aim for a sample of around 2,000 cases according to de Vaus (2014: 78). Beyond 2,000 cases there are few statistical benefits relative to resources used to collect the sample, but samples beyond 2,000 cases can boost under-represented groups of interest and allow for more representative sub-samples in the analysis phase such as an age or ethnic cohort.

Sample size should also accommodate anticipated response rates associated with various modes of survey implementation. For example, for a desired final simple probabilistic sample of 1,000 individuals and an anticipated non-response rate of 35–40% the final sample would need to be somewhere between 1,525 and 1,700 cases derived from the sampling frame.

Types of samples

Both probabilistic and non-probabilistic sampling have a variety of types that are necessary to achieve the aims of the research. Non-probabilistic sampling types are relatively simple to enact. Probabilistic sampling on the other hand can be incredibly complex and requires various mathematical skills and ways of accessing varied populations properly to have a chance at attaining representativeness.

Probabilistic sampling

There are numerous forms of probabilistic sampling that are used by survey researchers to attempt to achieve a representative sample. An important consideration associated with a probabilistic sample is the accuracy of the sampling frame and the desired size of the sample. The various forms of probabilistic sampling reflect increasingly sophisticated attempts to gain accurate representative samples from large and complex populations depending on the aims of the research.

Important aspects of **probability sampling** and representativeness are the confidence level and confidence interval. The confidence level denotes how confident we can be that the sample is an accurate representation of the population of interest. Most survey research assumes a 95% confidence level. The confidence interval is the margin of error for a measure based on the confidence level. In other words, how accurate is the sample in percentage terms if we adopt a 95% confidence level suggesting that whatever we find in the survey sample we can be 95% sure that it is within a particular margin of error relative to the real figure in the population and therefore determine its accuracy?

Let's consider an example to make this clearer. If our research is particularly interested in education levels and we know that our population comprises 31% of people who hold a degree, we would aim for around 30% of the sample to hold a university degree. For a sample size of 2,000 people then the margin of error would be 2.06% or ±2.06. This means that we would be 95% confident that the rate of degree holders in our sample is within 2.06% either side of the true rate of degree holders (28.94–32.06%) based on a sample size of 2,000, so quite accurate but not perfect. As sample sizes increase and decrease so too do the confidence intervals. To some extent this is guesswork, because we do not always know what the variation on a measure will be, although from previous surveys or other statistics we may have some idea. To calculate a confidence interval or margin of error, go to the companion website and use the calculator.

Random sampling

Basic or simple random sampling takes a sampling frame and aims to select a proportion of potential respondents from it to create the final sample. One way of achieving this is to nominate a sample fraction and calculate from it the number of respondents until the desired number of potential respondents is reached. If a sampling frame has 10,000 individuals and the desired number for the sample is 1,000, then every 10th individual is selected via a preferred method of random selection.

Stratified sampling

Stratified sampling is much the same as random sampling but emphasizes a special attribute or a number of attributes that might be of interest to the research, such as remote geography, ethnicity, or age groups. The sampling frame is then stratified along these lines to ensure that attributes of interest such as these are accurately represented.

Cluster sampling

Cluster sampling, otherwise known as multi-stage cluster sampling, is a highly complex form of sampling that large-scale survey designers use to make a sample as representative as possible. For complex populations such as large cities and whole nations, this kind of sampling, or a variant of it, is the preferred sampling method. This form of sampling is actually based on a number of samples that are constructed from various geographic blocks or 'clusters' such as different areas within cities or nations, and layered with various stages that aim to reflect the social variation in the population.

With all forms of probabilistic sampling there are occasions when key demographics or respondents with attributes of interest are missed. In such circumstances, researchers aim to collect what is known as a booster sample: a targeted increase in a population of interest to the research. This can often be people of certain ethnic backgrounds or who live in remote areas who are often under-represented in survey research.

Non-probabilistic sampling

Recruiting potential respondents is a key issue for sampling, but especially for non-probabilistic sampling. There are various ways in which survey researchers attempt to gain access to specific populations for the purposes of **non-probabilistic sampling**. Researchers will attempt to target organizations whose members will be relevant to the research with a simple notice in a newsletter, newspaper, or posted on a noticeboard in a relevant community centre. With the advent of electronic communication and social media, various groups can be contacted directly with the details of the intended study to recruit potential respondents.

Contacting important people such as leaders, office holders, or others with influence and power within a group is also a strategic step to encourage as many people as needed to take part. These people often have sufficient influence so as to be able to commend a survey project to other members of the group. This was my experience of gaining access to the Buddhists I was interested in. I made contact with a leader of the centre, who was happy for the research to proceed and encouraged others to take part through notices in the centre's newsletter. Another way to access members of specific groups is to offer something in return. Survey research can provide a group with data that they can use to apply for community grants, gauge active membership, or evaluate services and activities. Offering such services in exchange for access to a group is a worthwhile endeavour.

Convenience sampling

Convenience sampling is simply as the term implies, convenience, in that whoever the researcher can find to complete the survey, completes the survey. This is the street corner survey, or increasingly someone who posts a survey on social media. Whoever passes by sees the survey and is interested can undertake it. Certainly, various filters can be applied to the survey to restrict some people from attempting it, such as specific social attributes and/or other criteria, but essentially the convenience method is about enticing anyone within a zone of traffic, be it actual or virtual, to take part.

Snowball sampling

This is synonymous with qualitative research methods such as interviewing but can equally be employed for the collection of quantitative data. Snowball sampling operates on the premise that the recruitment of one respondent can facilitate access to others. If you are able to have one person fill out the survey, you can ask them to recommend it to others, and for these others to further recommend it etc., and so the sample grows like a snowball collecting more snow (data) as it rolls on. It is different from convenience sampling to some extent, because it is often used to access people with specific attributes. For example, snowball sampling has been used effectively to access specific ethnic groups, through leisure, religious, or other social organizations. Once some respondents have been recruited, the researcher then asks the respondents if they can pass on the details of the project to other relevant individuals, thereby increasing the sample.

Mode of administration and sampling

From the above descriptions we can clearly see that there are connections between the types of mode of survey administration and the types of sampling available that consequently produce certain data quality and representativeness or lack thereof. For example, web-based surveys, while cost and time efficient in many instances, have problems with representative samples due to bias against people who are not connected to the internet, or who are but whose email addresses are difficult to access. The construction of accurate sampling frames based on email, websites or social media is also extremely difficult for certain populations of interest such as a nation. Telephone survey modes are also increasingly problematic as we have seen. The face-to-face and mail-out survey modes can be impacted by access to addresses. Sampling problems such as these can be overcome, but often at great expense and often with the use of increasingly sophisticated technical means. The relationship between survey modes, sampling, and access to respondents is one of the fundamental challenges for survey research now and in the future. This is not such a problem for contained or connected populations in or attached to organizations, however, where contact of potential respondents is through a database.

From survey questions to survey construction

Moving on from sampling, other important aspects of survey administration are its aesthetic design, question arrangement, and style. In a previous chapter we discussed the construction of survey questions as single items, or as multiple items with the aim of adequately measuring concepts and producing valid and reliable data. Where you locate questions and how you arrange different questions on a survey can impact how respondents answer your questions and subsequently the quality of data.

Answer category arrangement: Religion question on the Australian census

The Australian government conducts a census of the population every five years. The Australian census carries a question about religious identity. From 2011 to 2016 the increase in the percentage of those who indicated 'no religion' was 8% (from 21% in 2011 to 29% in 2016). This is about double the percentage of respondents who indicated 'No Religion' from 2006 to 2011, and from previous censuses in recent years. One claim for the dramatic increase in those citing 'No Religion' is that in 2016 'No Religion' was the first response category on the list of responses to what is a closed-ended question. What do you think? Something to do with the question arrangement and response order, or more to do with real social or demographic changes?

Putting a survey together

In this section we consider another series of perhaps less obvious but equally as important survey administration issues. The structure, look and feel, and usability of a survey can go a long way to ensuring maximum response rates, reducing measurement error, and gaining better quality data. Below are five key aspects of survey construction that contribute to maximizing response rates and data quality.

Sequencing

Should attention be paid to the order of questions in a survey? The sequencing of questions or question order in a survey is a very important aspect of survey administration. 'A questionnaire should be organized much like a conversation', according to Dillman et al. (2014: 157), therefore the sequence of questions needs to follow a logical order in terms of topic or concept measured. Essentially this means that the questions (more than one most of the time) that measure a concept should be listed together in a group in sequential order one after the other, as opposed to a random or arbitrary ordering of questions that measure vastly different concepts. Dillman et al. (2014) cite two reasons for this: (1) questions are easier to answer if ordered logically because a respondent can think through the topic without having to switch attention to something completely different; and (2) a random or arbitrary ordering of questions appears as unprofessional.

Some guidelines for question sequencing follow:

- Ensure that all questions that are related to a concept are in the same bank, section, or module of questions.

- If related to the same concept but measure different dimensions or sub-dimensions of a concept, then questions should be divided up into sections reflecting the different dimensions or sub-dimensions.
- Introduce question sections with a brief statement informing respondents about the next section. For example: *In this section we'd like to learn a bit more about some of your important attributes*.
- Aim to reduce questions that may produce more 'socially acceptable' answers with a lead-in statement which is not emotive. For example: *It is very common for many people to experiment with drugs, especially when they are young. Have you ever taken an illegal drug?*
- Commence a survey with questions that are not difficult to answer or are not overly sensitive.
- Place demographic questions towards the end of the survey, especially questions concerning income.
- Ensure that there is a general open-ended question at the end of the survey that asks respondents if they have any further thoughts on any of the topics that the survey sought to measure that may be important to the research, and invite respondents to comment on how they found completing the survey.
- Insert a question towards the end asking if the respondent would be willing to be involved in any follow-up research such as an in-depth interview or focus group to gather qualitative data (if this helps or is desirable for the research).

There are some important differences between paper and web surveys for question sequencing. The most important problem of question sequencing for web surveys according to most scholarship is that the most important question is the first one. If the sequence of questions should reflect a conversation, then the first question should be like the opening of a good novel, of sufficient interest and intrigue, or at least a question that is not too challenging or confronting, so as to keep respondents turning the pages and reading (and answering!).

More specifically, there are potential consequences for data quality associated with the arrangement of question categories and with how questions are sequenced themselves. The ordering of answer categories in closed-ended questions can be highly consequential to the quality of data and to the resulting statistics. Consider the example concerning religion and the Australian census. In an arrangement of answer categories, the placement order of given categories can influence the way in which responses are recorded, especially for answer categories that are arranged vertically, which can be taken intuitively as indicative of some sort of hierarchy.

Similarly, another important consideration of sequencing of questions is the possibility of what is known as **question order effects**, a form of measurement error, that can inflate or deflate patterns in the data and potentially compromise validity and reliability. The notion of question order effects suggests that some questions in a module can influence how other questions in the module are answered (Blasius and Thiessen, 2012; De Leeuw et al., 2008) based on the arrangement of certain questions potentially inducing certain sets of answers for the rest of the module (for a very interesting discussion about the World Values Survey see Tranter and Western,

2010). Essentially question order effects potentially lead or influence a respondent into inflated positive or negative responses due to positioning. For example, if a module of questions in a survey begins with a question about how well or poorly a leader is performing and then asks a series of questions about how respondents feel about political or social issues, the answers about the leader may influence how the respondent thinks about the other political or social questions.

Layout

How should questions be laid out on a page, be it a paper page or a webpage? There are two aspects of layout that are important: the number of questions on a single page; and how navigable the page is. I discuss the question of looks below under aesthetics. Here I consider the number of questions and navigability.

The key to a successful layout is clarity. Clarity in this instance means not too many questions on a page, but not too few either. So, what is 'not too many questions' and what is 'not too few'? Most survey experts suggest an upper limit of 10 questions per page, but if clear and set out in proportion some pages can house up to 15 or 20. This assumes that questions are one or two lines in length with a series of response categories under them or besides them in a grid formation. Some questions such as those that have scenarios or vignettes with open-ended answer response categories will need more space. A long list of Likert scale questions (20 or more), even short questions, can induce a comatose-like state wherein a respondent simply checks off the same response all down the page. The example in the figure below is from the Household Income and Labour Dynamics in Australia Survey and is a good example of a clear layout for a self-complete survey.

Answer categories are also an important aspect of question layout. Answer categories where possible should always be listed vertically and not horizontally in paper and web surveys for purposes of clarity and discernment. However, there is a need to avoid having too long a survey that extends for pages and pages, so discrete banks of Likert questions can effectively carry answer categories horizontally and be clear to the respondent.

Layout should also include instructions for respondents. Any survey will require at least some basic instructions for respondents to follow to complete the survey properly. Self-completion surveys (Figure 8.5) especially require sometimes detailed instructions for respondents about how to indicate an answer – by circling, crossing, marking, and numbering closed-ended questions, or if open-ended questions to write an answer – and more detailed instructions for navigating the survey. General instructions can be listed at the front of the survey, or on the first page of a paper or web-based survey, and more specific instructions directly above the module of questions where necessary. No self-completion survey should be too difficult to fill out, so there should not be the need for lengthy notes on instructions.

B13 **Now some questions about family life.**

Please indicate, by crossing one box on each line, how satisfied or dissatisfied you currently are with each of the following relationships. The more satisfied you are, the higher the number of the box you should cross. The less satisfied you are, the lower the number of the box you should cross.

If the question does not apply to you, cross ☒ *the "Does not apply" category.*

	Completely dissatisfied									Completely satisfied		Does not apply
How satisfied are you with:	0	1	2	3	4	5	6	7	8	9	10	
a	your relationship with your partner?	0	1	2	3	4	5	6	7	8	9	10	
b	your relationship with your children?	0	1	2	3	4	5	6	7	8	9	10	
c	your partner's relationship with your children?	0	1	2	3	4	5	6	7	8	9	10	
d	your relationship with your stepchildren?	0	1	2	3	4	5	6	7	8	9	10	
e	how well the children in the household get along with each other?	0	1	2	3	4	5	6	7	8	9	10	
f	your relationship with your parents?	0	1	2	3	4	5	6	7	8	9	10	
g	your relationship with your step-parents?	0	1	2	3	4	5	6	7	8	9	10	
h	your relationship with your (most recent) former spouse or partner?	0	1	2	3	4	5	6	7	8	9	10	

(Continued)

Figure 8.5 (Continued)

B14 And how satisfied are you with the following aspects of family life?
Again, please indicate, by crossing <u>one</u> box on <u>each</u> line, how <u>satisfied</u> or <u>dissatisfied</u> you
currently are.

If the question does not apply to you, cross ☒ *the "Does not apply" category.*

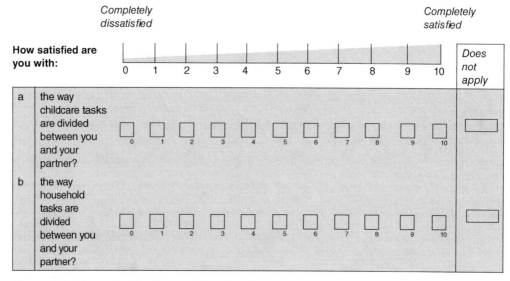

Figure 8.5 Example of self-completion layout

Source: Self Completion Questionnaire, *Household Income and Labour Dynamics Survey* in Australia
Wave 16, page 7

Duration

The duration or length of a survey is a contentious issue. On the one hand researchers
will need to include as many questions as it takes to measure concepts adequately, on
the other hand there is potential for respondents to become daunted with and turned
off a survey that is too large and long, resulting in missing data and/or poor data
quality. Although the above would appear intuitive, research into the length or duration of a survey according to de Vaus (2014) is ambiguous. As a guideline, however,
it is better to include all of the questions needed rather than compromise by leaving
some out, even if this causes the duration of time to complete the survey to be longer.
If respondents do not answer some questions due to the survey's length then so be
it. Even then, many of the sample may answer them, but if those questions are not
there due to concerns over the survey's length then the data can never be collected.
Principles associated with the sequencing of questions should maximize the potential for a fully completed survey, however. Having stated this, the researcher should
reconsider key components of what is to be measured and aim for as efficient a list of
questions as possible to minimize possible duration issues. Consider again, especially,
the dimensions of concepts and how many indicators they need to best answer the

research questions. Further, a researcher should consider whether relevant data can be gleaned from other sources, especially community-level data such as house prices, crime levels, or economic data.

To some extent duration and its problems depend on the needs of the survey and the mode. Most surveys, even larger ones, usually do not take much more than 30 minutes to complete, and many survey designs aim to be under 15 minutes, but there may be cause for surveys to be longer. Larger surveys can be carried out successfully for longer durations when interviewers are present. It is much more difficult to keep the attention of respondents who are completing self-administered surveys. One strategy to overcome this possible problem for longer paper and web surveys is to break up the survey into phases: for example, phase A or 1 at one time and phase B or 2 at another. If each phase is around 20 to 30 minutes this may make a very large survey more appealing and convenient to complete, though this approach does extend the length of fieldwork for the researcher.

Navigation

Navigation of a survey is different from the sequencing of questions, although related. The progression of answering questions through successful navigation in a survey for respondents needs to be very clear. Not all questions will be relevant to all respondents and some respondents may be required to answer some questions and not others, and then return to other questions later in the sequence. Many social surveys use filter questions to steer respondents with specific attributes or experiences to exclude partially or include respondents who meet specific criteria relevant to the research, such as have children living at home, or who commute to work via cycling, or some such attribute relevant to whatever is being measured. Clear instructions as indicated above will greatly assist correct navigation.

Again, the key here for successful survey progression is clarity. This is also especially important for paper and web-based surveys where respondents self-complete. However, survey progression is also important for face-to-face and telephone surveys that use trained interviewers who read from a schedule. Progression aids effective navigation of a survey through clear instructions. These can be written, but they can also be provided through sets of symbols.

Besides explicit instructions, a common form of specific navigation of a survey is through filter questions. Filter questions often instruct respondents to attempt a question based on certain conditions. For example, any filter questions will resemble the following:

Q 26. Have you ever given birth?

(1)   Yes (if yes, then please answer Questions 27 through 30)
(2)   No (if no, please go to Question 31 and continue the survey from that question)

The survey is seeking to isolate or filter respondents with special or specific attributes or experiences for a certain purpose. They differ from questions that aim to measure attitudes. For example, a question about attitudes towards birth could be relevant to all respondents irrespective of experience:

Q 31. To what extent do you agree that giving birth in a hospital is safer to giving birth at home?

Aesthetics

Another means of trying to ensure a maximum response rate and ensure data quality is to make the survey instrument visually attractive. For face-to-face and telephone surveys aesthetics are not an issue because questions are read out to respondents. The look and feel of a survey is pertinent to mail-out and web-based surveys, however, where respondents self-complete and engage visually with the survey. Efforts that make a survey aesthetically pleasing give the survey a professional look and feel and can assist respondents to feel that their contributions to the survey are important, which of course they are. In line with Dillman et al.'s (2014) notion that a survey is a conversation, is that the conversation extends to the visual. Aesthetics in survey construction are important but they do need to be within certain restraints.

Here are three guidelines for thinking about aesthetics and survey construction:

1 *Neutrality*: a survey is a scientific instrument, so it should attempt to maintain a neutral tone in look and feel but also be aesthetically pleasing.
2 *Clarity*: as a visual experience a survey is mostly words and should be clear and readable.
3 *Professionalism*: the more professional looking a survey, the more invested respondents will be.

For web-based and mobile devices there exist numerous built-in templates for attractive survey design. Many survey design programs such as Qualtrics and Survey Monkey allow users to configure and customize survey questions' look and feel through a host of image and colour schemes. These programs also allow the inclusion of company or organizational signs, logos, colours, and banners onto the interface of a web-based survey. There are numerous instructional guides for users of these web-based survey programs, but some key points about what kind of aesthetics should be used are below.

Clarity

Most of all, the look and feel of the survey should be clear. Aesthetic concerns can defeat the practical aspects of survey administration if the survey – however visually beautiful – is hard to read or follow. The survey as a practical visual experience will be mostly words, so images need not crowd a page but aim to complement the layout. Importantly surveys are sequential in progression and require respondents to proceed in a desired order. Greater response rates and better quality data are well aided by clear visual indicators and markers directing respondents to question paths and answer categories, such as arrows and pointers.

Colours and images

Colours of objects can stimulate particular impacts on our behaviour according to some psychologists, which is why many fast food companies have at least some red in their logos and outlets (red is supposed to trigger hunger). It has not been determined yet if the use of specific colours in a survey produces greater or lesser response rates and better or worse quality of data, but the colours and images you choose can go some way to presenting a clear, engaging, and professional-looking survey. For most professional surveys lighter shades should prevail. Lighter shades contrast darker colours for words, and as the greater proportion of documents have this colour scheme or contrast between light and dark then there will be the benefit of familiarity, making the survey easier to read.

For many surveys that are paper based, they can be 'introduced' with cover pages (both front and back) that allow a range of colours and images to represent the organization or the study itself or both. Symbols can also be used here. The page arrangements that present the survey questions are mostly under-stated and presented in a lighter colour backgrounding the darker colour questions. A colour production with appropriate images will add an aesthetic quality and further professionalism to the survey.

Colours can also be an important aide for navigation of the survey. Generally green and red are used to denote when to progress appropriately, and if you have made an error or not completed a section. These colours are universally acknowledged and accepted as generally symbolizing correct progression or not. In many web-based surveys, questions or pages or sections can light up in red, warning respondents. Some find this to be an overly aggressive approach to survey instruction, yet mostly effective.

Font

Fonts for some are the object of near cult worship. You may not feel the same way about them, but they can make an important aesthetic difference to the look and feel of your survey. Given that the survey experience for respondents is mostly reading words, fonts can make important contributions to clarity, readability, as well as the general look and feel of the survey. Fonts, much like other aesthetic concerns, also contribute to a survey looking and reading as professional, which means that some fonts are perhaps best avoided, unless the survey is for a specific organization, sample of the population, or purpose such as young people, users of particular services, or for particular industries. Consider the readability of some fonts shown in Figure 8.6.

As you will have noticed, there are various problems with fonts such as Broadway, Edwardian Script, and Kristen ITC that would exclude them from representing survey questions. A font should be clear and uncrowded and somewhat neutral in tone. Among the examples below, Times New Roman is clear, neutral, and is also a common font that people recognize and are used to. Beyond Times New Roman are fonts such as Calibri, Arial, and Courier New that are clear, neutral, and professional, as shown in Figure 8.7.

Times New Roman:

To what extent do you agree or disagree with the following statements – people like me don't have any say in what the government does

Broadway:

To what extent do you agree or disagree with the following statements – people like me don't have any say in what the government does

Edwardian Script:

To what extent do you agree or disagree with the following statements – people like me don't have any say in what the government does

Kristen ITC

To what extent do you agree or disagree with the following statements – people like me don't have any say in what the government does

Figure 8.6   Contrast between Times New Roman and inappropriate fonts for survey questions

Calibri

To what extent do you agree or disagree with the following statements – people like me don't have any say in what the government does

Arial

To what extent do you agree or disagree with the following statements – people like me don't have any say in what the government does

Courier New

To what extent do you agree or disagree with the following statements – people like me don't have any say in what the government does

Figure 8.7   Highly legible fonts for survey questions

Font size is another consideration. How large should the font be? Most documents are set with 11 or 12 point font. In web-based surveys font size can be adjusted in the settings to allow those who need to read in a larger font to do so. Key words in a question can also be **emboldened** and *italicized* to draw attention to specific aspects of the question.

There are some practical aspects to keep in mind when contemplating the aesthetics of a mail-out survey. Like many other aspects of survey design, aesthetic considerations are also subject to resources such as money, time, and capacity. With modern technology and computing, however, a lack of resources can be overcome somewhat. For mail-out surveys, booklet formats are popular and can be produced with minimum cost through packages such as Microsoft Word and Excel. If a budget permits, then a graphic artist can be engaged to format and design an aesthetically pleasing survey. A booklet is relatively easy to create with a template, is compact, restricts the number of questions on a page, and can be navigated relatively easily. Most booklets will be double sided, reducing printing.

YOUR SURVEY

Administration checklist

Below is a checklist for the various tasks that need to be discussed and decided upon with respect to survey administration.

Division of labour: do you have a schedule of who will do the following?

Check the sample frame and final sample particulars
(contact details: addresses, emails) ☐

Arrange mail-out and collection of returned completed surveys ☐

Construct and collate the survey (using a web-based platform
or paper booklet) ☐

Write the cover letter and follow-up notes ☐

Enter and store data as they are collected ☐

Mode: have you decided which mode, based on the sample,
capability, cost, and time?

Which is most feasible given your resources? ....

Can you have a mixed mode survey? ☐

Sample: do you know who your sample is? ☐

Which population? ....

What characteristics of the population are relevant to the research? ....

Have you organized the sampling frame and final sample with the group you
are working with and the population you are interested in? ☐

(Continued)

Can you construct a representative sample for a population? Will a convenience sample do? ....

Sequencing: have you followed the suggested sequence of question order?   ☐

Do you have filter questions?   ☐

Are they labelled clearly as such and instruct respondents clearly which questions to complete and which questions to avoid, based on clear criteria?   ☐

Do they allow respondents effectively to drop in and out of the survey?   ☐

Layout and aesthetics: how does the survey look? ....

Are clear instructions included?   ☐

Is it clear and easy to read?   ☐

Are the pages too crowded with questions?   ☐

Are the questions in a clear and neutral font?   ☐

Does it look professional? (Ask classmates or colleagues.)   ☐

Are you able to make it look aesthetically pleasing without compromising clarity or navigability? (Again, ask classmates or colleagues.)   ☐

Is the survey easily navigated?   ☐

Are there problems or confusion with how the survey is sequenced?   ☐

Codebook: have you compiled a codebook?   ☐

Putting the survey into the field

Once the survey is completed it is time to put the survey into the field. If you are working with an organization then it may be able to help you with administering the survey to its clients or customers.

Depending on which mode you have chosen or are using, send off the surveys, make the calls, or start the emails. Make sure someone is on hand to collect and collate the returned surveys as they are sent back. You may need to wait a week or two before most of the surveys are completed and returned. After that time, send a reminder letter to those in the sample who have not completed the survey to attempt and return it. Given your time constraints, do not wait too long before moving on to preparing a dataset and doing some analysis.

You may create a basic website or social media pages about the survey to promote it, or seek permission to promote the survey through your university's or college's social media platforms.

If using a web-based app or program such as Qualtrics or Survey Monkey, log in and check completed surveys regularly. Review and resend survey link or URL.

Key knowledge and skills

This chapter has introduced and considered the main elements involved in the administration of a survey highlighting some of the more important key practical concerns of survey design. Key knowledge and skills in survey administration include the following:

- A fair division of labour between survey team members to organize and perform all of the tasks associated with survey administration.
- Introducing the survey via a cover letter, clear instructions for completing the survey, and provision for assisting respondents with queries about the survey or the research it is associated with.
- Construction of a sample of an appropriate size that is either probabilistic or non-probabilistic, and that also acknowledges a margin for sampling error, confidence level, and confidence interval.
- How the survey will be administered to respondents, subject to resources and capabilities. Which mode is preferred, accessible, and meets the needs of administration: face to face, telephone, mail-out and return, or web-based/mobile device?
- The survey's compilation and structure also need careful consideration for clarity and professionalism. Attention needs to be paid to layout, navigation, and duration.
- The look and feel of the survey should be clear, neutral, and professional and take into account the role of colours and fonts.

Note

1 The United States Census is partly based on a sample instead of the whole population. Given that the current population of the United States is around 330,000,000, the cost of a full census would be astronomical.

Further reading

The most comprehensive guide to the various administrative components of a survey is Dillman et al.'s *Internet, Phone, Mail, and Mixed-Mode Surveys*. Dillman et al. provide detailed consideration of many key administrative components of survey administration such as aesthetics, compilation issues, incentives for respondents, cover letters, and more. Dillman et al. also do an excellent job of discussing the various problems and prospects of various modes of survey administration. For a very good overview of the web-based survey mode see Toepoel's *Doing Surveys Online*. Sampling is a very important specialist topic and covered by most texts on survey design. However, sampling becomes very mathematically complex very quickly. Two texts that give excellent insight into the many aspects of sampling and are accessible is Blair and Blair's *Applied Survey Sampling* and the chapters that deal with sampling in Part V of Wolf et al.'s *The SAGE Handbook of Survey Methodology*.

Full text references:

Blair, E. and Blair, J. (2015) *Applied Survey Sampling.* London: Sage

Dillman, D., Smyth, J., and Christian, L. (2014) *Internet, Phone, Mail, and Mixed-Mode Surveys: The Tailored Design Method* (4th edn). Hoboken, NJ: Wiley

Toepoel, V. (2015) *Doing Surveys Online.* London: Sage

Wolf, C., Joye, D., Smith, T., and Fu, Y.-c. (2016) *The SAGE Handbook of Survey Methodology.* London: Sage

 Discover the digital resources for this chapter, including reflective questions, case studies, and templates, at https://study.sagepub.com/aarons

Nine

Survey Design and Data Analysis: From Questions to Data and From Plan to Action

Once a survey has been administered and the completed surveys have been returned, a data set is created. This chapter covers:

- Creating a data set with completed returned surveys
- Entering survey data into a data analysis program
- Preparing survey data for analysis
- Matching survey data through indicators to analysis types
  - Univariate
  - Bivariate
  - Multivariate

What is to be done once your data have been collected? This chapter outlines how to prepare data for analysis (Figure 9.1) through the construction of a data set. The chapter also introduces the main techniques of data analysis within the context of the principles of survey design. While the chapter does not provide detailed instructions for actual data analysis, it aims to outline a guide for discerning how survey design is related to data analysis to answer research questions. It is here that the front end of survey design meets the results of the survey to answer the research questions, exemplifying how conceptual models inform survey design. The chapter also links indicator design to data needs through thinking about data analysis.

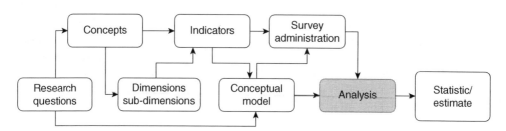

Figure 9.1   Survey design process: analysis

Creating a data set

The first step in preparing data for analysis (despite it not being particularly analytic) is to create a data set from your returned surveys. Many researchers use data analysis programs such as SPSS, Stata, SAS, R, Excel, and a host of other programs. Essentially, they perform the same functions and most have the same procedures for entering data. SPSS is a common and user-friendly data analysis program so the examples used in this chapter will be derived from that one. If you only have access to a program other than SPSS there are numerous guides available to assist you in creating a data set.

There are two ways to create a data set in programs such as SPSS, corresponding to the modes of survey administration. The first way is to import the data from another file into the program of choice. If your data have been collected by an agency it will prepare files for you in various formats that you can simply import into your program and begin using it. If you have collected the data yourself from survey software such as Survey Monkey or Qualtrics, you can also import the files in readable format from these programs to programs such as SPSS to perform more complex analyses. For face-to-face, electronic, web-based, and telephone modes of survey administration with computer capabilities the data set will usually be automatically created with each completed survey. These procedures are not difficult and the software you use for data collection should provide you with instructions on how to import data sets to various analysis programs. Despite the data being 'ready' when imported to a program such as SPSS, you may have to make some key changes to the format of the data for them to make sense and be amenable to analysis.

Enter survey data

The second way of creating a data set is to do so manually. This is mostly associated with the mail-out and return mode of survey administration, but pen and paper are still used in some cases even for face-to-face and telephone interviews necessitating manual entry of data. For many survey projects that are on a tight budget and have lower sample sizes this is not overly burdensome, but for larger projects manual data entry is somewhat time consuming and tedious. Familiarization with manual entry is important even if your data are imported from another file because you will probably need to reorder or change the dataset with appropriate labels, descriptions, and values at some point before analysis, and most definitely during analysis.

SPSS data and variable windows

In this section you can follow the descriptions and instructions with the completed surveys you may have designed and administered or download the completed surveys that come with the text. If you have your own surveys from another source in need of data transcription, you can of course use them should you have access to data analysis software.

SPSS and similar packages are just big spreadsheets that begin with a series of blank cells that are filled in with numbers, labels, and descriptions. On opening SPSS you will see two gridded windows with lots of empty cells, one is called the *data view window* (Figure 9.2) and the other the *variable view window*, as in Figure 9.3. Note the tabs highlighted at the bottom left of the screenshots. The two windows are interactive in that once you enter characters in one they will appear in the other. The actual data from a survey are entered into the data view window and its labels, values, and other particulars are entered into the variable view window.

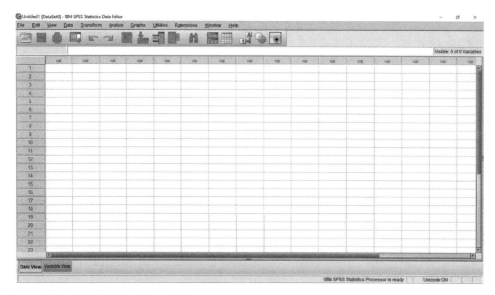

Figure 9.2 SPSS Data View window

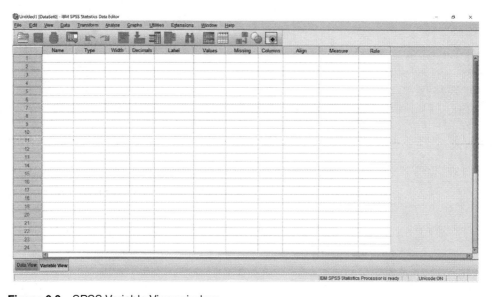

Figure 9.3 SPSS Variable View window

Working with whichever survey that you choose, begin by giving each completed survey an ID or case number, from 1 to however many completed surveys you have. If your data set is imported from another program you can create an ID in SPSS by adding a variable and completing the labelling details. Let's start with the Variable View window to begin creating the variables. The variables, you will recall, are the data versions of the questions on the survey. Looking at the variable view window you will see columns and rows. I will be working with the Arts Centre and Gallery Patron Survey (ACGPS from here on) (be sure to download the codebook). Take a look at the first column in Figure 9.4. In the first cell underneath 'Name' I will enter the name of the variable 'ID' for identification as shown in Figure 9.5. ID and the accompanying number in Figure 9.5 in the data view window of SPSS represents each individual completed survey composing the data set.

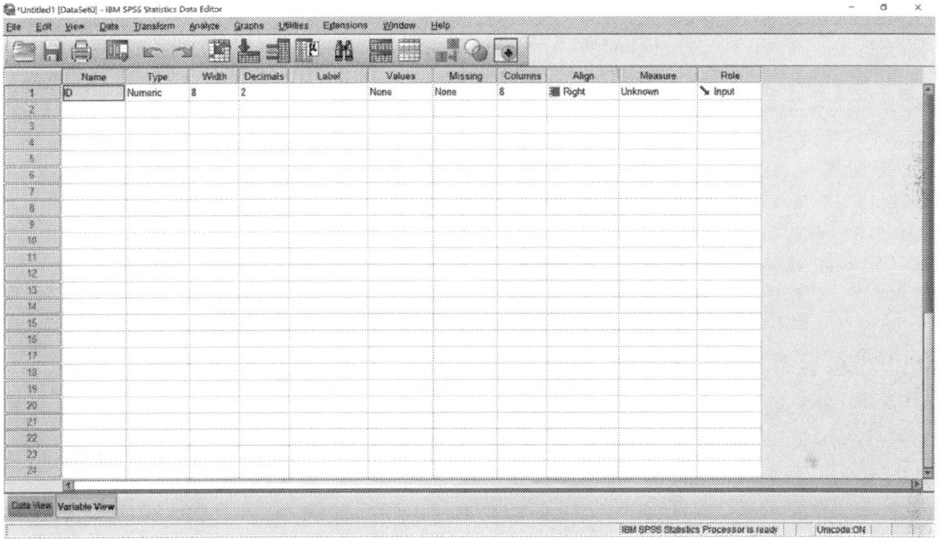

Figure 9.4   ID variable creation

In the data view window, I have highlighted the variable as it appears after we have entered the details in the variable view window. In the data view window enter in the cells the case or ID numbers as shown in Figure 9.5; these represent each individual completed survey and are good practice for cross-checking if there is an error in data entry for subsequent variables.

Continue on with the codebook and begin entering in the other variables. Figure 9.6 elaborates on the first example with a proper variable – the first question in the ACGPS. There are some more things to note in Figure 9.6. Firstly, there is more detail we need to supply the variable view window in SPSS with. In the 'Name' column we need to give the variable a nickname or shortened coded variable (as indicated in the codebook under the column called 'Name'). We have called this variable 'ExRating', short for exhibition rating. The names need to be short and without spaces to comply with SPSS's character limits and syntax. You can call your variables whatever you want, so long as they make sense and remind you and other users what they are about. In many large-scale surveys with hundreds of variables they are

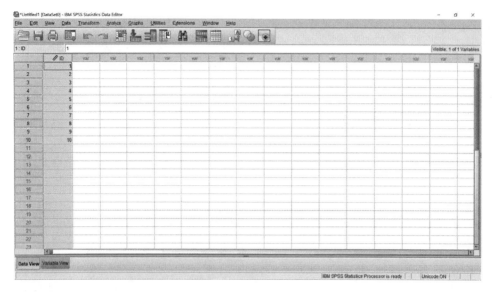

Figure 9.5　Data View for ID variable

often algebraically coded with a letter to denote a section or module of questions, and a number sequence to differentiate the individual variables within them, such as A1.1, A1.2, A1.3, etc. In concert with the codebook, this makes the data much easier to navigate in SPSS.

Secondly, after recording a name, you need to enter something in the 'Label' column. Many SPSS users simply input the survey question or an abbreviation of the survey question, as I have done here. Thirdly, after you have labelled the variable, you need to enter 'Values', namely the codes for the answers to your questions. In the case of question 1 we have four values that correspond to the four answer categories accompanying this question. The codebook indicates the codes. Enter them in the 'Values' cells by clicking the relevant cell and assigning the score in the 'Value' bar and its description the 'Label' bar. For example, '1' = 'poor'. Once you have entered the value and the label, click 'Add' and SPSS will lock it in. You can change and remove values and labels, as the buttons indicate. Figure 9.7 shows the values and labels entered.

Finally, you have to tell SPSS if there are any missing values associated with this variable (for when respondents do not answer a question) via the 'Missing' column by clicking the cell in the Variable row. Missing values are often coded out of sequence with the other values so they are conspicuous. For the ACGPS we have chosen '99' to denote missing data (but any number can suffice so long as it is recognizable). Figure 9.7 shows where to enter the score for missing data. Enter the 99 then click 'OK'. Sometimes there are more than one type of missing data.

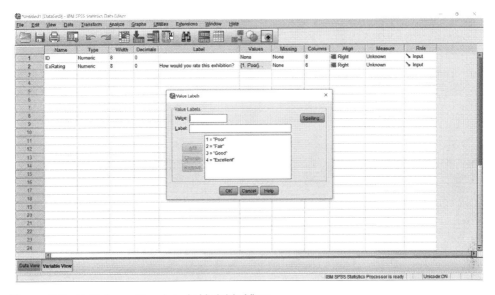

Figure 9.6 ExRating with values in Variable View

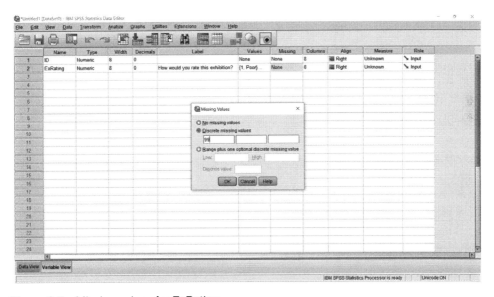

Figure 9.7 Missing values for ExRating

Turning to the data view window, we can see via the highlighted column in Figure 9.8 that our variable 'ExRating' is listed at the top of the column. After we have named and labelled the variable and entered the values with corresponding labels, we then type in the answer numbers as they were recorded on the survey for each respondent adjacent to the ID numbers and in the 'ExRating' column. The values that the first 10 respondents have indicated on the surveys for this question have been entered into SPSS as shown by Figure 9.8. Respondent 1 for example indicated that the exhibition was 'excellent', which we have coded as '4', therefore we type '4' into the cell. Respondent 3, however, thought the exhibition was 'poor', as indicated by the '1', and so on.

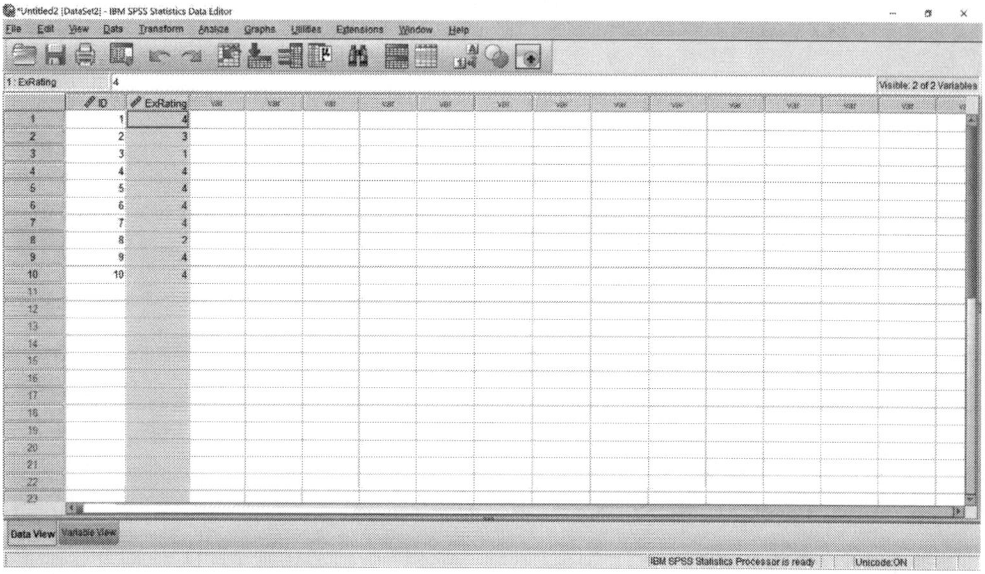

Figure 9.8 ExRating in Data View window

Eventually your data set will look like the screenshots in Figures 9.9 and 9.10 that show both the complete variable and data view windows. There are four additional variables that I have added to the data set that are displayed in the first figure (bottom four). These are derived from the answer categories from questions 3 and 7 on the survey. Note that in question 3 there is an answer category called 'Other' which allows respondents to add a relevant category to a nominally closed-ended question. Very often respondents do indicate via words (qualitative data) what this 'Other' is. In this case we have two respondents who have learned about the exhibition opening from sources not listed in the survey: a public notice and another directly from the artist. Similarly, we have taken the sub-categories from question 7, after filtering out those who indicated that they did not follow the gallery's activities on social media and created three other variables from them, corresponding to the three forms of social media the survey sought to measure. These extra variables are necessary as they are essentially different questions.

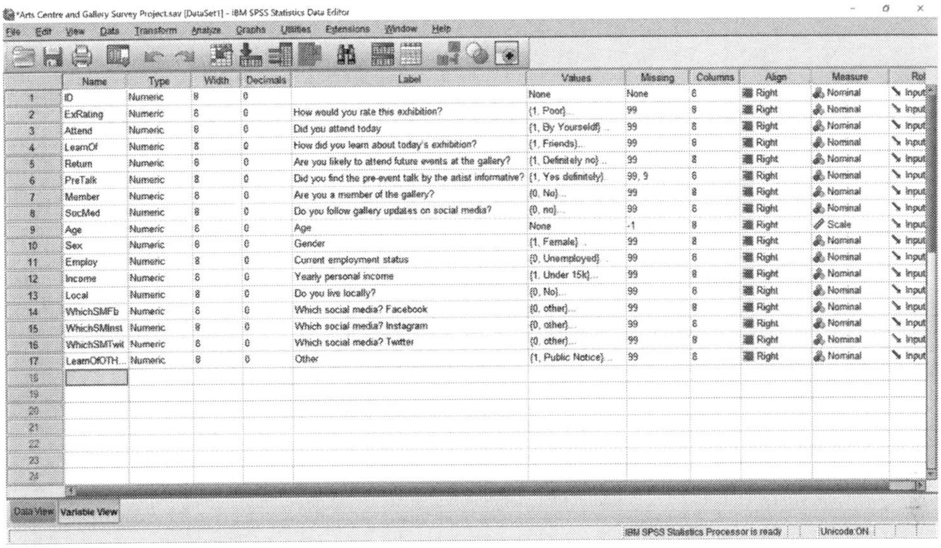

Figure 9.9 Completed data set – Variable View

Having created the 'shell' of our data set with appropriate names, labels, and values, we now enter the data from the surveys into the spreadsheet via the data view window in the corresponding cells for each variable for each survey until complete. We will do 30 cases with 17 variables to keep it light. Imagine having to do this for a sample of 2,500 cases and around 300 complex variables! In Figure 9.10 you can see a partial screenshot from the completed data set in the data view window.

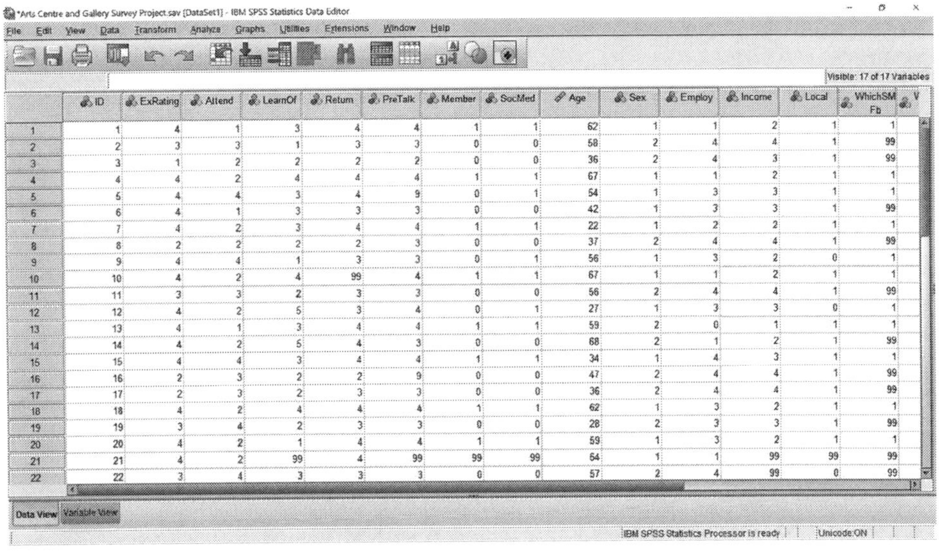

Figure 9.10 Complete data set – Data View

Preparing data for analysis

Once your data have been entered, save them! You will then need to check them for entry errors. Checking for errors is crucial as the analysis can be severely impacted by data entry errors. Error checking is best done via consultation with the codebook. In smaller surveys such as the one we are using here, this does not take much time. Errors can still be undetected after you have checked and can be found through data analysis. If during analysis something is not making sense, you have odd outliers, or is counterintuitive to your knowledge of a concept or a measure, then this could be a red flag to check data entry, coding, and missing data. Cleaning data also involves minor jobs such as changing the decimal places on a variable (see the 'Decimal' column in the variable view window). This allows numbers to be extended or contracted depending on the needs of the analysis and the type of data used. Currency, time, or certain fluid measurements for example may require many decimals (most social science data will not), changing the labels or names of variables, and coding appropriately.

The most important aspect of cleaning and preparing data is to make them amenable to analysis. Survey data are fiddly. In their original state, once entered into a software package such as SPSS, they may appear to look fine, but often may be in need of some form of change or restructuring to make them more amenable to efficient and effective analysis. Changing or restructuring survey data often involves reducing or collapsing them, or increasing and compounding them, so they are more suitable to clearer analyses, without compromising their quality or representativeness. A good rule for survey data is parsimony, that is the lesser, the better, to the point where you are still communicating complete answers to questions with your data, but they are not unreadable due to their size or volume. Below are some common forms of preparing data for analysis by changing them via common preparatory steps that researchers commonly do to make data analysis more efficient and effective.

Recoding

Recoding data concerns changing the codes on a variable to make it more amenable to most kinds of analysis. Recoding can be simply **reverse coding** (changing a variable's codes from 4, 3, 2, 1 to 1, 2, 3, 4), but more often involves reducing a variable's coding categories from a large number to a smaller, more manageable number to make analysis easier and clearer. Consider a variable such as age in years, for example. Age is often measured by asking respondents simply how old they are, to which respondents answer with their age in years: 68, 19, 54, and so on. This is a valid and reliable measure of age, but the problem with this kind of measure when it comes to analysis is that it produces as many answer categories as there are ages, from 18 to 100 for example.

In a large sample therefore, we will have far too many answer categories to use the variable efficiently and effectively in most instances. What researchers do with such variables is reduce the answer categories by recoding the variable into a smaller number of categories. So, a recoded age variable often reduces or arranges the various single ages into category ranges such as 18–30, 31–40, 41–50, 51–60, etc. From a potentially very large range of age scores that are relevant but awkward to use, we can create a more streamlined and efficient variable, without losing the essence of the concept we are trying to measure. Recoding such as this changes the nature of the variable, however, in this case from an interval measure to an ordinal measure due to age ranges coded from 1 to 7, for example. This can have consequences for more advanced forms of analysis, yet having the original variable with its natural codes allows us to perform certain kinds of analysis, so we tend to measure age with questions and answers that allow the full range.

Another common practice is to collapse the categories of Likert scales that measure levels of affectual agreement with a statement or proposition. Recall that a Likert scale will typically have five, but often seven, or at times even eleven answer categories, coded 1–5, 1–7, or 1–11. We certainly may be interested in the extremes of Likert scales, and can simply elect to highlight these, but often it is acceptable and informative to report simply on proportions who agree or disagree with the statement or proposition in question. A five-point Likert scale, for example, can then become a two-point scale consisting of values 'agree' and 'disagree', often with the omission of the neutral category if included in the question. The same holds for seven- and eleven-point Likert scales.

Recoding does take some thought and should follow a logical process, however. Categories and codes should not be randomly assigned in the creation of a new variable. One of the problems of recoding a variable such as age for example is where to begin and limit categories. If we create, say, 18 to 36 as our first recoded age category and call it 'younger', there is the possibility that we mask over some important differences in the attributes and life experiences of respondents, as 18 year olds and 36 year olds can be very different. Yet we may not be able to recode age groups too finely due to sample numbers. A succinct guide is to do one of two things:

1   Divide the sample evenly into thirds, quarters, or fifths, and so on.
2   Construct categories based on specific attributes that are plausible.

Recoding age

This example should illustrate the points above. The **frequency distribution** in Table 9.1 is long and cumbersome, so we will recode it. There are over 20 categories that we need to reduce. But we can discern from the ages listed that the majority of the sample is older, so the gallery is doing OK with older members of the community, not so well with the young. There are a few younger attendees in the sample, but the majority of the sample are over 40. This is supported by the mean age, which is 50.83.

Table 9.1 SPSS output: Age frequency distribution

		Frequency	Percent	Valid Percent	Cumulative Percent
			Age		
Valid	18	1	3.3	3.3	3.3
	22	1	3.3	3.3	6.7
	27	1	3.3	3.3	10.0
	28	1	3.3	3.3	13.3
	34	1	3.3	3.3	16.7
	36	2	6.7	6.7	23.3
	37	1	3.3	3.3	26.7
	42	1	3.3	3.3	30.0
	47	1	3.3	3.3	33.3
	48	1	3.3	3.3	36.7
	49	1	3.3	3.3	40.0
	52	1	3.3	3.3	43.3
	54	1	3.3	3.3	46.7
	56	2	6.7	6.7	53.3
	57	1	3.3	3.3	56.7
	58	2	6.7	6.7	63.3
	59	2	6.7	6.7	70.0
	61	1	3.3	3.3	73.3
	62	2	6.7	6.7	80.0
	64	1	3.3	3.3	83.3
	67	2	6.7	6.7	90.0
	68	1	3.3	3.3	93.3
	69	1	3.3	3.3	96.7
	72	1	3.3	3.3	100.0
	Total	30	100.0	100.0	

To recode age here we need to make a decision about how to divide the distribution into discrete categories that make conceptual sense and statistical sense. For example, with age, conceptual sense means valid categories of younger to older, and statistical sense means enough cases in each category to allow analysis. In larger samples with more even distributions, age is recoded into discrete categories such as 'Young' or 'Millennial', 'Middle aged' or 'Gen X and Y', 'Older' or 'Baby Boomer', and 'Oldest' or even 'Silent Generation'. Whatever the designations, the categories must make some sense and have enough cases to be fit for some analysis (at least over 10 cases). So how would we go about dividing our sample? I suggest that given the average age is 50, and we have so few cases, we divide along the average and state two categories of over and under 50.

Composite measures: Scales and indexes

Another common form of data preparation is to create composite measures. Composite measures are a common form of data preparation that combine various single items into a new single measure to measure a concept better and capture the various dimensions of more complex concepts. The combination of several variables to create a scale or index often represents what researchers call a latent or emergent variable, that is a measure that has an underlying unity that the scale or index brings out. Scales and indexes should have construct or conceptual validity, that is they make theoretical or conceptual sense and are not a random collection of measures, and statistical validity, usually given via a composite measure statistic such as an 'alpha score'. Composite measures can also be changed with a variety of statistical means to reflect the needs and uses of the measure, such as reverse coding, weighting, and standardizing. There are two forms of composite measure, a scale and an index. Many researchers use these terms interchangeably, but to some there are important differences which I highlight here.

Scales

In many surveys, depending on the complexity of the concept of interest to be measured, there will be more than one indicator for the concept in the survey. Scales (and indexes) can be created at any time during the analysis phase, but researchers usually have scaled items in mind when the survey is being designed, and therefore are planned with sets of questions that are easily combined before analysis occurs. Scales are often designed as indicators and constructed as variables through the use of a uniform question format that denotes a latent and unifying theme or concept. For example, in many social surveys there will be a module of questions that will ask respondents how much trust or confidence they have in various social and political institutions such as Parliament, the courts, universities, the military, religious organizations, and so on. Each item will attempt to measure a number of dimensions of the same concept (trust or confidence) expressed usually in the same way, such as '*Please indicate the level of confidence you have in the following institutions:...*'. The construction of a scale involves combining these measures into one measure to create a robust or summary measure of the concepts of trust or confidence.

Indexes

Indexes are very similar to scales in that they combine a number of items into a new single measure, yet they differ from scales according to DeVellis (2012) because they are derived from different question formats. Even though they may not appear to be related as dimensions of a concept due to their derivation from different question types, index items share a common *effect*, and can be employed to measure it. For example, in a research project I was involved in I created an index of factors predicting 'precarious employment' which combined variables as different as type of work done, ethnicity, level of education, income, and citizenship. A scale is usually perceived to have greater conceptual validity embedded in the question design (such as the scale assessing trust or confidence in institutions stated above). Index creation therefore needs to be judicious in that the items that are combined should demonstrably relate to the latent concept as it is discussed in theories and previous research. In my example, the literature and theory concerning the concept of 'precarious employment' identified these disparate attributes (Standing, 2014), so there was some rationale and justification for combining them into an index.

Demographic variables

In addition to age, other demographic or social background variables can be recoded to make analysis more efficient and effective. Common variables in surveys whose response categories can balloon into large numbers of values making analysis cluttered are demographic variables such as income, ethnicity, religion, occupation, political party, and social or leisure group affiliation. These are all often very important variables to survey research and are nearly always recoded to reduce the categories. Income, like age, if recorded in the survey as a precise or rounded amount such as $67,908/$67,000, is often recoded into categories that denote 'low', 'mid range', and 'high'. Religions and ethnicities in surveys need more informed recoding to reflect appropriate groupings accurately. For example, in many surveys that ask about religious identity, many respondents state their exact religious group. For a religion such as Christianity, there are hundreds of groups that are Christian, but are Christian in very different ways. We may recode along the lines of Catholic, Protestant, and Orthodox, but within these broad categories are many different types of Protestants, such as mainline, evangelical, and progressive. Within Orthodox Christianity there are Greek, Russian, Ukrainian, and others. Ethnicities present the same challenges and are grouped across geographic region or combined within a relevant nationality. We do potentially lose some quality of experience and possibly some variation in attitudes that may occur if these categories are allowed to stand, but very few of these separate religious or ethnic groups would have enough cases to qualify statistically as an independent group in most samples. Occupations are many and diverse also. Often researchers recode and collapse similar occupations based on industry, skills, qualifications, and earnings. For example, many manual professions are often recoded as 'blue collar', 'manual', or 'semi-skilled' and many clerical and professional jobs as 'white collar', 'skilled', or 'professional'.

Recoding demographic variables such as religion, ethnicity, and occupation requires knowledge of the specific domain as they represent complex groupings that make amalgamation sometimes difficult. In building knowledge of a specific domain, it is always a good idea to refer to the previous literature that uses some kind of classificatory system if recoding. Appropriate recoding and clustering of groups can also be learned through various national and international statistical agencies that have detailed guidelines and rationales for recoding variables in various ways.

Dummy variables

Dummy variables are variables used in a special kind of analysis called regression, that is a technique mostly used in multivariate analysis and some bivariate analysis. A dummy variable is a variable that is recoded to reduce the categories of an item from many categories to two, usually to reflect that something is or is not, as '1' and '0'. The aim of creating dummy variables is to create an interval-level variable from a variable that was not one originally.

Missing data

Missing data presents a unique problem in the preparation of variables for analysis. Missing data are the result of respondents not answering survey questions. What do you do about missing data when preparing your data for analysis? Firstly, it depends how much data is missing. If there are only a few cases or a small proportion of data missing, it is usually fine to proceed with analysis. It is when a significant proportion of the sample is not represented that problems for analysis can occur. For example, many respondents under-report measures such as income in social surveys. In some instances, there can be 30% or over that is missing. This is a proportion that impacts the representativeness of the sample, leaving the sample biased. There may be many people from very wealthy backgrounds and from very poor backgrounds that refuse to indicate their income in a survey; there does not seem to be much stigma if you are somewhere in the middle, however.

There are numerous statistical approaches to overcome this problem, which I will not consider here. However, a common way of dealing with missing data is to supplement the cases without an income figure or score with the average income or score from the remainder of the sample and have the average stand in as the response for the missing cases. The other approach is not to use the measure if it is not essential. Another common form of overcoming missing data is to create sample weights. **Weighting** variables allow the sample to be changed so as to account for large amounts of missing data. There exist a number of ways to create weights making the sample more representative of a population. (For a good overview on weighting of survey data see Pfeffermann (1996) and Kalton and Flores-Cervantes (2003).)

Qualitative data

Coding qualitative answers or word answers is another task in preparing the data set for analysis. Most often, the qualitative responses are one word or short phrases that can and should be translated into numeric form for ease of analysis. Most qualitative responses in surveys are worded responses to questions that provide an 'other' category or are open-ended question answers. In many instances they will represent a nominal variable, but not always. In our survey of gallery attendees we have only two cases in which qualitative answers need to be coded into quantitative responses. At times there is no need to quantify qualitative responses and they can stand as important descriptive additions to the statistics that the survey generates.

Once you are satisfied with the state of your data, by considering and acting on the above, you are ready to begin your analyses. As you work with data, you may want to change or modify them further to prepare them for further analyses. The important point here is that survey data in their raw or natural form are often in need of some changing to make them more amenable for analysis and to assist in overcoming problems such as missing data. An important point regarding question and answer formats that produce data that usually need recoding is that recoding to condense a variable can always be done, but you cannot recode to expand a condensed original variable. Variables with numerous categories such as age in years are valuable for more advanced analysis such as multiple regression. So keep these kinds of question and answer formats in your survey design – you can always recode the data once you have them.

In the next section we will cover some basic types of analysis. The section will not go into depth regarding analysis of survey data as there are many excellent guides and texts for learning analysis. Further, it is not the intention of this book to teach data analysis, but it is important to consider how survey design translates concepts through the data it is designed to collect into statistical findings through the kinds of analysis that answer research questions. In other words, data analysis techniques answer the question of how do we transform the broad concepts we began with into empirical findings that answer our research questions? The full scope of survey design therefore needs to include frameworks for the analysis of data born of the concepts a survey seeks to measure.

Matching data to analysis types: How survey design translates to data analysis

I used the phrase 'descending the ladder of abstraction' (see Chapter 4) earlier to describe the process of operationalizing concepts as a fundamental aspect of survey design. Within the survey research process, data analysis represents a parallel notion of transition, from plan to action! In the analytical phase we are testing not just whether or not our research questions and hypotheses can be answered coherently (to some extent irrespective of the results), but also if the survey worked, net of the various errors. Did the survey measure what we wanted it to measure, and did it measure what we wanted it to measure for those who matter? In analysing survey data, we aim to discover if proposed relationships amount to something approaching actual relationships via the data that then allow us to learn or approximate some form of truth or reality, and at the same time learning whether these relationships are built on solid foundations or are perhaps due to limitations and errors.

Answering questions

The most fundamental aim of analysing survey data is to answer our research questions and/or test our hypotheses. But just how does survey data answer questions? The answer may appear obvious, but we need to appreciate some key considerations before we begin analysis. The first consideration is to identify what we need from the data. This we can do by virtue of our research questions and conceptual models. Again this may appear obvious but there are many ways in which we can do this, so how do we discern what to do? We can ask ourselves the following questions based on our models, questions, and objectives. Firstly, do we need to assess and/or summarize just one variable, or many variables separately? Do we need to establish, explore, or test relationships between two or more variables? If so, how many variables do we need to use in order to test our relationships properly, given the theoretical and conceptual frameworks that are associated with our research? Secondly, what are the limits or possible errors associated with measurement that may compromise how we can analyse our data and consequently answer our research questions? How do we identify and amend variables that are deficient? And thirdly, exactly which analytical technique should we use to best get what we need from the data the survey has collected?

How question types enable analysis

In addition to being guided by conceptual models, data analysis as a further consequence of survey design is either enabled or restricted by the question and answer types that a survey employs to measure a concept. The variety of question types that we encountered in Chapter 6 have consequences at the analysis stage, as was mentioned. How we ask and score broadly translate into how we can analyse and what we can learn. Indicators, as questions and answers, carry implicitly the various levels of measurement that our variables qualify as. From these levels of measurement certain kinds of analysis are conventionally deemed 'admissible' and others 'inadmissible' (Stevens, 1946). Recall that the logic of quantitative research is about comparing various quantifiable levels, such as strong and weak, high and low, more or less. The extent to which we can demonstrate such differences for various states of human activity and thought is dependent on the types of questions we ask and which answer categories we allow. Compare for example a question that allows 'yes' or 'no' and 'strongly agree to strongly disagree (two categories versus up to eleven). In the following sections I will discuss this point to show how analysis is guided by different levels of measurement.

Univariate, bivariate, and multivariate

Data analysis proceeds on three levels, univariate, bivariate, and multivariate, each level of analysis corresponding to different kinds of research question or objective. **Univariate analysis** is the analysis of one variable, bivariate two variables (an IV and DV), and multivariate analysis more than two (IVs and DVs). Of course, which level of analysis (and specific analytical techniques) you need depends on the questions you have proposed. The greater majority of research using survey data is bivariate and/or multivariate, because most survey research aims to explore or test relationships between IVs and DVs, but univariate analysis is still important.

Univariate

Univariate analysis is helpful, useful, and informative but really only as a preliminary or entry point to a more complex research problem or set of problems. I will consider here three important uses of univariate analysis associated with survey design and survey research:

1   Checking the representativeness of the sample
2   Distributions of variables
3   Basic patterns associated with attitudes, opinions, states, behaviours, and attributes

Univariate analysis helps us understand the representativeness of a survey sample by comparing key demographic variables against established benchmarks such as those produced by a population census. All that is needed in statistical terms is the percentages of key demographics of the sample. However, 'key demographics' can mean different things to different research projects. Often large social surveys aim to capture representative samples of age, gender, and geographic location, social class, and educational attainment.

Distributions of variables

Univariate analysis is principally used to examine the distribution of various variables, either in preparation for further analysis or to establish a pattern in and of itself. A distribution is simply how the answers to the survey questions varied among the respondents. There is a lot we can learn from distributions. Distributions of a range of states, behaviours, attributes, or attitudes can be compared over time, or considered at one point in time. This is useful because we can track change or have a snapshot of the state or phenomena, but it does not allow us to attempt to explain it empirically or describe it in much detail. Assessing the distribution of a variable also informs the researcher about the 'shape' of the variable, that is if it is 'normal' or skewed, if it has a lot of variation or not, and whether it has missing data or not.

A distribution of a variable is gained through a technique called a 'frequency distribution' in SPSS. A frequency distribution as generated in a data analysis program such as SPSS displays the distribution, variation, or spread of answers across the answer categories of a variable in a number of ways. A frequency distribution will answer a question such as what people think or feel and to what extent they think or feel it, for one variable, or what they have or not have and what the difference is between them. Consider the gallery data we have seen and the example below.

What did gallery patrons and attendees think of the exhibition they attended? The frequency distribution gives us a snapshot of what respondents thought. We learn that there were no missing data, everyone answered the question, and the greater majority of those who attended the exhibition opening responded 'excellent' to the question. How do we know this? The frequency distribution gives us the distribution of responses in a few important forms, so let's take a closer look (Table 9.2).

Table 9.2 SPSS output: frequency distribution for 'ExRating'

How would you rate this exhibition?

		Frequency	Percent	Valid Percent	Cumulative Percent
Valid	Poor	1	3.3	3.3	3.3
	Fair	5	16.7	16.7	20.0
	Good	5	16.7	16.7	36.7
	Excellent	19	63.3	63.3	100.0
	Total	30	100.0	100.0	

The frequency distribution for the 'ExRating' variable shows four columns that SPSS gives as its essential output. 'Frequency' gives us the counts of respondents for each answer category, that is how many individuals recorded what answer on the survey. The next column is 'Percent', which displays the proportions of respondents who indicated which category, then there is the 'Valid Percent' column, which displays the same information but accounts for missing data by adjusting the percentage based on a revised total (not necessary here because we have no missing data), and finally the table displays the 'Cumulative Percent' column, which adds the percentage of each category to the preceding percentage up to 100%. So, clearly, we can see that 19 individuals of the sample of 30 indicated that they thought the exhibition was

'Excellent'; this represents 63% of the total sample (as seen in the 'Percent' column). Conversely the gallery staff and artist would no doubt be pleased with the fact that only one respondent thought the exhibition to be 'Poor', with smaller minorities of the sample indicating the exhibition to be 'Fair' (16.7%) to 'Good' (also 16.7%). There is more good news for the artist and gallery, however, if we consider the 'Cumulative Percent' column. If we take the figure in this column that corresponds to the category 'Fair' we see 20%; this is derived by SPSS adding the 3.3% for 'Poor' and the 16.7% of 'Fair'. From this the gallery can state that 80% of the sample thought the exhibition was 'Good' or 'Excellent'. It is a matter of perspective!

Univariate analysis can assist us in establishing a strong rationale or important benchmark for phenomena associated with a research problem that then urges the researcher to ask more complex questions requiring bivariate or multivariate analysis. Often snapshots produced by simple univariate analysis from surveys can produce evidence of profound social or economic change that has taken place over time. Change for example in the rates of world poverty as mostly drawn from household surveys measuring income (earlier years in the chart below are from estimates) give us an excellent long-term view of what change has occurred, without, however, informing us how or why it occurred, as Figure 9.11 from the Our World in Data website displays (note the operational definition of poverty here). There are many examples such as these across many different measures that highlight the use of univariate analysis.

World population living in extreme poverty, 1820–2015
Extreme poverty is defined as living on less than 1.90 international-$ per day. International-$ are adjusted for price differences between countries and for price changes over time (inflation).

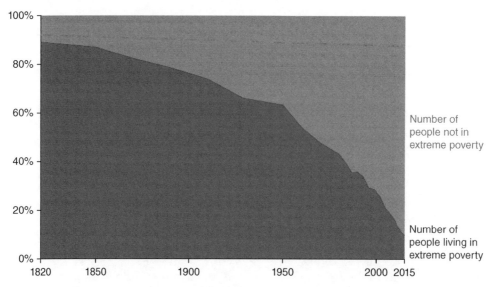

Source: OWID based on World Bank (2019) and Bourguignon and Morrisson (2002)   OurWorldInData.org/extreme-poverty/ • CC BY

Figure 9.11   Univariate chart of global poverty

Source: Our World in Data

Univariate data

The most common statistics used in univariate analysis are basic percentages or pro-portions of a sample on a given measure. We can use what are called counts, that is the exact number of respondents who indicated an answer to a question, but this is less effective in analysis because of sampling differences: more or less responses for one group do not always mean that an attribute or attitude is higher or lower than another.

Other common univariate measures are also what is known as descriptive statistics or summary statistics. Descriptive or summary statistics are averages such as the mean, median, and mode, also known as measures of central tendency. These statistics give us a summary position on a variable and like percentages can be compared over time to assess the rate of change. Further descriptive statistics that indicate variation and change include standard deviations, the variance, and range.

Frequency data for a single variable can also be displayed visually with a range of charts. Commonly researchers use what is known as a histogram (Figure 9.12) to dis-play the frequency and variation of a variable for a sample.

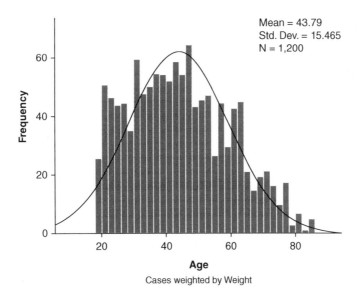

Figure 9.12 Histogram: age

Source: World Values Survey Wave 6

The normal distribution

When we first look at a variable in SPSS we are interested in its distribution, that is how the frequencies of answer categories among the sample are distributed. For exam-ple, how many of the sample and in what proportion answered 'yes' or 'no', 'agree', 'strongly agree', or 'disagree', and so on? Statistically there is an assumption that all of the categories will be relatively evenly distributed (what we call the normal distribution, where 95% of cases fall within 1 or 2 standard deviations from the mean), but in real-life research they are disproportional or in some state of skewness or kurtosis: that is, tending more towards the extremes of the answer categories at times (if half or more than half of the sample answered strongly agree, for example). To make some sense in research terms, we rely on questions being answered differently by different people in a survey. This accounts for variation in a variable that is then displayed in the analysis and explained by IVs, such as different levels of income related to different levels of education as we have seen. However, some variables do not display much variation; that is, most of the sample may feel the same way about a statement, record the same or similar attributes, and demonstrate the same or similar behaviours. Otherwise there may be items that have a large amount of missing data, for which we can do statistical repair work in the form of weighted items. The normal distribution looks like a bell curve as in Figure 9.12 with most cases clustered around the mean.

Frequency distribution

Having entered our data, the first step in data analysis is to generate a frequency distribution. Take a look at the instructions for performing a frequency distribution in the HOW TO box.

──────────── HOW TO: Frequency distribution in SPSS ────────────

Click 'Analyze'

Click 'Descriptive Statistics'

Click 'Frequencies'

Select the desired variable from the variable list on the left, click the arrow to position it in the 'Variable Box' (the box on the right of screen)

For descriptive statistics click the 'Statistics' button on the top right

Select the 'Mean' and/or others

Click 'OK'

Bivariate and multivariate analyses

While univariate analysis has its uses, it is really at the bivariate and multivariate levels that the data really begin to give us answers to our research questions. Bivariate means two variables, multivariate more than two. It is at this level of analysis that we can make sense of DVs and IVs that are the components of our questions, theories, and the concepts in our models. It is bivariate and multivariate analyses we have in mind when we are designing surveys to measure complex concepts that we propose will be related. Surveys often require numerous measures that are at least ordinal and often interval/ratio to allow the research to best explore empirically and establish statistical relationships between them.

In **bivariate analysis** we take one IV and attempt to establish its influence on a DV through a conceptual model leading to an analytic strategy, as was flagged in Chapter 7. In SPSS or similar programs, we can do this in a variety of ways, the most common forms of which I outline below. In this section I will cover:

- Testing research questions, hypotheses, and conceptual models through analysis.
- The logic of relationships.
- Cross-tabulation and other forms of data presentation.
- Establishing a relationship.
- Assessing a relationship.

Covariance

Before we consider an example, a brief word about the logic of relationships first. It is important to appreciate that the basis of bivariate and multivariate relationships is the notion of covariance. Covariance is the phenomenon attributed to the commensurate change in variables that informs us of the possibility of a relationship between an IV and a DV. In other words, as one variable changes, or varies across its categories, so too does the other (recall independent variable dependent variable). This is what the arrows in our models indicated and what the data should show if there is a relationship. Covariance suggests a relationship, but not necessarily a causal relationship.

Testing research questions, hypotheses, and conceptual models: An example

Let's look at a classical example of a bivariate relationship that attempts to answer a research question and test a **hypothesis** and a model with survey data. Consider the conceptual model below. We have seen it before. Now it is time to put it to the test. We will do that with what is known as a cross-tabulation. Most bivariate analysis is composed through the creation of cross-tabulations, a form of analysis that you will be familiar with if you have seen a table with data, even if you have not heard of the term before. Cross-tabulations are a statistical form of the conceptual model in that there is an IV and a DV. The data in the cross-tabulation inform us whether or not our propositions and hypotheses represented by the model are supported by variations in the IV across the DV. Cross-tabulations can also be thought of as two frequency distributions woven together to display any possible changes in the DV because of or associated with the IV.

In the example below we can see the various components of survey design relevant to our example laid out and assembled ready for data analysis. We have a model with concepts, question/hypothesis, the survey questions with answer categories, and the prepared data.

_____ An Example of the Components of Survey _____
Design in a Research Problem

Research question: Does the level of education impact the level of income?
Hypothesis: The higher the level of education, the higher the income.
Model: As in Figure 9.13.

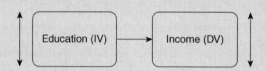

Figure 9.13   Basic conceptual model of education and income

Data/variables/indicators: World Values Study 2014

Independent: *'What is the highest educational level you have attained?'*

Answer categories and coding:

       No formal education = 1

       Incomplete primary school = 2

       Complete primary school = 3

       Incomplete secondary school: technical/vocational = 4

       Complete secondary school: technical/vocational = 5

       Incomplete secondary school: university preparatory = 6

       Complete secondary school: university preparatory = 7

       Some university-level education without degree = 8

       University-level education with degree = 9

Recoded: 1–3 = 1 'Primary school or less'

       4– 6 = 2 'Some high school'

       5–7, 8 = 3 'High school and some university'

       9 = 4 'Degree'

Dependent: 'On this card is an income scale on which 1 indicates the lowest income group and 10 the highest income group in your country. We would like to know in what group your household is. Please specify the appropriate number, counting all wages, salaries, pensions, and other incomes that come in.'

Answer categories and coding: Lower step = 1; Second step = 2; Third step = 3; Fourth step = 4; Fifth step = 5; Sixth step = 6; Seventh step = 7; Eighth step = 8; Ninth step = 9; Tenth step = 10

Recoded: 1–3 = 1 (Low)

4–6 = 2 (Middle)

7–10 = 3 (High)

The data are from the World Values Survey which is easily downloaded from the project's website. We can also presume that we have thoroughly researched the theory on economic differences and have developed and tested our questions and are satisfied with their validity and reliability. After we plug in the data we run the analyses and create a cross-tabulation. The statistics in this example are straightforward percentages.

Table 9.3   SPSS output: cross-tabulation education (recoded) and income (recoded)

| | | | \multicolumn{5}{c}{IncomeR * EDUC Cross-tabulation} | | | | |
| | | | \multicolumn{5}{c}{EDUC} | | | | |
			Primary school or less	Some high school	High school some uni	Degree	Total
IncomeR	Low	Count	8187	3771	8855	2032	22845
		% within EDUC	41.3%	28.4%	23.2%	13.3%	26.4%
	Middle	Count	8987	6748	20468	7751	43954
		% within EDUC	45.3%	50.7%	53.7%	50.7%	50.8%
	High	Count	2669	2781	8812	5504	19766
		% within EDUC	13.5%	20.9%	23.1%	36.0%	22.8%
Total		Count	19843	13300	38135	15287	86565
		% within EDUC	100.0%	100.0%	100.0%	100.0%	100.0%

What to look for? How to interpret? In our 'cross-tab' produced in SPSS (Table 9.3) we have the IV in the columns (Education level) and the DV (Income) in the rows (both have been recoded by collapsing some categories, making for a more readable and interpretable table). It is an excellent idea simply to make a rule for yourself to have the IV in the columns and the DV in the rows for all analyses. We are interested in how the different groups in the columns, that is the different educational levels, compare across the income levels in the rows. Variation, and therefore influence, is apparent when we find percentage differences across the different income levels for the different education levels (you can compare the percentages with the counts to see how percentages make more sense in establishing a relationship). So, looking across the first row ('low income') we can see that there is 41.3% of the sample with an elementary (primary) school education or less that are in this income group, compared with only 13.3% of those with at least a college or university degree. The pattern, if continued, should reveal that as we read across the rows for the higher income steps, they should include greater proportions of those with higher education levels. And that is what this table in fact displays. Compare 'low income' with 'high income', wherein only 13.3% of those with an elementary education or less are represented, compared with the 36% of those who have a degree from a university or college.

Establishing and assessing a relationship

This variation demonstrated by the percentage differences between the categories of the IV supports our hypothesis that the higher the level of education, the higher the income. Convention suggests that if there is at least a 10% difference between the categories, then we can state there is a relationship or association between the IV and the DV. While I will not demonstrate exactly how, researchers aim to assess the relationship statistically to be confident of this association, so there is a need to ask some more questions of the data that help us confirm our hypothesis and critique our conceptual model. What sort of relationship is it (that is, in what direction is the association), does education predict income, or does income predict education? How strong is it, that is how good a predicator of income is education? And is it a relationship that is likely to be observed in the broader population or, in other words, is this relationship just a product of a biased sample?

Measures of association

An important feature of the relationship between an IV and a DV is the direction and the strength of the relationship. If we can establish that there is a pattern between two variables with some basic percentage differences, we will want to know how strong it is, and in which direction it is. We can answer these questions statistically with what are called **measures of association**, which summarize the relationship. Bivariate relationships consist of various combinations of different levels of measurement, such as nominal and interval, ordinal and ordinal, and so on, and will therefore require different measures of association to account for the type of statistics that they generate. Many texts on data analysis have useful charts listing the most appropriate measures of association for the different combinations of levels of measurement. (For a concise chart for various statistics and levels of measurement for bivariate analyses see de Vaus, 2014: 291–292.)

Statistical significance and inference

Having noticed a relationship between an IV and a DV, how do we know whether or not the relationship is a result of sampling error, and therefore not generalizable to the broader population? In addition to descriptive statistics and measures of association, a bivariate relationship is often tested for statistical significance to ascertain the level of sampling error and establish inference. Statistical significance is based on the assumption that there is no relationship between the variables in the population; this is expressed as the '**null hypothesis**'.

Statistical significance is expressed by what is known as a 'p' value, or probability value. Conventionally most disciplines that use survey data accept p values, p levels or significance levels from less than 5% sampling error written as '$p = <0.05$'; this means that there is less than a 5% (5/100) chance the relationship is due to sampling error. Many relationships can also be 0.01, that is a 1% percent (1/100) or 0.001 or .01% chance or 1/1000.

Beyond cross-tabulation

There are numerous ways of performing bivariate analyses in addition to cross-tabulations. All, however, follow the same logic of covariance and the same aims of trying to establish an association or test a hypothesis or model.

Comparison of frequencies

Another bivariate example below considers the impact of gender (and specific age cohorts) on the frequency of sex over a 12-month period. The data are not presented as a classical cross-tabulation, but act like one through a comparison of frequencies, in that as the IV (gender) is differentiated, the DV changes in variation (frequency of sex). The other thing to notice about the example below is that the key IV, gender, is nominal, so it does not strictly change in terms of being higher or lower or more or less, but it does change on its own terms to the extent that gender is differentiated.

One of the most discussed patterns of the 2018 General Social Survey (for the United States) was the decline in how often Americans were having sex between 1989 and 2018. This pattern was evidenced by one variable that asked whether the respondent had had sex in the past 12 months. The overall decline (using the whole sample in the analysis) in Americans who 'had sex within the last year', is 4%, up from 19% in 1989 to 23% in 2018 according to analysis from the *Washington Post* (Ingraham, 2019). On digging a little deeper into the sample the more intrepid analysists noticed that an age-ing population may account for some of the decline, but surprisingly the main changes were with the young, young males to be precise. We can see from Figure 9.14 that in the 10-year period between 2008 and 2018 the rate of young men aged between 18 and 30 reporting that they had not had sex (in the previous 12 months) had very nearly trebled from a low of 10% in 2008 to a high of 28% in 2018. The pattern is in the same direction for young women also, but the rate of decline is not as high.

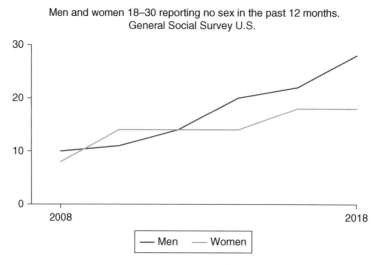

Figure 9.14 Sex and gender for younger people in the United States

Source: The General Social Survey. The General Social Survey (GSS) is a project of the independent research organization NORC at the University of Chicago, with principal funding from the National Science Foundation

This finding has generated a lot of commentary with researchers theorizing and hypothesizing why this pattern has occurred, illustrating the value and limits of bivariate analysis and how data are linked to theory in survey research. Explanations range from young men still living with their parents to their spending too much time playing video games. There are no data (yet) to substantiate any of these explana-tory claims, but a specific survey design could easily test such a theory. So, we know through bivariate analysis that there is a pattern of interest, and we may have some theories about why it has occurred but no real evidence for them. From here bivari-ate and multivariate analysis can test possible causes and influences on the pattern of interest according to various theories and propositions, providing the data allow. For example, if the GSS had measures about the extent of video game playing and whether young men of the ages of interest are still living at home with their parents.

──────────────── HOW TO: Cross-tabulation in SPSS ────────────────

Click 'Analyze'

Click 'Descriptive Statistics'

Click 'Crosstabs'

Select desired IVs and DVs from the variable list on the left. Select IV first and click the arrow to position it in the 'column', then select the DV and put it in the 'row' box

For percentages for columns, click 'cells' and then check the 'column' option in the box labelled 'Percentages'

For measures of association and inferential statistics click the 'Statistics' button on the top right

Select desired statistics

Click 'OK'

Scattergrams

Scattergrams are another attractive and efficient way of presenting bivariate analysis. One advantage a scattergram has over a cross-tabulation is that we can see instantly if there is a relationship between the IV and DVs without having to read a series of numbers due to the pattern and shape of the 'scatter' of the cases. A scattergram is composed of an X and a Y axis. In bivariate terms the X is the DV and is the horizontal axis, and the Y is the IV training up and down the vertical axis. A scattergram uses the same statistics as other bivariate analyses to assess any relationship found. Another advantage of the scattergram is that a researcher need not recode variables to perform the analyses, indeed the broader range of response codes can make a pattern clearer. Scattergrams, however, should only be performed with interval level data. In the example below it's important to note that we have used a different measure of education to the cross-tabulation above: namely, years of formal education instead of highest level of education. The measure for income is different also, namely amount per month, rather than per annum (this does not matter too much, however).

We can see clearly that as education rises (Y axis), so too does income (X axis) in Figure 9.15. Each dot in the scattergram is a respondent in the survey or case and the dots trend in a direction and form a pattern. The relationship is usefully summarized with a 'fit line' or 'trend line' that graphically and statistically summarizes the relationship. The relationship is linear and positive and the equation in the middle of the chart tells us that each year of education above the average of 11.48 years is worth an extra 570 euros per month for the French.

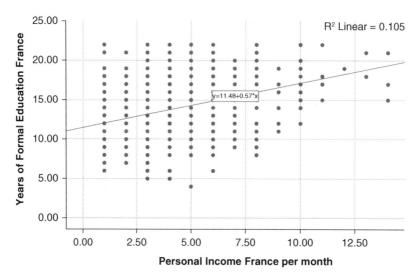

Figure 9.15 Education and income in France scattergram

Source: World Values Survey Wave 6

Comparison of means

Another form of bivariate analysis that is an abridged form of a cross-tabulation is called a comparison of means. There are a number of techniques which compare means of a variable such as income across two or more groups for the same sample, or different samples, at the same time, or at different times. For variables that have large numbers of categories such as income, an elegant way of analysing them is to use a summary measure such as a measure of central tendency and then compare it with others. Table 9.4 is a comparison of means for a measure of life satisfaction for a group of countries from the World Values Survey. Rather than present a table with a very large number of cells based on the DVs' 7-point scale of satisfaction for 22 countries, the comparison of means is easy to read and effectively conveys a lot of data, allowing a clear comparative snapshot of the variation in life satisfaction reporting across the countries.

Table 9.4 SPSS output: comparison of means

Report

Q30 Life in general: How satisfied on the whole?

Country ISO 3166 Code (see c_sample for codes for the sample)	Mean	N	Std. Deviation
AT-Austria	2.46	1199	1.009
TW-Taiwan	2.74	1953	1.108
HR-Croatia	2.83	1022	1.152

Country ISO 3166 Code (see c_sample for codes for the sample)	Mean	N	Std. Deviation
CZ-Czech Republic	2.92	1404	1.160
DK-Denmark	2.63	1018	1.011
FI-Finland	2.69	1059	1.066
FR-France	3.03	1468	1.180
HU-Hungary	3.38	1006	1.016
IS-Iceland	2.37	1368	1.192
IL-Israel	2.57	1261	1.194
JP-Japan	3.29	1568	1.361
MX-Mexico	2.84	973	1.340
NZ-New Zealand	2.64	1343	1.025
PH-Philippines	2.42	1192	1.091
RU-Russia	3.21	1514	1.205
SK-Slovak Republic	3.01	1404	.982
SI-Slovenia	2.64	1047	.955
ES-Spain	2.72	1725	1.077
SE-Sweden	2.58	1115	.940
CH-Switzerland	2.35	1066	.866
TH-Thailand	2.96	1460	1.102
GB-Great Britain and/or United Kingdom	2.77	1562	1.131
Total	2.79	28727	1.145

Source: World Values Survey Wave 6

Correlation and linear regression

Further to establishing a relationship between two variables via a cross-tabulation, scattergrams, comparing frequencies, or comparing means, researchers often use correlation analysis and linear regression to examine bivariate relationships. These techniques use more sophisticated statistics but the logic of covariance between the two variables to explore and test relationships still holds. Correlation is measured between 1 and 0 and 0 and −1. The closer to 1 or −1, the stronger the relationship, meaning that 1 or −1 explains all of why something occurs, such as education being entirely responsible for income variation. A correlation of 0.324 is moderate, meaning it certainly has influence, and it is positive (meaning that as education levels rise, so to do incomes), but there are other potential influences that may also be important in determining why income differences exist between groups. This is apparent in the correlation coefficient of 0.324 (Table 9.5) which states that education explains about 10% (0.324 squared x 100) of the variance or differences between the income groups. This point again highlights the limits of bivariate analysis. What else might be important and plausible to explain further the differences in income beyond education? A final point about correlation is the 'Sig. (2-tailed)' figure of 0.000; this means the correlation is significant and that is due to a 1 in 1,000 chance of sampling error.

Table 9.5 SPSS output: bivariate correlation of years of formal income and personal income for France

Correlations

		Years of Formal Education France	Personal Income France per month
Years of Formal Education France	Pearson Correlation	1	.324**
	Sig. (2-tailed)		.000
	N	1380	1089
Personal Income France per month	Pearson Correlation	.324**	1
	Sig. (2-tailed)	.000	
	N	1089	1176

**. Correlation is significant at the 0.01 level (2-tailed).

Source: World Values Survey Wave 6

Multivariate analysis

In this section I briefly describe some of the key details concerning multivariate analysis. **Multivariate analysis** is a suite of complex analytical procedures that allow the researcher to test numerous IVs against a DV. This level of data analysis builds on bivariate techniques through adding complexity to the analysis to test more complex conceptual models, but does so using the same analytical logic of covariance. Given the complexity of human behaviour, we can assume that there may be competing influences on why various behaviours, states, or attributes occur and are different for different cases in a sample. It is this complexity that multivariate analysis attempts to replicate so as to clarify the various strands of influence and causation. Multivariate analysis proceeds to assess how well individual items predict changes in the DV, but also how clusters of IVs predict changes in DVs through various models. Multivariate analysis needs to be planned for in the survey design phase, and this is one of the reasons that many surveys can include hundreds of questions, supplying indicators enough to allow the research to explore and test numerous influences at the analysis stage. The more complex the research questions, the more complex the conceptual model and the more items needed in the survey to perform the analysis adequately.

Types of variables used

Statistics is a dynamic discipline – there are innovations and differing interpretations about data and methods all the time, and this is a good thing. There is an interesting debate about levels of measurement and their use in various data analysis techniques among statisticians. There are similar contests about statistical significance. Conventionally, however, both bivariate and multivariate analysis of survey data follow what is known as the linear model. Survey data typically require interval-level data to perform multivariate analyses. There is an important difference between DVs in different types of multivariate analysis.

Let's take our example of education and income further as we did in Chapter 7 with a complex conceptual model (Figure 9.16). While we see that there is a relationship between education and income as judged from the bivariate analysis, there may be a range of other factors that are associated with high or low income as well. Education is one factor, but in the bivariate table above there were still proportions of people who bucked the expected trends, such as the 15% of the elementary or primary school level or lower who recorded high incomes, or the 13.3% of respondents in the degree level category who registered low incomes. While there might be a relationship between education and income, it might not explain *all* or even most of the differences between people's incomes. How might we better explain these differences? What about class backgrounds, the type of work someone does, whether they are a man or a woman, where they live, whether they have children or not, their age, their ethnicity, and various aspects of home life, in addition to their education?

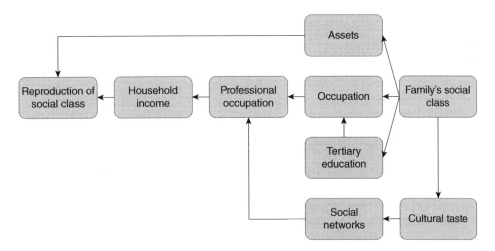

Figure 9.16 Complex conceptual model of the reproduction of social class

Recall the more complex conceptual model presented in Chapter 7 (Figure 7.9), reproduced here. Multivariate analyses consider all of these possibilities as individual items, or as clusters of items as independent models. The IVs are seen as predictors of the DV with some acting as better or stronger predictors than others, through what we call correlation coefficients (a statistic that displays the covariance between the variables). The most frequent form of multivariate analysis is called multiple regression. Below I outline the three most important multiple regression analyses used for survey data.

We can gain further insight into the development of the concepts that were high-lighted in the case studies presented in Chapter 5 also, by considering how data are used through techniques such as multivariate analysis. Dimensions, sub-dimensions, and further sub-dimensions of a concept such as poverty with 15 dimensions may have appeared to be overdoing it, but after taking analysis procedures such as multiple regression into account, it means that researchers can assess a large number of measures together and separately, and make judgements about which are the most powerful and impactful influences on states such as being in poverty. The same is true for the concepts of homelessness and middle class. The more sophisticated and differentiated the definition, and the more measures included in the survey, the more sophisticated the analysis can be.

Ordinary least squares regression

Ordinary least squares regression (OLS; I will refrain from explaining what is ordinary, least, and square about this technique) concerns the DV. If the DV is continuous, or interval (as income is), then OLS is the most appropriate form of multivariate analysis. This method is used for income, age, and other DVs that might be in the form of a scale.

Logistic regression

Logistic regression differs from OLS in that the DV is not continuous but binary: usually a variable whose response categories or whose recoding indicate a simple yes or no, high or low, has or has not. An example is whether people have voted in an election or not. The analytic logic is the same as OLS, however, in that the IVs are assessed independently or in clusters to assess their impact on the DV.

Multilevel regression

A further multivariate technique is multilevel regression, such as structural equation modelling, hierarchical linear regression, and other impressive-sounding pieces of statistical kit. The idea in multilevel regression is that you can test IVs that represent different units of analysis within the same models to ascertain which level is the better predictor, or how different levels of measurement combine to describe variation. For example, in analysing income differences, we might specify between individual-level predictors such as education level, gender, age, occupation, personality, genetics, and non-individual-level indicators such as country one lives in, household composition, community (postcode or zip code), school zone, type of school, and others.

Table 9.6 summarizes some of the most common data analysis techniques and the level of measurement for variables in a survey that are commensurate.

Table 9.6 Summary of data analysis and levels of measurement

Data analysis technique	Level of measurement of variable	Modification needed or variable requirement
Univariate		
Frequency	Nominal, ordinal, interval/ratio	
Mean	Ordinal, interval/ratio	
Median	Ordinal, interval/ratio	
Mode	Nominal, ordinal, interval/ratio	
Bivariate		
Cross-tabulation	Nominal, ordinal, interval/ratio	
Comparison of frequencies	Nominal, ordinal, interval/ratio	
Scattergram	Interval/ratio	Original coded data, not recoded data
Correlation/linear regression	Interval/ratio	Nominal and ordinal data can be converted through recoding into 'dummy variables' making ordinal variables 'interval/ratio'
Multivariate		
Ordinary least squares regression	Dependent variable is interval/ratio	Nominal and ordinal data can be converted through recoding into 'dummy variables' making ordinal variables 'interval/ratio'
Logistic regression	Dependent variable is nominal or ordinal but with only two categories such as 'yes' or 'no' (or sometimes referred to as 'dichotomous')	Nominal and ordinal data can be converted through recoding into 'dummy variables' making ordinal variables 'interval/ratio'
Multilevel regression	Dependent variable is interval/ratio	Ordinal data can be converted through recoding into 'dummy variables' making ordinal variables 'interval/ratio'

—————————————————— YOUR SURVEY ——————————————————

Preparing data for analysis

This section is concerned with how you will prepare your data in readiness for data analysis. As this is not a data analysis text and I have only suggested a few basic procedures in this chapter, I will not go into great detail about analysis here.

Choose a data analysis program to use, such as SPSS, and manually enter the data as the examples earlier in the chapter demonstrated. If your completed surveys are web based and collated automatically, then transpose the data into the data analysis software.

If you have used a mail-out and return survey or have paper surveys, mark them 1 to however many you have for a record.

(Continued)

Create names, labels, values, and record missing data for your data set in accordance with your codebook.

Enter the data, check over for data entry errors. If you have a lot of data, break up this task with team members.

Run some frequency distributions and consider how the data look – are they skewed, is there a lot of missing data, are there outliers (for example, if the question is a Likert scale from 1 to 5 and there is a 12)?

Recode relevant variables such as age, create scales or indexes (check a data analysis guide for this), and run some frequency distributions on new variables.

Begin to test some relationships proposed by your conceptual model using cross-tabulations.

Prepare a basic report, use the data for any assignments set, and present the findings to relevant parties.

Key knowledge and skills

This chapter has considered some of the most common forms of data analysis collected from surveys after data from a survey have been collected. Key knowledge and skills associated with creating a data set include the following:

- Creating a data set with the completed surveys in data analysis software such as SPSS manually or by importing a data file from another program.
- Organizing, cleaning, and preparing data in preparation for data analysis inclusive of labelling and valuing variables, entering data, checking for data entry errors, recoding, creating scales and indexes, and checking distributions of variables.
- Appreciating the relationship between question and answer formats for indicators, coding, scoring of answer categories, levels of measurement, and the types of analysis variables are suited to.
- Answering research questions, hypotheses, and testing conceptual models performed through various data analysis techniques in SPSS or similar programs.
- Bivariate and multivariate techniques of data analysis to test and establish relationships between IVs on the DVs through statistical patterns, thereby empirically answering research questions.

Further reading

There are many, many, good guides on using SPSS and other computer programs for data analysis. Two in particular, however, include sequential steps from creating a data file to more complex data analysis: Julie Pallant's *SPSS Survival Guide* is perhaps the most up-to-date, clear, and accessible SPSS user guide, but Earl Babbie et al's. *Adventures in Social Research* is similar in scope and a great resource for beginning data analysis.

Full text references:

Babbie, E., Halley, F., Wagner, W., and Zaino, J. (2016) *Adventures in Social Research: Data Analysis Using IBM SPSS Statistics* (10th edn). Los Angeles: Sage

Pallant, J. (2020) *SPSS Survival Guide* (7th edn). Melbourne: Allen & Unwin

Discover the digital resources for this chapter, including reflective questions, case studies, and templates, at https://study.sagepub.com/aarons

Ten

Pulling It All Together: A Survey Design and Survey Research Example

The aim of this chapter is to illustrate how each stage of the survey design process must be connected in order to produce quality survey data necessary for research. This chapter covers:

- How the various stages of the research process must be properly linked and applied
- How the complete survey design process is put into practice with a real example
- How to think like a survey designer

Each section of this chapter will correspond with the themes of the earlier chapters and the specific stages of the survey design process. Throughout, I will refer to the details of my scholarly example. It will help you to identify precisely each stage of the survey design process and to follow the development of the survey design via the examples. My further aim in this chapter is to help fire the survey design imagination by discussing details about the background to the research and the ways in which I developed concepts and measures, gained access to a sample, worked on the survey's administration, and considered the various limitations and errors of the research as a real-life example of survey design. Hopefully the combination of formal process and informal 'doing' or practice will inspire you to think of and frame your own projects.

For the example in this chapter, I will use my work on Australian Buddhists, aspects of which I have shared throughout the text but will more fully discuss in integrated stages here. The survey evidenced an honours year thesis as well as two publications in professional journals. The journal articles can be downloaded from the companion website and I recommend reading them as you read the chapter. Do not be too concerned if you cannot understand some of the data analysis, it is the stages of survey design and research process that are important. I hope that this is a useful and encouraging example for two reasons: (1) that you can confidently trace and recognize how the various phases of survey design are interrelated and emerge in the research; and (2) that designing a survey need not be a project that requires huge resources such as time, money, and very large samples for it to produce excellent evidence upon which good research is based.

Surveying Australian Buddhists: Perspective, context, purpose

It is important to recall that my study of Australian Buddhists was discipline specific – sociological – and that this discipline has its own discourses and concepts. You do not need to be a sociologist to understand the example in this chapter, however, as the process of developing a social survey is the same across disciplines, but we sociologists do have our own jargon that can be difficult to interpret for the uninitiated. Having stated that, I have endeavoured to explain the examples and process with as little socio-jargon as possible. The research, as you will recall from Chapter 4 on concepts, is situated within specific perspectives and theories within sociology. Contexts are also important to this research; my context here is academic or basic research. The research is not applied or relevant to any industry or policy setting, and the purpose is to explore and test through measurement some theoretical ideas in sociology. These parameters structure the way the research is pursued, and importantly how the survey design process associated with it evolved.

The topic

As the research process often begins with the deliberation of a topic, so shall this example. As you will recall, topics are broad and vague and in need of refinement. Topics are formal research areas, but also often have personal appeal to researchers. The combination of personal appeal or interest and formal area of study is true in my example. I was and still am interested in religion personally and as a social institution that impacts on how people behave. I was also interested in social change that produces different forms of social behaviour (which I also still am), as I have discussed earlier. A lot of media attention as well as sociological research had gone into the changing nature of religious affiliations in western countries such as Australia during the last quarter of the twentieth century and into this one. That people in these societies were searching for alternative spiritualities to the established religions in them was becoming an increasingly important phenomenon and meaningful topic in sociology, as it had to some extent in psychology and religious studies.

Modern social life has allowed all kinds of opportunities for social and cultural change for many people. The rise of leisure, cheap travel, and cultural traffic of ideas and philosophies are a key part of contemporary religious searching. Many thousands of westerners have travelled to Asian countries in search of something as well as a holiday. They have also read widely, attended workshops, done yoga, and listened reverently to figures such as the Dalai Lama. Western societies have also seen their traditional cultural and social institutional moors loosened. Individuals have not felt compelled to follow certain social or cultural traditions such as belonging to a religion, where in previous ages they did as something quite natural and expected from family and community. There was a widely held belief and solid prediction that what we know as the west would shrug off religion and spirituality as a childish superstition belonging to another time. Yet for many the search for some kind of spiritual meaning continued.

One of the main forms of this change was the increase in the proportions of Australians (as well as Americans, British, and Europeans) who were becoming or taking a serious (and not so serious) interest in 'alternative' spiritualities from the 'east'. This was anecdotal, impressionistic, as well as an empirical pattern (as indicated by the national census). There was not a lot of research on western interest in specific forms of alternative religions in sociology, but quite a lot on this kind of religious and spiritual change in these societies. As a topic, it really began to gel in my mind that what was little researched in a specific sense and also of increasing popular and scholarly interest could be an interesting and timely project.

The topic needed further refining. Who, where, and what about a western turn 'eastwards' was I going to study? On a personal level, I was one of those people who were searching along with the multitude of others. I dabbled a bit in Buddhist meditation, took courses in religious philosophies, and attended a Buddhist Centre in the community where I was studying. These confluences both personal and scholarly, at a certain time and in a certain place, helped form the topic of my honours dissertation and the research that flowed from it.

Refining the topic

From these broad social and cultural changes, I focused on western interest in Buddhism. It was a timely choice. The Dalia Lama had visited Australia in 1996 and I went along to a packed stadium to hear him talk. Martin Scorsese had directed the lavish biopic about him called *Kundun*. Celebrities such as Richard Gere were constantly in the media discussing their Buddhism. Buddhism had captured the imagination of the arts world also: the National Gallery of New South Wales had an enormous exhibition of Buddhist and Hindu artefacts that ran for some months. Not far from Sydney in a place called Wollongong, a huge Buddhist Centre was being built to be a centre of pilgrimage. There was also an active and well-established group of Buddhists right where I was.

I was interested certainly in why Australians were embracing Buddhism, but as a sociological study I was not interested in the specifically personal circumstances of Australian Buddhists, as much as the social and cultural conditions that might have produced them – and if there were any patterns to how this group behaved that could be linked to various social changes and group attributes. As a religion that was 'displaced' in the sense of it being transplanted to a new context, I was also interested in how these Buddhists practised this religion, and what of it they believed and did not believe, given that some tenets of the religion are at odds with some western worldviews and ways of living. These were important considerations, because Buddhism in the Australian context, as it might be in a British, European, or American one, represents a very different cultural and social context to that in Thailand, Tibet, or Sri Lanka.

Previous research

What has been done before, and how might it guide what you want to do now? For me these were questions that had no answer, yet many answers. There was precious little previous research in sociology on westerners, such as the Australians I was interested in, becoming Buddhists or engaging with Buddhism. Certainly nothing group orientated or quantitative from a survey, outside of the census, and the census did not offer much other than head counts. There was plenty of popular interest as I have mentioned. There were also plenty of journalistic accounts of individuals who had taken up Buddhism or had practised forms of Buddhist meditation, and some autobiographical experiences of individuals who had converted to Buddhism or incorporated Buddhism into their religious identities. There was a history of Buddhism in Australia (Croucher, 1989) that outlined some of the broad social changes such as immigration since the 1970s, and the take-up of Buddhism and Buddhist practice by some westerners who had travelled to places such as Nepal, Thailand, and India, but scant substantive sociology. This left me daunted, but also excited because I could attempt to fill in a gap in the research.

Sociology of religion in general, however, was a major sub-discipline with countless signposts pointing to how I might think about doing this research. The literature in the sociology of religion at that time had some major themes that resonated with my topic. Among them was a theme called 'new religious movements' that was characterized by changing religious identities and practices, the decline of traditional institutional religions in the west, individualism, and alternative spiritualities consistent with what I have described above about western social and cultural change. The 'new religious movements' work seemed to frame what I was interested in quite well as various studies described and attempted to explain this form of social and cultural change. The literature in the sociology of religion was also replete with numerous studies over time that measured key concepts such as religious identity, belief, and practice.

Why a survey?

In Chapter 1 we considered why researchers used surveys. What kind of data can we collect and what kind of research do we produce from using a survey? Very common in my discipline is research based on similar topics to mine that relies on a range of qualitative interviews with people to grasp what meanings, experiences, and motivations are behind a social phenomenon. This way of enquiry produces very interesting and scientifically valid research and reaches into the more personal experiences and meanings of individuals in specific social contexts. For many this is the best way to understand certain aspects of human behaviour.

For many it is topics such as this that cry out for qualitative research into the various meanings people give for profound life changes such as converting to or engaging in a religious tradition. Indeed, some of my lecturers were somewhat incredulous that I wanted to and then had collected survey data on such a topic, one that was usually seen as best understood with qualitative data providing rich description and nuanced interpretation. But I was thinking of asking different questions to those that require answering with qualitative data, and the project had different aims than to try and understand personal meaning and motivation.

There were three principal scholarly reasons why I choose a survey to collect data for this project, and one instrumental reason. Firstly, I wanted to collect data about a whole group and capture the social background composition of Australian Buddhists and determine if any social pattern to Buddhist identity existed. Were these people middle class, were they mostly women or men? What level of education did they possess? What jobs did they do etc.? Essentially, I wanted to know who was a Western Buddhist? Secondly, I wanted to benchmark quantitatively Buddhist practice, belief, and identity in a non-traditional context, for a whole group, and not for just a few individuals. This would inform how new religious movements were structured. How committed are Buddhists to Buddhism? And how does one practise Buddhism in modern Australia? Thirdly, I was also interested in the relationships between these components, as my models below show, and to test the various theories that attempted to explain the rise of interest in such religions.

There was not anything known about the social backgrounds and cultural experiences of people who were interested in Buddhism, beyond Hollywood celebrities such as Richard Gere, so there was a chance to produce new knowledge about a relatively new sociological phenomenon. Nothing was said, in scholarly circles at least, about how these Buddhists practised this religion in a non-traditional Buddhist country such as Australia, or to what extent people felt they belonged or had incorporated Buddhism into their identities. Survey research into these questions (not for Buddhism, however) has a long tradition also and produced very reliable data evidencing various patterns.

For these reasons, manifesting as my research questions and conceptual models, I decided that a survey was the best methodology to collect the data required. There were other benefits to using a survey that presented solutions to problems between researcher and researched and resources. Using a survey, I contended, could also produce data that the Buddhists themselves could use, which they did to improve access to events run by the Buddhist Centre. I felt this was a way of exercising ethical and reflective research practice. Moreover, I could attempt to overcome the practical problems of the honours year of time and money by designing a survey and collecting a lot of useful data inexpensively and quickly and have a unique and useful data set on an area of sociological research that was gaining a lot of interest. Finally, I was interested in developing my skills in survey research and data analysis, which have proven beneficial for my career thus far.

Research questions

After refining the topic of 'eastern religions and western societies' to considering Australian Buddhists, my research questions were in line with the reasons I chose a survey to collect the data I needed to do the research. In line with what we have covered in Chapter 3, I was interested in groups, and also interested in quantifying experiences such as how often these Buddhists meditated and how often they read texts. For the purposes of the thesis I posed some general exploratory research objectives, as follows.

How do Australians practise Buddhism? To what extent are Australian Buddhists committed to Buddhist practices and beliefs? Do Australians identify with Buddhism much like the consumerist and New Age models in the literature suggest? Is attraction to Buddhism for Australians anything to do with a problematic western identity?

From these basic questions that the survey data addressed in my honours thesis, my supervisor helped me focus on the most interesting and sociologically valuable findings to evidence two research papers that were eventually published in very good sociology journals. The first paper, called *'Choosing Buddhism in Australia: Towards a Traditional Style of Reflexive Spiritual Engagement'*, was a broad report on the religiosity of Australian Buddhists with a strong focus on the style of engagement, that is how Australians practised Buddhism and incorporated it into their identities. Did they engage with it as the New Age and new religious movements theories had suggested? Using a survey enabled the research credibly to test a leading theoretical strand in the sociology of religion at the time. The second paper, *'Looking East: An Exploratory Analysis of Western Disenchantment'*, was a more focused analysis on the notion of interest in Buddhism being associated with a questioning of western identity. This paper aimed more at an explanation of why individuals might be interested in Buddhism from the perspective of large-scale social change. The research for both papers was refined to produce key questions and hypotheses appropriate for survey design, as Chapter 4 describes.

In 'Choosing Buddhism' general research objectives were pursued such as:

1 *What spiritual style characterizes people who choose to engage with Buddhism? A New Age approach or a traditional style?*
2 *For those who are more orientated towards a traditional style, how important are social factors in patterning commitment?*

In 'Looking East' two hypotheses were considered:

1 *Those individuals involved in an eastern religion will be more disenchanted with a western vision of self-identity than individuals in general.*
2 *Among individuals who are involved in eastern religion, the highest levels of disenchantment with a western vision of self-identity will be found among the most deeply engaged.*

Theoretical frameworks

My research questions, as are any research questions, were connected to theoretical frameworks that are employed sociologically to explain empirical patterns. The patterns

I was aiming to identify and measure with my survey data were religious practice, belief, and identity of Australian Buddhists. The key theoretical framework relevant to this research was what I had dug up in the literature: principally the theories on 'new religious movements' including the rise of the 'New Age', patterns of individualization, the decline of traditional religious institutions, globalization, and the emergence of multiple religious identities in conditions of profound social change. This line of theorizing stated that picking and choosing religions in the west had become commonplace due to their availability and transmission through cultural, communicative, and economic networks. The 'New Age' had become a consumerist experience wherein people bought and sold religious traditions like groceries and, once used for a certain purpose, they were then thrown away. Terms such as 'spiritual supermarket' (Roof, 1999) characterized how researchers thought about the changes and their impact on the religious lives of individuals in western societies. What emerged from this body of work was a fundamental question about the style or type of engagement with Buddhism that could be evidenced from the survey data.

In a similar vein, sociology of religion also theorized about how religious institutions work to attract and retain adherents and sell their 'products' to potential 'customers'. Religions were as much a commodity as anything else, and people 'bought' and 'sold' them in a 'market', often depending on what they were looking for. So, there was a consumerist behaviour model that might explain why Australians were becoming Buddhists, which was called 'rational choice theory', after the economic behaviour model. The Buddhist Centre I attended was active in matching want and need with product along these lines. It was very active in attracting funds for projects, dynamic in extolling the virtues of Buddhism for busy, tired, and stressed urban lives, and presented Buddhism quite distinctly as an alternative to other forms of religion and spirituality.

Another theoretical framework that proved to be relevant to westerners engaged in Buddhism was around personal identity and the nature of 'eastern' society. The classical German sociologist Max Weber theorized a general mind set termed 'disenchantment'. For Weber, as society became more and more rational and efficiently planned (like many western societies had come to be), things became more certain but less 'magical', less effervescent, and less engaging, resulting in a kind of mechanical and unreflective dullness. Religions among other things could become institutions of re-enchantment, especially where science, rationality, and materialism could not explain or satisfy areas of life that individuals felt were important and meaningful. Weber's theory was a general theory, but the personal literature of westerners having a new lease on life as a result of finding and engaging with Buddhism could represent something important for understanding the growth of western interest in Buddhism.

The theoretical frameworks for this research were used in a combination of deductive and inductive data theory procedures. I wanted to test whether the more commodified and throw-away aspects of the 'new religious movement' held for Australian Buddhists.

I also wanted to test Weber's idea around disenchantment, although that idea was a variation on a theme and came later. And I wanted to benchmark Australian Buddhist identity, practice, and belief.

By now hopefully you will have some idea of how this process of clarification and refinement works in the mind of a researcher, a very junior one in my case at that time. How topics arise, how they are refined, how life and circumstance can influence ideas, the rationale behind a survey, and the kinds of questions it can answer, work in the mind of a survey researcher and inspire survey design. I think all researchers are slightly different in how they might come to their research ideas in survey research, but they more or less do the same things as I have described to this point. Some steps might be in different order, but the process of descending the ladder of abstraction aims at the same outcomes. Below I discuss the process and work of operationalizing concepts and measurement leading to the design of the survey and the collection of the data.

Concepts, dimensions, and indicators

Having refined my topic, distilled some key research questions, decided on a survey, and identified some relevant theoretical frameworks, the next step was to identify and clarify the concepts I needed to measure. The bulk of the clarification and operationalization work here was around the concept of religion, and more precisely Buddhism. In addition to religion I identified a chorus of additional concepts that were relevant to the research but common to social surveys and easily operationalized, such as personal identity, social background, and demographic attributes.

The key challenge for this survey was to clarify and operationalize religion by considering 'western' Buddhism as a dimension of it, which had not been done before. Here I confess to perhaps many forms of possible measurement error and accept the limitations of the survey method. If other researchers were to attempt to measure Buddhist identity, practice, and belief, I have no doubt that there would be some sharp criticism of the measures that I have employed in the research, despite the deep thought and consultation that went into the operationalization of these concepts. That is a natural part of research. No one has to this point, so I am the expert for now!

Measuring religion in a survey, however, has been done many times before and entails numerous dimensions. There were four dimensions that I found to be relevant as discerned from the literature upon which I modelled my research. The first was religion itself, a definition for which I really was not going to bother with, but there was a crucial sub-dimensional aspect to the concept of religion here. I had to consider the specific type of Buddhism that the Buddhist Centre practised and adhered to, somewhat displaced and transmitted from its traditional context as it was. Buddhism as an institution is as diverse, complex, and elaborate a religion as any of the other major faiths, and its practices, beliefs, and traditions are well established within various cultural and ethnic contexts that relate its manifold varieties. I was not measuring Buddhist identity, practice, and belief essentially but some variation or specification of them, in a place that was very different from where Buddhism had traditionally taken root as an institution. As a philosophical aside there is a school of thought that suggests Buddhism is not a religion at all, but more like an 'ethical philosophy'. Defining religion is really very difficult, and to some extent counterproductive, so I simply treated it like a religion and attributed to it the dimensions that other sociologists had identified with religions such as Christianity. Hence my point about limitations and possible measurement error.

The second dimension was identity. That is, is someone religious? If so, what religion(s) do they identify with? People can be 'interested' in a religion but not feel they belong to it; similarly they can belong to one formally but not really be that active within it. This was a really important dimension in the light of the theory of 'eastern' religions such as Buddhism in western contexts as essentially consumer items that most people picked up and put down when it suited them, against the usual trend of a religious identity lasting a lifetime. Religious identity in western societies could be multiple. There is nothing stopping someone from identifying with as many religions as they desire. Religious identity has relative strength such as being formally accepted into a religious community or organization through an initiation, ceremony, or formal ritual of some sort acknowledged by the community, or was religious identity merely self-identification? Religious identity could be formal but weak, informal but strong, formal and strong, informal and weak.

The next concept was religious practice or religiosity, sometimes also stated as 'commitment', that is what one does as a member of a religious group, day to day, week to week, or year to year, and how often do they do what they do? In Christian, Jewish, or Muslim terms, this is how often one prays, attends religious services, reads religious texts, fasts, goes on pilgrimage, and/or does whatever the religion requires them to do at whatever rate they are required to do it. What do Buddhists do? What do lay Buddhists do? What do lay Australian Buddhists do who also do school runs, coach football, work in hardware stores and hospitals, and who mow their lawns and feed their cats, apart from what Buddhist monks and nuns do? How do they practise, and to what extent do they practise? Religious practice is not just about what, but to what extent. Practice or doing can also be strong or weak, high or low, a lot or not a lot. These considerations give us a way to measure more or less commitment or engagement. Measuring religious practice in the sociology of religion has reflected a mostly Christian institutional model, with church attendance, prayer, and scriptural reading as key dimensions. I have developed the concept of Buddhist spiritual practice from this model. To some extent religions are the same in that their adherents display general patterns of religious action. To what extent my operationalization of the concept in a Buddhist context is valid and reliable is somewhat unknown, but what Buddhists actually practise is not necessarily a great mystery.

Next is belief: what do religious adherents believe about their religion and what their religion teaches them about the relationship with the wider world, themselves, and other people? This is usually within the confines of the religious philosophical or doctrinal system itself. All of the great religious traditions have teachings and doctrines that instruct the faithful, and which they should believe to be considered fully integrated into the religious group and worthy of whatever rewards or benefits the religion bestows. Religious belief is never usually black and white, however, and surveys have shown that many religious people do not always believe everything that they are required to by their religions. Was it the same for Australian Buddhists, given the theory that the western engagement with Buddhism is perhaps not formal or binding and more consumerist and fluid? What indeed were these Buddhists supposed to believe? And do they believe what they are supposed to? Belief is again another way of measuring commitment, engagement, or involvement as it also can be thought of as strong and weak, high and low, or more or less. Clarifying a concept such as Buddhist belief requires some knowledge of Buddhism, which I have, without being an expert. Buddhism as I have stated is a complex and intricate religion and the beliefs associated with it reflect this. Adding to this is the fact that there are many different kinds of Buddhism. There are some forms of Buddhist belief, however, that are central to all forms, from which I was able to produce measures.

These were the core concepts associated with the religion I was interested in. They do follow a model of previous research into religions that are not Buddhism. Their clarification was attempted by reading, discussions, and experience, however, an immersion in the context hopefully lent some insight into how to measure some important dimensions of engagement with Buddhism. You will notice that in the research papers that used the data my co-author and I change the names of these concepts slightly, but they are still the same and use the same measures. In the papers we write about 'commitment', 'engagement', and 'involvement' (different ways of saying religious identity, practice, and belief); we also discuss concepts such as 'multiplicity' and 'reconstruction' with regards to religious identity, practice, and belief. I also measured some other concepts that were much easier to clarify and operationalize. They appear below.

Self-identity

Self-identity was a concept operationalized through relating what people considered important to their own sense of self. Components of self-identity are key aspects of self, pertinent to the notion of living in a western society. There are numerous dimensions to self-identity such as economic, political, familial, and cultural.

Disenchantment

Disenchantment was operationalized as disenchantment with a western identity. This concept was not measured directly but something of a latent concept realized through implication by the negative responses to some of the items that measured self-identity.

Social background

Social background entailed what we call the 'usual suspects' and included what are known as achieved and ascribed attributes such as: gender, age, educational levels, occupation, income, and political persuasion.

Conceptual models

Conceptual models for both papers were quite simple and a modified version of them are presented here which accurately represents the mechanism behind the research in both papers. The conceptual models are not included in the research papers, but implied. The reasoning behind them is adequately described in the papers, however.

For 'Choosing Buddhism' (Figure 10.1) we were not really investigating sets of relationships between variables, with the exception of explaining whether those who indicated a traditional style of engagement with Buddhism was due to social factors. Rather the aim was to establish whether a form of behaviour existed – traditional religious style – against what a lot of the theory had suggested.

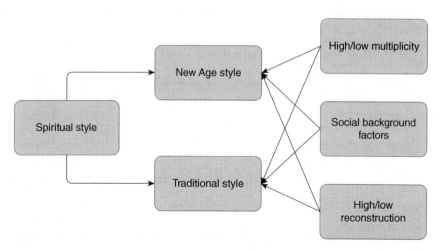

Figure 10.1   Conceptual model for 'Choosing Buddhism'

In 'Looking East' (Figure 10.2) the heart of the research was the pursuit of relationships between variables to investigate theories associated with contemporary religious and spiritual identity, such as a variation of Max Weber's concept of disenchantment. These relationships were not proposed as causal but we suggested they were correlated. The models are constructed with the quantitative research in mind that suggests that as one variable changes, so too does the other: the more disenchanted, the more involved, for example.

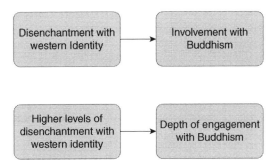

Figure 10.2   Conceptual model for 'Looking East'

Operationalization

Having identified and attempted to clarify the core concepts that were relevant to my research questions and emerging models, I then had to develop indicators for inclusion in the survey that would measure these concepts. Below I describe how I operationalized the concepts I was interested in and list the indicators that I eventually used in the survey.

Measurement error, reliability, and validity

A crucial aspect of survey design common to all surveys is measurement error, reliability, and validity. There are no guarantees that I have avoided measurement error in my survey of Australian Buddhists. I had little time or resources to run a pilot study; the questions were not the subject of cognitive interviewing either. I had little feedback therefore from potential respondents as to whether they understood the questions. Leaving aside concepts such as identity, social background, and disenchantment, which were all operationalized using tried and true measures, the main concepts that the survey attempted to measure, and measure for the first time, were at some risk of being invalid and unreliable. However, the survey was made available to select members of the Buddhist Centre primarily in accordance with the demands of the ethics application, but also for the consideration of the leaders of the Buddhist Centre to affirm the content of specific practices and beliefs that the Centre taught or were fundamental to Buddhism and confirmed by them. The members of the Buddhist Centre were not experts in survey design, but they knew a lot more than me about Buddhism. This was my attempt to limit measurement error and make some effort towards establishing reliability and validity for these measures. Further research, comparison, and better preparation would enable the measurement of these concepts to evolve.

Religious identity (engagement/involvement)

The survey included five questions to measure religious identity. Two pertained to how one sees oneself in religious terms, at one time before the respondent encountered Buddhism, and at the time of completing the survey. These questions aimed to measure whether or not a respondent had changed their religious identity from something else or nothing to Buddhism, or had remained whatever they were after being involved with Buddhism. Another question asked how important Buddhism was to how they saw themselves, and two more that were aimed to measure a formal commitment to Buddhism and a measure of potential life commitment.

1 *Before developing your interest in Buddhism at this time, what was your religious preference?*
2 *What is your religious preference?*
3 *Have you ever been initiated as a Buddhist?*
4 *Have you ever seriously considered the possibility of becoming a [Buddhist] monk or nun in the future?*
5 *How important is Buddhism in describing how you see yourself?*

Questions 1 and 2 were open ended, questions 3 and 4 offered yes and no as answers, and question 5 was a Likert scale format: *1, very important; 2, fairly important; 3, not very important; 4, not at all important.*

Religious belief (engagement/commitment)

This proved to be a challenging concept to develop indicators for, given the complex and intricate nature of Buddhist belief; however, there are central tenets of Buddhism that all forms of Buddhism acknowledge as fundamental to identifying with and practising Buddhism. The first of these is called the Four Noble Truths and the second is the Eight-fold Path. Each of these teachings contains propositions that a Buddhist perhaps should agree with. These might be thought of as similar to the Nicene Creed or the Ten Commandments familiar to a more formal identity as a Christian. In addition to these doctrines there are other aspects of Buddhist philosophy such as reincarnation and impermanence that are also key aspects of the Buddhist worldview and teachings that may be challenging or at least unfamiliar to western adherents.

I laid out a range of ordinal measures for the Four Noble Truths. The question wordings were taken from an English translation of a Buddhist text.

The answer categories were: *1, fully agree; 2, partly agree; 3, don't agree; 4 don't know.*

1   *Do you agree that all life is filled with suffering and unsatisfactoriness?*
2   *Do you agree that the cause of such suffering is craving, desire, and a thirst for pleasure and existence that leads to rebirth?*
3   *This cause then can be eliminated by the cessation of craving and desire, and the cultivation of non-attachment?*
4   *The path or way that leads to the cessation of suffering is the Noble Eight-fold Path?*

For the eight questions measuring how important respondents thought the various components of the Eight-fold Path, the answer categories were a Likert scale adapted to measure level of importance rather than agreement: *1, very important; 2, fairly important; 3, not very important; 4, not at all important; 5, not applicable.*

1   *To have the right views or beliefs accepting the Four Noble Truths, and the impermanence of existence?*
2   *To have the right attitude, favouring the goal of renunciation, goodwill, and harmlessness?*
3   *To practise the right speech, avoiding lying, slander, and gossip?*
4   *To practise the right conduct or bodily action upholding moral discipline?*
5   *To practise the right livelihood that avoids work that harms sentient beings?*
6   *To develop the right effort or motivation to follow the path?*
7   *To develop the right mindfulness, involving self-awareness of body, feelings, and thoughts?*
8   *To develop the right concentration or meditation leading to wholeness of mind?*

These questions carry some potential measurement errors, and some of them are technically double and even triple barrelled. There were two reasons I did not divide them into a series of sub-questions. Firstly, their core is concerned with a single aspect of behaviour extolled by Buddhist teachings such as speech, livelihood, effort, and mindfulness. These core attributes are singular and capture the essence of the belief; what comes after them are mere examples that are repeated often, although there are variations. While these are core teachings common to many forms of Buddhism, they are also complex and what they actually mean is the subject of much debate; this is common to many religious teachings from any religious tradition. To some extent belief, however, is predicated not necessarily on complete understanding of what a teaching suggests, but a measure of faith that they are the right way to act or be, irrespective of their precise meaning. Such are the challenges of clarifying and operationalizing a concept such as religious belief! These questions were merely my way of measuring some aspects of Buddhist beliefs in a survey. Other researchers may have other ways of attempting this, based on their knowledge of the religion and what they think to be important. This is how survey research progresses, and part of the challenge of survey design. Secondly, to some extent there was a practical consideration of breaking up this module of questions which would extend the survey into many more questions, potentially making the survey less tolerable and more confusing to respondents.

Religious practice (engagement/commitment)

The next challenge was to design a series of items that would measure Buddhist practice, or Buddhist religiosity. Much like the complexity of belief, what stands as practising or 'doing' Buddhism is multilayered and detailed. Further, given the many different forms of Buddhism, there exist many different forms of practice, all held as legitimate. Here I was led by the Buddhist Centre and designed the questions on what the Centre offered and suggested to members about practising, which were mostly basic practices for a lay community of people and not specialized and more complex practices associated with more professional (monks and nuns) or experienced Buddhists. A point here concerning validity is important. Operationalizing Buddhist practice from the Buddhist Centre's programme and suggestions may compromise the validity of the measures used to operationalize this concept because they may not reflect practices of other Buddhist traditions. However, the measures are mostly general and not specific, so I would argue that they could be claimed as valid. Again, more research, more debate, greater testing, and more progress. These practices had two sub-dimensions: *personal*: meditation, ethical practices, study; and *communal*: participation in the activities of the Buddhist Centre.

Personal:

Meditation

How often, if at all, do you meditate?

1 Everyday; 2 Once a week; 3 About once a month; 4 Several times a year; 5 Never

Do you have a statue of the Buddha in your home?

1 Yes; 2 No

Do you use the statue to help you meditate?

1 Yes; 2 No

Ethical practices

How often do you eat meat?

1 Never; 2 Occasionally; 3 Regularly

How often do you drink alcohol?

1 Never; 2 Occasionally; 3 Regularly

Study

Here is a list of different types of reading material which you might come across in the course of advancing your understanding of Buddhism. Could you please circle the number which indicates how often you read the following type of material about Buddhism.

Magazine articles

Introductory books

Advanced books

Sutras (Buddhist scriptures)

1 Every day; 2 Once a week; 3 About once a month; 4 About once a year; 5 Never

Communal:

Have you ever participated in a meditation retreat at the Buddhist Centre?

1 Yes; 2 No

Are you a financial member of the Buddhist Centre?

1 Yes; 2 No

Do you do any voluntary work at the Buddhist Centre?

1 Yes; 2 No

When Buddhist teachers are visiting the Buddhist Centre how often do you attend their teachings?

1 Always; 2 Occasionally; 3 Never

How often do you take part in the weekly activities run by the Buddhist Centre?

1 Every week; 2 Occasionally; 3 Hardly ever; 4 Never

Self-identity

Numerous social surveys ask respondents what they consider to be important in describing who they are and how they see themselves. You do not have to reinvent the wheel for every concept. The following questions I drew from previous surveys on identity. They are ordinal measures that use a Likert-type scale.

The questions took on the same format for each aspect of self-identity: *How important is...in describing how you see yourself?*

The answer categories were: *1, very important; 2, fairly important; 3, not very important; 4, not at all important; 5, not applicable*

Personal identity was further divided into sub-dimensions including:

- Nation/community/political: *Australia, the state (such as Victoria), the town or district, political party*
- Personal details: *age, ethnicity, gender, family*
- Economic identity: *occupation, professional association, social class, trade union*
- Leisure: *sporting club*

Disenchantment

From these measures of self-identity five were chosen in line with the literature on western identity to measure the latent variable disenchantment with western identity: *Australian, Political party, Ethnicity, Gender, Age.*

Open-ended questions

I offered some open-ended questions throughout the survey, but at the end of the survey I left a blank page for respondents to comment on the survey or give any of their thoughts about their experiences of Buddhism. My supervisor suggested I should do this as it is good practice. So, I did. Usually many respondents do not take up the offer to respond because by the end of a survey the last thing they may want to do is contribute to an optional question. However, I received a lot of very interesting comments, some about the survey and some about the Buddhist Centre, but most about the impact Buddhism had had on the lives of the respondents to that point. Some comments were accompanied by multi-page letters that gave me a privileged insight into how Buddhism was a transformative experience for some people and gave their lives profound meaning after a period of personal trauma and confusion. Some of these comments became valuable qualitative data informing the study about the nature of engagement with Buddhism. Importantly some of these data gave me a space to think about the human stories informing the research.

Sample

Gaining access

The sample for my study was a specialized one. It was an open group in terms of participation, but also a group with a hierarchy, governance, and various forms of power that decided how people belonged. Most groups with whatever purpose are the same. I could have simply written to the Buddhist Centre and asked it if I could survey its members, but groups are not so trusting of strangers, and ethically it would have been highly problematic. I had to gain access to the group.

I mentioned earlier that I dabbled in Buddhist meditation. I did, and I did before I thought of the idea of studying Australian Buddhists as a part of my honours year in sociology. Most Wednesday nights at a church hall in the town where I was studying, for about six months before my honours year, I went along and listened to a Buddhist monk (himself an Australian of Jewish heritage who used to be a doctor) give talks on Buddhist themes, and then he would guide us in meditation for around an hour. The class was small, warm, and friendly, and the sessions were very interesting. The sessions were run by a local Buddhist Centre as a part of its community engagement. At the same time, I was taking undergraduate courses in the philosophy of religion, and Buddhist and Hindu teachings were a very interesting part of the curriculum.

Over the weeks I attended the meditation sessions I learned a lot and enjoyed the sessions very much. Towards the end of that year I had it in my mind that I would like to study the Buddhist Centre's members for the purposes of the project. I came to know the director of the Centre quite well and discussed the idea with him. I then sent a formal letter to him and the other members of the council that managed the Buddhist Centre explaining the study and its purposes for their consideration. After reviewing my request, they were happy for me to have access to the Centre and its members as the focus for my honours study. Later, when I had worked out that I wanted to use a survey, they commended me and the survey to their members as a project worthy of their time and consideration. I had gained access to the group and could go on to collect the data, upon approval from the university ethics committee.

The sample for my study entailed the whole population of a Buddhist Centre, but it was not representative of the wider population of Australian Buddhists, because I had not sampled the many other Buddhist Centres that exist in Australia, or individuals who might be Buddhist but had no affiliation to a group. Not being representative was not a major disadvantage in one sense, though I had to exercise caution over the interpretation of the results and their generalizability. The Centre assisted in sending out the surveys using the addresses from their database, ensuring confidentiality and anonymity. From memory the total sampling frame was over 400 individuals, from which 333 were chosen. I received 169 completed returns, a response rate of just over 50%, which was a pleasing result given the survey mode.

Survey mode

The survey mode was mail-out and return. I was a poor honours year student and the internet was only in its infancy. There was an intense labour of survey administration to make my timelines after I had designed the survey and completed my other coursework as a part of my honours year. The survey's look and feel were not aesthetically pleasing ones, but a pretty dull MS Word document, truth be told, with grid box questions all down the pages. Resources were a restraint on the look of the survey, so I went with a staid but clear black and white interface. However, the pages were not crowded with questions, and question and answer formats were clear. The questions were arranged in an order that reflected the concepts so that they were banked together; this gave respondents some clarity about what the survey was trying to achieve. In order to get the survey out, give respondents a chance to complete it, and return it via mail in time for me to construct the data set and get moving with the analysis and write up, I had a very intense few days of printing, collating, packing, and delivering. I spent one night photocopying until around 1.30 a.m., and friends helped me carry a few boxes containing the loose sheets of the surveys back to my accommodation afterwards. The survey was around 14 pages long. I spent another day stapling the pages together, gathering return envelopes, and collating the introductory letters. Friends assisted with packing the 300-odd envelopes with a copy of the survey, an introductory letter, and a return envelope. Once that was all done, I delivered the surveys to the Buddhist Centre who then affixed the names and addresses of its members to the envelopes and posted them out.

Data administration

In the next couple of weeks after the surveys had been sent out they began to return with their precious cargo. I had no time to post follow-up surveys, but I had received a good response rate. Most surveys were returned within two weeks; after four weeks there were few and then no more returned surveys, although I did receive one or two in November after my thesis had been submitted, too late for the thesis but they could be added to the sample for the articles. I have no idea why they suddenly appeared. As soon as they came in, I began constructing the data set in SPSS, as the previous chapter demonstrated. After entering the data manually, checking for data entry errors, and preparing my data I was in a position to begin the analysis.

Data analysis and research outputs

In this final section I will not discuss the honours thesis, but the two professional research papers that were evidenced using the survey data. The research papers distilled the key findings of the thesis and framed them more precisely around key debates in the sociology of religion literature. Here I am aiming to show how survey design is applied to the final product, an output of research, and without going into the technical specifics of data analysis techniques. In doing so I also aim to relate how using a survey and the way it was designed allowed me to make a meaningful, if modest, contribution to this area of the sociology of religion. What you should notice about the survey design and the analysis after reading the two papers is the flexibility of the data: that is, using data in various ways to answer the questions. This is a really interesting aspect of quantitative data collection that I feel to be something of a hidden feature of survey design.

'Choosing Buddhism'

We chose an analytic strategy that allowed us to best answer the research questions and illustrate our models. In 'Choosing Buddhism' we used univariate, bivariate, and multivariate techniques and also a wide selection of data for various aspects of the paper (Table 10.1).

Table 10.1   Data and analysis for 'Choosing Buddhism'

	Univariate		Bivariate	Multivariate
Variables	Practice	Belief	As for univariate	Latent variable: 'high commitment'
	Meditation	Four Noble Truths		
	Reading	Eight-fold Path		
	Initiation	Reincarnation		Some social background measures
		Impermanence		Age, income, occupation, education
	Demographic			
Format	Original		Collapsed/ recoded	Recoded into dummy variables
			Scaled	Dependent variable nominal
Techniques	Frequency distributions		Cross-tabulations	Logistic regression
	Recoding			
Use	Description of the sample		Reveal different levels of commitment	To measure a range of independent variables against the dependent variable
	Distribution of identity, practice, and belief		To create variables to test whether commitment was socially structured	To test if high commitment was socially patterned
	Distribution of Buddhist identity types			
Result	The analysis established the finding that the sample was traditional in religious style and not New Age as the theories suggested		Variation in commitment and development of latent variable for multivariate analysis	Buddhism mostly middle class and no social factors were found associated to different levels of commitment

Univariate analysis allowed us to consider the characteristics of the sample and the distributions of key variables, such as Buddhist identity, practice, and belief, that measured the concepts of engagement and style. Univariate techniques convinced us that most of the sample were identifying and practising Buddhism not in a New Age style as the theories suggested, but via a more traditional style.

Bivariate analyses allowed us to continue to investigate this notion of traditional style v. New Age style by combining sets of variables and concepts: the two key areas of Buddhist practice, matched with Buddhist belief. We combined these two key concepts and created an index, and this allowed us to find sub-samples of differently committed Buddhists based on different levels of engagement. From there we were able to create new variables and sub-samples and investigate whether Buddhist commitment was related to social background.

For multivariate analysis we used logistic regression to test whether social background factors had any impact on the level of commitment to Buddhism. The DV was nominal or categorical.

The level of measurement for the majority of our variables was ordinal. This level of measurement afforded greater potential variance across the concepts. We were then able to assess a range of different levels and rates of engagement and commitment. In analytical terms these variables allowed us to pursue bivariate and multivariate techniques. The question and answer formats gave us data that allowed the research to explore and attempt to answer more complex questions.

Theories and data

The findings in 'Choosing Buddhism' made the use of a survey very worthwhile. We had found that, for Australian Buddhists, the pattern of religious engagement was more traditional. This was a challenge to a lot of the theory that attempted to explain involvement in 'eastern' religions like Buddhism as a pattern of multiple religious identities and reconstructed teachings that were easily disposed of. The caution, however, is to do with the sample, which is not representative, so we cannot claim that this is a feature for all Australian or western Buddhists. Yet at least a benchmark had been set and some questions asked of the theory.

'Looking East'

Our hypotheses and models in 'Looking East' were more focused than in 'Choosing Buddhism'. The data were employed to consider whether disenchantment with a western identity was somehow associated with greater levels of engagement in Buddhism. We used mostly bivariate and multivariate techniques in that paper (Table 10.2).

Table 10.2 Data and analysis for 'Looking East'

	Univariate		Bivariate		Multivariate
Variables	Practice	Belief	Self-identity	Religious identity	Latent variable
	Meditation	Four-Noble Truths	Social class	Practice	Western social identity
	Reading	Eight-Fold Path	Australian	Belief	Gender
	Initiation	Reincarnation	Political party		Age
		Impermanence	Ethnicity		Politics

	Univariate		Bivariate		Multivariate
			Gender		Education
			Age		
Format	Scaled	Scaled	Original	Scaled	Scaled
Techniques	Frequency distribution	Frequency distribution	Cross-tabulation		Factor analysis
					OLS regression
Use	The frequency distributions assisted with constructing the independent variables for later multivariate analysis		The cross-tabulation compared key aspects of self-identity between western Buddhists and Australians in general	Cross-tabulation also allowed the comparison of importance of self-identity factors between highly and weakly committed Buddhists	The regression analysis further tested the different levels of Buddhist commitment on western self-identity controlling for a series of social background experiences
Result	There was significant variation in the sample for Buddhist commitment allowing the research to pursue hypothesis 1		Cross-tabulation showed that there was significant variation between western Buddhists and Australians in general on the importance of self-identity factors	Cross-tabulation showed differences in importance of western self-identity factors between highly and weakly committed Buddhists	The regression analysis showed that differences in importance of a western self-identity existed even when social background factors were introduced, lending some support to hypothesis 2

Univariate analysis played a small but important part in the paper. A table of frequency distributions allowed us to compare the sample of Buddhists against Australians in general concerning the level of importance ascribed to a set of self-identity indicators. This established that there was some difference between how Australians in general and our sample of Buddhists reported self-identity. Again, univariate analysis was beneficial for establishing an empirical position from which more sophisticated and complex questions could be addressed with the data.

Bivariate analyses allowed us to establish the pattern of religious involvement associated with disenchantment with a 'western' identity, through some cross-tabulations. Bivariate analyses also allowed us to test the second hypothesis concerning the level of engagement and level of disenchantment with a 'western' identity.

Once the bivariate analyses had established that there was a relationship between engagement in Buddhism and disenchantment with a western identity, multivariate analysis allowed us to test further the idea that disenchantment was associated with stronger levels of commitment and engagement by adding a series of social background control variables to the analysis.

Theories and data

The paper found some cause to consider explanations of why it was that some people had been attracted to 'eastern' religions such as Buddhism. We attempted to answer this question sociologically and not necessarily as an aspect of personal experience or individual motivation, as important as those perspectives may be. We found Max Weber's theory of disenchantment a very interesting and useful theoretical framework to attempt to explain the social reasons behind the emergence of western Buddhists. The data allowed us to test this idea empirically with both hypotheses supported, but hypothesis 2 was only partially supported.

Summary

This chapter has illustrated how a survey research project is thought through and performed from inception to publication, going through all of the steps involved in survey design to produce the research eventually. The survey of Australian Buddhists is a modest survey, indeed we state as much in both the papers I have reviewed for the examples in this chapter. Modesty should not be confused with a lack of quality, however. Even modest surveys can provide data useful enough to contribute meaningfully to professional research outcomes if they are designed well and adhere to the survey design process. The various stages of survey design throughout the text are summarized and illustrated here. Each survey project is unique even though the process is the same, meaning that different problems and challenges are encountered in every stage for each project, but each stage is a necessary step towards good research. The end results of diligent and process-led survey design are usually rewarding. Above all, survey design shares with all research that special feeling of discovery and the sense that one is contributing to knowledge.

Glossary

Bivariate analysis   the analysis of two variables: an independent and dependent variable to establish or test a relationship

Census   a survey that collects data from an entire population, without the use of a sample

Closed-ended question format   a set of pre-defined and given answer categories on a survey question

Codebook   a document that records and lists in a specific order the questions, labels, sequencing, and scoring of answer categories for all of the questions in a survey

Coding   the organization of answer categories of a survey question into numeric scores or textual themes and question sequencing in numeric or alphanumeric order in a survey

Cognitive interviewing   a form of pre-testing of survey questions to establish validity and reliability that uses an interview and discussion format between researchers and potential respondents

Concept   a key general idea or abstract mental construct that a survey aims to measure, often associated with a theory

Concept validity   that the concept a survey is designed to measure is relevant to the stated research question

Conceptual model   a graphical representation of a research question and the proposed statistical or analytic relationship between various concepts relevant to the research question

Content validity   the assessment of a measure of a concept to ascertain whether the measure adequately covers the meaning of a concept

Correlation   a specific relationship between an independent and a dependent variable such that the direction and strength of the relationship is clear

Criterion validity   the assessment of a new measure of a concept against an old measure of a concept

Cross-section   a study design that uses a unique sample to collect survey data at one specific time only

Cross-tabulation   a data analysis technique and the output thereof that tests a possible relationship between an independent and a dependent variable simultaneously

Curvilinear   a relationship between an independent and a dependent variable that does not present consistent variation like a linear relationship, but displays the influence of an independent on a dependent variable inconsistently through different points of variation between variables resembling a U-shaped curve

Data quality   the quality of data acquired from a survey to answering research questions and representing substantive relationships between variables taking into account the various sources of error associated with survey design

Deductive research   research that commences with a theory and then tests the theory with data

Dependent variable   a variable whose change or variation is attributable to an independent variable or independent variables. Also, the variable in a research question or conceptual model for which changes are proposed to be related to via (a) stated independent variable(s)

Descending the ladder of abstraction   a description of the process in survey design of the development of an abstract concept into a statistic or estimate through a survey question

Descriptive statistics   a series of statistics that summarize a variable through univariate analysis

Dimensions   related but differentiated components of a broader concept

Direct relationship   a relationship between the independent and dependent variable without an intervening variable

Disc by mail   a mode of survey completion wherein a respondent is sent a survey to complete and return that is stored on a disk allowing completion on a computer

Double-barrelled question   a question that contains two key objects of interest making the question ambiguous

Dummy variable a variable created through recoding to change the level of measurement from nominal or ordinal to interval for the purposes of some forms of data analysis

Estimate the statistic the survey aims to find for a specific research question or dependent variable

Evaluation a form of research design using a survey that measures the effectiveness of a service, product, or change in circumstances

Experimental design a form of research design that uses a survey to pre- and post-test respondents prior to and after an intervention or change in circumstances

Feeling thermometer a question format that measures metaphoric 'temperature' associated with a subject, person, or group, usually with a metric that is between 0 and 100

Filter question a question that filters out, blocks, or purposively steers respondents with or without one or more specific desired or relevant attributes for part of a survey

Frequency distribution a method of data analysis and the output thereof wherein the distribution of the answer categories in statistics and raw numbers of a single variable are displayed

Hypothesis a research statement or proposition of expected results or relationships that are tested with survey data

Independent variable a variable that influences or produces change or variation in the dependent variable or is proposed to influence or produce change in the dependent variable in a research question or conceptual model

Index a composite measure that combines two or more variables of different types relevant to or indicative of an underlying concept to create a new variable

Indicator a question in a survey, also referred to as an item, measure, or variable

Indirect relationship a relationship between two variables that is mediated or linked via a third variable

Inductive research research that commences with data to build or test a theory

Inference a statistical state such as a p value from a significance test to denote that what is observed in a sample is likely to occur in a population and is not likely to be the product of sampling error

Interval variable   a level of measurement of a variable that is defined by precise and meaningful numeric differences between categories

Intervening variable   a variable that connects and establishes an indirect relationship between a proposed independent and dependent variable

Leading question   a question that is worded so as to produce possibly a positive or negative bias in the mind of a respondent artificially affecting the way in which a question is answered

Level of measurement   the different kinds of variables based on the kinds of ranking of numeric differences between answer categories that produce specific kinds of data appropriate for different forms of analysis

Likert scale   a question format that measures affectual or emotional response to a statement via a scale of agreement and disagreement

Linear relationship   a relationship that suggests that as the independent variable changes, so too in similar proportion does a dependent variable in a consistent manner indicative of a straight line

Longitudinal survey   research design that uses independent samples or the same sample to collect data at two or more times

Measurement error   various means of inaccuracy associated with measurement that do not produce reliable or valid estimates or statistics of the concept in question, such as poor question construction

Measures of association   statistics that indicate the strength and direction of a relationship between two variables

Missing data   questions in a survey for a case or cases that have not been answered

Multilevel modelling   a method of data analysis wherein data representing different units of analysis are part of the same model

Multivariate analysis   a suite of data analysis methods that assess statistical relationships between two or more independent variables against one or more dependent variables

Nominal variable   a level of measurement of a variable in which there are no meaningful numeric differences or rank order between categories

Non-probability sample   a form of sampling that is not mathematically or probability based and does not qualify to infer findings to the broader population

Null hypothesis a statistical assumption that two variables will not be related prior to analysis; a rejection of the null hypothesis is consistent with the notion of a relationship between two variables

Open-ended question format a question format that has no pre-defined answer categories and requires a respondent to answer on their own terms, usually with a written or textual response

Operational definition the stated selected criteria pertaining to dimensions and sub-dimensions of a concept and the measures developed for it through survey questions

Operationalization the process of refining an abstract concept into the survey questions consistent with an operational definition

Ordinal variable a level of measurement of a variable in which the response categories indicate general rather than specifically meaningful numeric differences or rank ordering between categories

Path analysis a data analysis method and form of conceptual modelling that analyses and proposes numerous direct and indirect relationships between independent and dependent variables

Pilot test a form of pre-testing of a questionnaire to identify any problems with the survey questions

Plausibility relates to how realistic proposed or observed relationships are in terms of theoretical explanatory power

Poll a type of survey in which a small number of focused questions are asked of a sample of respondents to gain estimates on a specific issue

Population the total number of units of analysis such as individuals of interest to a survey research project from which a sample can be taken

Probability sample a suite of sampling methods that are based on the mathematical probability that every case in a sampling frame has an equal chance of being selected in a sample. Examples include random, stratified, and cluster samples.

Question order effect where the ordering or placement of questions can influence how respondents answer questions

Ranking question a question and answer format that enables respondents to rank categories in order of preference in relation to the other categories

Rating question   a question and answer format that enables a respondent to elect a single numeric rating within a category

Recoding   changing the coding of variables during data analysis, such as collapsing or amalgamating categories or reversing the coding of a variable to make a variable more amenable to analysis

Reliability   consistency of respondents' answers to the same question in the same or similar contexts over time assuming the nature of the question does not change

Replication   a study that attempts to reproduce the same or similar results of a prior study in another context such as a different national or community setting at a different time

Representative   pertaining to a sample's nearness to an actual population in terms of the proportions of particular characteristics or demographic attributes represented in a sample, such as age groups, gender proportions, and geographic units

Research design   the specific form and process of a research project structuring data collection

Response rate   the rate or percentage of a sample that completes and returns a survey

Reverse coding   recoding a variable so that the codes for the categories are exactly the reverse of their original codes

Sample   a selection or proportion of a population for the purposes of data collection

Sampling error   the rate or proportion of discrepancy or difference between a sample and the population on a given attribute signified by a statistic such as the standard error

Sampling frame   a full list of the unit of analysis, such as individuals or households from which a final sample is drawn

Scale   a composite measure that combines related indicators of a common underlying concept to form a new variable

Scattergram   a bivariate data analysis method and output for the analysis of two interval-level variables

Semantic differential   a rating format question that presents a continuum between two stated extremes stated as adjectives, such as excellent and poor

Statistic   a number that is produced for a measure or question that indicates or summarizes a meaningful position or state regarding a phenomenon

Sub-dimension   a specific aspect or related but differentiated component of the dimension of a concept

Survey fatigue   apathy associated with completing surveys due to over-application of the method, leading to poor data quality

Theory   a set of propositions forming an explanatory mechanism of phenomena within a plausible context, consisting of relational concepts

Unit of analysis   the level or element of respondent represented in a survey sample, such as an individual, a household, or community

Univariate analysis   forms of data analysis or outputs thereof that consider only one variable

Validity   the state when a question measures what it is supposed to measure

Vignette   a brief description of a scenario or situation to provide the context for a survey question

Weighting   statistical procedures used for compensating for missing data to reduce sampling error

References

Aarons, H. (2012) 'Consumption' in Beilharz, P. and Hogan, T. (eds) *Sociology: Antipodean Perspectives* pp 313–317. Melbourne: Oxford University Press

Aarons, H. (2018) 'Moral Distinction: Religion, Musical Taste, and the Moral Cultural Consumer'. *Journal of Consumer Culture*. Available at https://doi.org/10.1177/1469540518787584 (Accessed 29 June 2020).

Aarons, H., and Phillips, T. (1997) Experience of Buddhism Survey. La Trobe University.

Abramowitz, A. and Teixeira, R. (2009) 'The Decline of the White Working Class and the Rise of a Mass Upper-Middle Class'. *Political Science Quarterly*, 124 (3): 391–422

Alkire, S. and Santos, M. E. (2014) 'Measuring Acute Poverty in the Developing World: Robustness and Scope of the Multidimensional Poverty Index'. *World Development*, 59: 251–274

Anderson, B. (2007) *Imagined Communities: Reflections on the Origin and Spread of Nationalism*. New York: Verso

Australian Bureau of Statistics (2012) Information Paper – A Statistical Definition of Homelessness. Catalogue No. 4922.0. Canberra: Australian Government Publishing Service

Babbie, E., Halley, F., Wagner, W., and Zaino, J. (2016) *Adventures in Social Research: Data Analysis Using IBM SPSS Statistics* (10th edn). Los Angeles: Sage

Bauman, Z. (2000) *Liquid Modernity*. London: Polity Press

Beck, A. T. (1972) *Depression: Causes and Treatment*. Philadelphia: University of Philadelphia Press

Belli, R., Traugott, M., Young, M., and McGonagle, K. (1999) 'Reducing Vote Overreporting in Surveys: Social Desirability, Memory Failure, and Source Monitoring'. *Public Opinion Quarterly*, 63 (1): 90–108

Bennett, T., Emmison, M., and Frow, J. (1999) *Accounting for Tastes: Australian Everyday Cultures*. Melbourne: Cambridge University Press

Bennett, T., Savage, M., Silva, E., Warde, A., Gayo-Cal, M., and Wright, D. (2008) *Culture, Class, Distinction*. London: Routledge

Bessell, S. (2015) 'The Individual Deprivation Measure: Measuring Poverty as if Gender and Inequality Matter'. *Gender and Development*, 23 (2): 223–240

Blair, E. and Blair, J. (2015) *Applied Survey Sampling*. London: Sage

Blank, R. (2008) 'Presidential Address: How to Improve Poverty Measurement in the United States'. *Journal of Policy Analysis and Management*, 27 (2): 233–254

Blasius, J. and Thiessen, V. (2012) *Assessing the Quality of Survey Data*. London: Sage

Blumer, H. (1931) 'Science Without Concepts'. *American Journal of Sociology*, 36 (4): 515–533

Bouma, G. (1973) 'Beyond Lenski: A Recent Critical Review of "Protestant Ethic" Research'. *Journal for the Scientific Study of Religion*, 12 (2): 141–155

Bouma, G. and Carland, S. (2016) *The Research Process* (6th edn). Melbourne: Oxford University Press

Bourdieu, P. (1984) *Distinction: A Social Critique of the Judgement of Taste*. Cambridge, MA: Harvard University Press

Bryman, A. (2015) *Social Research Methods* (5th edn). Oxford: Oxford University Press

Burkitt, D. P. (1980) 'Diseases of Affluence' in Howe, M. and Lorraine, J. (eds) *Environmental Medicine* (2nd edn). London: Heinemann

Cain, S. (2019) Women are Happier without Children or a Spouse says Happiness Expert. Available at https://www.theguardian.com/lifeandstyle/2019/may/25/women-happier-without-children-or-a-spouse-happiness-expert (Accessed 25 May 2019).

Chamberlain, C. and Johnson, G. (2001) 'The Debate About Homelessness'. *Australian Journal of Social Issues*, 36 (1): 35–50

Chamberlain, C. and Mackenzie, D. (1992) 'Understanding Contemporary Homelessness: Issues of Definition and Meaning'. *Australian Journal of Social Issues*, 27 (4): 274–297

Chamberlain, C. and Mackenzie, D. (2014) 'Definition and Counting: Where to Now?' in *Homelessness in Australia: An Introduction*. Sydney: New South Publishing

Charmaz, K. (2006) *Constructing Grounded Theory*. London: Sage

Connelly, R., Gayle, V., and Lambert, P. S. (2016) 'A Review of Occupation-Based Social Classifications for Social Survey Research', *Methodological Innovations*, 9: 1–14

Converse, J. M. (1987) *Survey Research in the United States: Roots and Emergence 1890–1960*. Berkeley: University of California Press

Croucher, P. (1989) *A History of Buddhism in Australia 1848–1988*. Sydney: University of New South Wales Press

Davis, J. (1985) *The Logic of the Causal Order*, Sage University Paper Series on Quantitative Applications in the Social Sciences pp 7–55. Beverly Hills, CA: Sage

De Leeuw, E. (2008) 'Choosing the Method of Data Collection' in de Leeuw, E., Hox, J., and Dillman, D. (eds) *International Handbook of Survey Methodology* pp 113–135. New York: Taylor & Francis

De Vaus, D. (2001) *Research Design in Social Research*. London: Sage

De Vaus, D. A. (2014) *Surveys in Social Research* (6th edn). St Leonards: Allen & Unwin

Deaton, A. (1997) *The Analysis of Household Surveys: A Microeconometric Approach to Development Policy*. Washington, DC: The World Bank

Delanty, G. (2009) *Community* (2nd edn). London: Routledge

Deming, W. E. (1944) 'On Errors in Surveys'. *American Sociological Review*, 9 (4): 359–369

DeVellis, R. (2012) *Scale Development: Theory and Applications* (3rd edn). Beverly Hills, CA: Sage

Dillman, D., Smyth, J., and Christian, L. (2009) *Internet, Phone, Mail, and Mixed-Mode Surveys: The Tailored Design Method* (3rd edn). Hoboken, NJ: Wiley

Dillman, D., Smyth, J., and Christian, L. (2014) *Internet, Phone, Mail, and Mixed-Mode Surveys: The Tailored Design Method* (4th edn). Hoboken, NJ: Wiley

Donkin, A. J. M. (2014) 'Social Gradient'. In *The Wiley Blackwell Encyclopedia of Health, Illness, Behaviour, and Society* (Eds W.C. Cockerham, R. Dingwall and S. Quah) doi:10.1002/9781118410868.wbehibs530

Durkheim, E. (1996) *The Elementary Forms of Religious Life*. New York: Free Press

Easterly, W. (2001) 'The Middle Class Consensus and Economic Development'. *Journal of Economic Growth*, 6 (4): 317–335

Ellis-Petersen, H. (2017) Available at https://www.theguardian.com/music/2017/jan/03/record-sales-vinyl-hits-25-year-high-and-outstrips-streaming (Accessed 10 April 2018).

Field, D. (1988) 'Perspectives on Homelessness' in Loft, J. and David, M. (eds) *Homelessness: An Annotated Bibliography of Australian Research*. Melbourne: Australian Institute of Family Studies

Fortune (2016) How One Pollster Correctly Predicted Both Trump's Victory and Brexit. Available at http://fortune.com/2016/11/11/pollster-brandseye-donald-trump-brexit-social-media/ (Accessed 8 April 2018).

Fowler, F. J. Jr (1995) *Improving Survey Questions: Design and Evaluation*. Thousand Oaks, CA: Sage

Gerth, H. H. and Mills, C. W. (1958) *From Max Weber: Essays in Sociology*. Oxford: Oxford University Press

Gibbs, J. and Blumer, M. (2010) *Social Measurement Through Social Surveys: An Applied Approach*. London: Routledge

Glaser, B. and Strauss, A. (1967) *The Discovery of Grounded Theory*. Chicago: Aldine

Goldthorpe, J., Llewellyn, C., and Payne, C. (1987) *Social Mobility and Class Structure in Modern Britain*. Oxford: Clarendon Press

Groves, R., Fowler, F. J. Jr, Couper, M., Lepkowski, J., Singer, E., and Tourangeau, R. (2009) *Survey Methodology* (2nd edn). New York: Wiley

Groves, R. M. and Lyberg, L. (2010) 'Total Survey Error: Past, Present, and Future'. *Public Opinion Quarterly*, 74 (5): 849–879

Heelas, P., Martin, D., and Morris, P. (eds) (1998) *Religion, Modernity, and Post Modernity*. Oxford: Blackwell

International Deprivation Measure (2018) *IDM Technical Update*. Individual Deprivation Measure. Available at https://www.individualdeprivationmeasure.org/resources/idm-methodology-update-condensed/ (Accessed 14 November 2019).

Ingraham, C. (2019) 'The Share of Americans not Having Sex Has Reached a Record High'. *Washington Post*. Available at https://www.washingtonpost.com/business/2019/03/29/share-americans-not-having-sex-has-reached-record-high/?noredirect=on&utm_term=.7dcbedf7acc6 (Accessed 14 November 2019).

Kalton, G. and Flores-Cervantes, I. (2003) 'Weighting Methods'. *Journal of Official Statistics*, 19 (2): 81–97

Marsh, C. (1982) *The Survey Method: The Contribution of Surveys to Sociological Explanation*. London: Allen & Unwin

Merton, R. (1968) *Social Theory and Social Structure* (2nd edn). New York: Free Press

Morton, M. H. and Montgomery, P. (2013) 'Youth Empowerment Programs for Improving Adolescents' Self-Efficacy and Self-Esteem: A Systematic Review'. *Research on Social Work Practice*, 23 (1): 22–33

NYCH (National Youth Coalition for Housing) (1985) *Shelter or the Streets: National Policies*. Melbourne: National Youth Coalition for Housing

Pallant, J. (2020) *SPSS Survival Guide* (7th edn). Melbourne: Allen & Unwin

Pew Research Center (2018) *Partisan Divides in Views in Many Countries - but Not North Korea*. Pew Research Center. Available at https://www.pewresearch.org/politics/2018/09/10/partisan-divides-in-views-of-many-countries-but-not-north-korea/ (Accessed 14 November 2019).

Pfeffermann, D. (1996) 'The Use of Sample Weights for Survey Data Analysis'. *Statistical Methods for Medical Research*, 5 (3): 239–261

Phillips, T. (2007) 'The Allure of Quantitative Data' in Walter, M. (ed.) *Social Research Methods*. Melbourne: Oxford University Press

Phillips, T. and Aarons, H. (2005) 'Choosing Buddhism in Australia: Towards a Traditional Style of Reflexive Spiritual Engagement'. *British Journal of Sociology*, 56 (2): 215–232

Phillips, T. and Aarons, H. (2007) 'Looking "East": An Exploratory Analysis of Western Disenchantment'. *International Sociology*, 22 (3): 325–341

Phillips, T. and Smith, P. (2000) *Incivility: The Rude Stranger in Everyday Life*. Melbourne: Cambridge University Press

Putnam, R. (2000) *Bowling Alone: The Collapse and Revival of American Community*. New York: Simon & Schuster

Reeves, R., Guyot, K., and Krause, E. (2018) *A Dozen Ways to be Middle Class*. Washington, DC: Brookings Institution. Available at https://www.brookings.edu/interactives/a-dozen-ways-to-be-middle-class/ (Accessed 14 January 2020).

Reeves, R., Rodrigue, E., and Kneebone, E. (2016) *Five Evils: Multidimensional Poverty and Race in America*. Washington, DC: Brookings Institution

Robinson, S. and Leonard, K. (2018) *Designing Quality Survey Questions*. London: Sage

Roof, W. (1999) *Spiritual Marketplace: Babyboomers and the Remaking of American Religion*. Princeton, NJ: Princeton University Press

Salkind, N. J. (2010) (ed.) *Encyclopedia of Research Design, Volume 3*. London: Sage

Scoboria, A., Kimberley, A., Wade, D., Lindsay, S., Azad, T., Strange, D., Ost., J., and Hyman, I. E. (2017) 'A Mega-analysis of Memory Reports from Eight Peer-reviewed False Memory Implantation Studies'. *Memory*, 25 (2): 146–163

Shaw, J. and Porter, C. (2015) 'Constructing Rich False Memories of Committing Crime'. *Psychological Science*, 26 (3): 291–301

Singler, B. (2014) '"See Mom, it's Real": The UK Census, Jediism, and Social Media'. *Journal of Religion in Europe*, 7 (2): 150–168

Standing, G. (2014) 'The Precariat'. *Contexts*, 13 (4): 10–12

Stanley, T. D., Carter, E., and Doucouliagos, H. (2018) 'What Meta-analyses Reveal about the Replicability of Psychological Research'. *Psychological Bulletin*, 144 (12): 1325–1346

Stevens, S. (1946) 'On the Theory of Scales of Measurement'. *Science*, 103 (2684): 677–680

Supported Accommodation Assistance Act (1994) Available at https://www.legisla tion.gov.au/Details/C2004A04835 (Accessed 11 February 2020).

Toepoel, V. (2015) *Doing Surveys Online*. London: Sage

Tourangeau, R. and Yan, T. (2007) 'Sensitive Questions in Surveys'. *Psychological Bulletin*, 133: 859–883

Tranter, B. and Western, M. (2010) 'Overstating Value Change: Question Ordering in the Postmaterial Values Index'. *European Sociological Review*, 26 (5): 571–583

United States Department of Housing and Urban Development (1984) *Report to the Secretary on the Homeless and Emergency Shelters*. Washington, DC: HUD Office of Policy Development and Research

Van de Poel, E., O'Donnell, O., and Van Doorslaer, E. (2009) 'Urbanization and the Spread of Diseases of Affluence in China'. *Economics and Human Biology*, 7 (2): 200–216

Wade, K., Garry, M., and Pezdek, K. (2018) 'Deconstructing Rich False Memories of Committing Crime: Commentary on Shaw and Porter 2015'. *Psychological Science*, 29 (3): 471–476

Wann, D. and James, J. (2019) *Sport Fans: The Psychology and Social Impact of Fandom* (2nd edn). London: Routledge

Watson, S. (1984) 'Definitions of Homelessness: A Feminist Perspective'. *Critical Social Policy*, 4 (2): 60–73

Weber, M. (2001) *The Protestant Ethic and the Spirit of Capitalism*. London. Routledge Classics

Weisberg, H. F. (2005) *The Total Survey Error Approach: A Guide to the New Science of Survey Research*. Chicago: The University of Chicago Press

Wilkins, R., Laß, I., Butterworth, P., and Vera-Toscano, E. (2019) *The Household, Income and Labour Dynamics in Australia Survey: Selected Findings from Waves 1 to 17*. Melbourne Institute: Applied Economic & Social Research, University of Melbourne

Willis, G. (2004) *Cognitive Interviewing: A Tool for Improving Questionnaire Design.* London: Sage

Wolf, C., Joye, D., Smith, T., and Fu, Y.-c. (2016) *The SAGE Handbook of Survey Methodology.* London: Sage

Woodward, I. (2007) *Understanding Material Culture.* London: Sage

Wright, E. O. (1985) *Classes.* New York: Verso

Zinnbauer, B. J., Pargament, K. I., Cole, B. S., Rye, M. S., Butter, E. M., Belavich, T. G., Hipp, K., Scott, A. B., and Kadar, J. L. (1997) 'Religion and Spirituality: Unfuzzying the Fuzzy'. *Journal for the Scientific Study of Religion*, 36 (4): 549–564

Index

Made in United States
Orlando, FL
04 January 2024